DANGER ROAD

Author's Web Sites

www.JPContini.com

www.DangerRoadTheBook.com

Individual copies: 1.800.957.6476

DANGER ROAD
A true crime story of murder and redemption

By John P. Contini

DANGER ROAD
A true crime story of murder and redemption

By John P. Contini

Printed in the United States of America
First Edition: May 2006
10 9 8 7 6 5 4 3 2

ISBN 0-9773174-0-4
ISBN 978-0-9773174-0-0

Cover design by Jeff Tidwell

Liberty
P R E S S

Danger Road is distributed
by Bookworld Companies.

For the Record

This book is based on the trial of Gilbert Fernandez, Jr. on charges of first-degree murder. The testimony and dialogue have been abbreviated and modified where necessary to consolidate timeframes and events, allowing for improved content flow. Where possible, testimony was reprinted verbatim from archived trial transcripts. Additionally, many of the events described are based on police reports, trial transcripts, newspaper articles, and the recollections and perceptions of the author, John P. Contini.

These recollections and perceptions have further been buttressed by recent interviews with former Fernandez case prosecutors Jim Lewis and Cindy Imperato; former court personnel members Mike Ruvolo, Denise Hughes and Beth Kessler; and trial spectators, including Reverend Dave Blood and Dr. Bill Kelly. Their comments have been reprinted verbatim in some instances and paraphrased in others, and there have been modifications made for space and esthetic reasons. In some cases, names have been changed to protect privacy. These alterations have caused no material changes to any aspect of this true crime story.

Reviews from Readers

DANGER ROAD rips the curtain off a high profile murder case that has the highest stakes possible: life or death. Then it takes you into the bowels of the justice system and on this journey you go from the darkest, coldest heart to the crowning glory of the human condition. DANGER ROAD is a searing and scintillating gawk at the truth about our legal system and ourselves.

John Contini proves that when you fight monsters you don't have to become a monster…you can become a man of God.

Howard Finkelstein
Broward County Public Defender
Help Me Howard Television Segment

John's work goes beyond just being another "true crime" book: It is a riveting morality treatise affording extraordinary insight into a homicide's rippling effects not only on the immediate participants, but on all who are touched by the ongoing waves of its horror — yet revealing hope that a measure of good can spring out of even the machinations of evil.

Brian Cavanagh
Chief of Homicide
Office of the Broward State Attorney

DANGER ROAD by John Contini is a great work of art which provides insight into the trial of a death penalty case.

Every lawyer and judge should obtain a copy of this brilliant book by a veteran attorney.

Alan H. Schreiber
The elected Public Defender
of Broward County from 1976-2004

A must read about Fort Lauderdale's "Cocaine Cowboy" era, rogue cops and ambitious young prosecutors cutting deals with "evil" to obtain a conviction. Tonight, read about a real life criminal defense attorney, who actually slugs it out in the courtroom, instead of listening to the television "talking head" lawyers, the "second-guessers," who have never tried a death penalty case.

H. Dohn Williams Jr.
Attorney at Law and a brother in "Law"

John Contini's new book is a great read for lawyer and non lawyer alike. It is fast paced, dramatic and real. He will become the John Grisham of real courtroom suspense writing.

Bob Stone
Attorney at Law

DANGER ROAD is a "must read" for an attorney or anyone interested in the law. This book shows how our legal system really works.

James Facciolo III
Attorney at Law
Professor of Behavioral Science and Legal Studies
Nova Southeastern University

As a trial attorney, I have precious little time to read for pleasure. However, I recently picked up a copy of John Contini's DANGER ROAD and could not put it down. I read it in one day. The story is compelling, as are the characters. The book reads like a movie, so you feel like you are a part of the actual courtroom drama.

Reed Tolber
Attorney at Law

John Contini has written a fascinating true crime book of one of the most high profile murder cases in Broward County history. In addition, he has managed to superbly display the psychology behind the tense moments in the courtroom with his frank disclosure of his own insightful self-talk during that time. It is as honest as it gets and I was not able to put the book down...and I already knew the ending!

Dr. Michael Brannon
Forensic Psychologist

"Wow!! I just finished DANGER ROAD. I could not put it down…"

Stephanie O'Neal
Christian Television Network

Reading DANGER ROAD made me feel like I was actually inside the investigation, the courtroom and the minds of the people involved in the crime.

Anita Mitchell
Senior Editor
Liberty Press Publishing

I see inmate Gil Fernandez on a regular basis. Other inmates respect him, prison guards respect him. We are spiritual brothers, me on the outside, Gil on the inside. Gil is so powerful that the other inmates give him their precious phone minutes so that he can comfort others. Gil is a man of God, he never wavers.

Minister Gerry James
Prison Minister, Kairos
Florida State Prison
Starke, Florida

I had the privilege of meeting with John Contini for lunch and got his book, DANGER ROAD. He took the time to write such a nice message and signed it. What a great guy. Just took a trip and read his book. I could not put the book down. I enjoy true stories and enjoyed the book very much. Mr. Contini is quite the writer with great expression!

Kerry Avila

A very powerful story of trial, tribulation and redemption. I am filled with awe at the prospect of meeting John Contini when he speaks at the University. He is a person of such strong spiritual conviction.

Dr. Ed Aqua
Director of Lifelong Learning
Nova Southeastern University

I thoroughly enjoyed John's book, DANGER ROAD. I had worked with Judge Tyson for many years and John described his temperament and personality perfectly. Having been a criminal attorney, both prosecutor and defense attorney for a combined 16 years it was truly enjoyable to "be in trial" again. John's book encourages you to feel you are a part of the case, whichever side you choose. John writes so passionately that you cannot put this book down!

Melinda (Mindy) Brown

Lawyer's true-life crime tale a sizzler. A book about the 1991 trial of an ex-policeman and bodybuilder accused of killing three men in the Everglades has become a must-read at the Broward County Courthouse.

Nikki Waller
The Miami Herald

After reading one chapter, I was hooked! I rearranged my busy schedule, even trading sleep for the opportunity to read more of this gripping true-life who-done-it! John presents a carefully crafted story, written with exquisite balance:

- the seamy side of life counterbalanced by compassion for all involved
- intense situations oozing with raw emotion counterbalanced with perfectly-timed injections of his witty humor
- lies spoken under oath counterbalanced with an honest view into what was going on in John's heart and mind throughout the trial

DANGER ROAD was both enlightening and disturbing. It was hard to deal with so much sin and the resultant pain generated in so many lives. John frankly revealed the full truth about the dark reality of death and destruction that is the outcome of sin; yet he consistently presented the counterbalance: murder *and* redemption. After reading Gil's uplifting letters at the end of the book, I could set it down with a mental picture of the victory of good over evil, a picture of the hard edges of justice softened by God's love and mercy.

Janice M. Valvano
Author of *Proof Positive*

DANGER ROAD reads like a novel with shades of John Grisham, Barbara Parker and Steve Martini directing the plot. DANGER ROAD is heart rendering, poignant and inspirational. The story is moving and unforgettable.

Richard R. Blake

Acknowledgements

Foremost, I would like to give thanks to Jesus Christ, to God the Father who made me, and to the Holy Spirit, who provides unending inspiration.

I would also like to thank…

Elizabeth, my sweet-spirited, Proverbs 31 wife, for putting up with me. I thank her for being tolerant about all the time I spent researching trial transcripts, meeting with prosecutors and court personnel, and writing and rewriting this book.

Gil Fernandez, for his permission to write about this painful time in his life, especially given that he expects no benefit from the publication of this book. I will be forever grateful to Gil for his unwavering inspiration and encouragement. I have yet to meet anyone who has gone through a greater transformation than him.

Luana Tringali, a nice young woman who was hurt because of my zealous defense of Gil Fernandez. Luana suffered victimization in this case, in more ways than one. In my desire to expose Mike Carbone's callousness and cruelty toward her, I disrespected her privacy in a way that also could be construed as callous and cruel. For that, I apologize.

Judge Cynthia Imperato and *Jim Lewis,* two of the prosecutors on the Fernandez case, and BSO Detective Joseph Damiano, for the time they took to meet with me. They helped me to fully appreciate their perspective on issues relating to this case. Our discussions over lunch were refreshingly honest and illuminating, even healing.

Doug Molloy, Chief Assistant Statewide Prosecutor on the Fernandez case. I appreciate his candor and perspective on this case, and his professionalism and class.

Denise Hughes, Beth Kessler and *Mike Ruvolo,* for their time and willingness to share information when we broke bread together to discuss the case. For their help and friendship, I'll always be grateful.

Sheriff Nick Navarro, for his time and thoughtfulness, and for selflessly sharing his recollections about the case.

Jeff Tidwell of *Homeward Media*, for going the Matthew 5:41 "extra mile" on his awesome cover design for DANGER ROAD — and also for his design of www.DangerRoadTheBook.com. There is nobody more responsive and more efficient than Jeff Tidwell.

Martha Blumel of *Envision Graphic Design*, for jumping in there with both feet at the eleventh hour to format this book and clean up the remaining mistakes caught by Janice Valvano and by Martha herself!

Mark Rienzo, the glue within the quintessential book printer, *Genesis Press* of Hialeah, Florida, for going that extra quality mile in printing DANGER ROAD! And were it not for Mark Rienzo, I would not have been introduced to Bookworld!

Carla Chadwick, my editor, for her advice and counsel. To her credit, Carla understood my refusal to allow for ghostwriting. She respected my need to use my own words and phraseology throughout DANGER ROAD, even as she felt that my "writer's voice" was at times "slightly irreverent." Her repeated e-mail inquiries (i.e. inquiring into details of possible interest to prospective readers) helped to prompt and guide me as I wrote and rewrote, even when I thought I was done!

My earlier writing teacher, Taigh White, was entirely right. "The art of writing is re-writing!"

Becky Schall, Edna Byrd, Gay Sparks, Steve Hodson, Kim Nicholls, Julie Bobikevich and *John Plough* of *Bookworld Companies*, for all their distribution efforts and success, and especially for encouraging me at the onset by signing on as DANGER ROAD's distributor.

Anita Mitchell, Senior Editor of *Liberty Press Publishing*, for her tireless efforts at the helm of Liberty's publishing and grass roots success to date.

Lorne Fisher, President of *Fish Consulting*, another high-end, successful public relations firm, for all the extraordinary effort and success in trumpeting this project and DANGER ROAD over the national secular media and wire services.

Susan Zahn, President, *Dave Bohon,* Vice President, *Leane Worthington* and *Krystal Colazzo* of *White Dove Communications Media* (WDC Media), the highly-acclaimed, faith-based public relations firm, for their commitment to excellence in their ongoing efforts and success in promoting DANGER ROAD throughout the Faith community.

Phil Lowry (owner and also a pastor!) and *Wes Jolly* at *Express Logistics,* the fulfillment center in Glasgow, Kentucky, for also going that Matthew 5:41 "extra mile" in shipping DANGER ROAD to the folks who order the book through www.DangerRoadTheBook.com.

Chris Herridge and his awesome staff at *Telelink Call Center,* St. John's, Newfoundland, for always being so helpful with the callers who order DANGER ROAD via 1.800.957.6476.

Pastor Larry Thompson of *First Baptist Church* of downtown Fort Lauderdale, for being a wonderful man and pastor, and for also causing DANGER ROAD to be sold and promoted at First Baptist's "Family Books & Music," its popular downtown bookstore; additional special thanks to *John* and *Shari Jones,* Music Ministers and worship leaders at First Baptist, for their friendship, encouragement and support during this project, and to *Marion Williams,* Manager of *Family Books & Music.*

Pastor Derrick Gillis of *Zoe-Life,* for extending his pulpit to me on Father's Day and allowing me the coveted privilege of sharing the gospel message of redemption and forgiveness with his church, and for also organizing and providing for a very special DANGER ROAD book signing event.

Reverend Dave Blood and *Pastor Bob Sands,* for allowing me the special honor and privilege of sharing the Gospel from their respective pulpits at *New Hope Christian Fellowship* in Port Charlotte, Florida and *Community Bible Church* (Formerly Griffin Road Baptist Church) in Dania Beach, Florida.

Bob D'Andrea and *Stephanie O'Neal* of *Christian Television Network* (CTN) and its nationally-renowned show, "The Good Life with Bob D'Andrea," for our sweet-spirited, nationally-televised interview and for Bob's tremendous, inspirational and public endorsement of DANGER ROAD!

Dede Hayes, Director of Programming at nationally-acclaimed *Cornerstone TeleVision,* for our wonderful and awesome live interview — and her very public endorsement of the book on "Focus Four," Cornerstone's internationally-televised show. I want to express the same gratitude to founder and President of Cornerstone, *Norma Bixler,* one of the sweetest women I have ever met. Her televised prayer — "in Jesus' name," that "DANGER ROAD will be a movie," was yet another huge encouragement.

Laurie Quinn, Janice Valvona, Mimi Hiller, Kristin Egan and host *Joe Watkins* of *Trinity Broadcasting Network* (TBN), for inviting me on several occasions to be a guest on "Praise the Lord," TBN's internationally-televised show and also on locally-televised "Joy in Our Town."

Dr. Ed Aqua of *Nova Southeastern University,* for his generosity in inviting me to speak to the undergraduate students, law school students and faculty at Nova Southeastern University and its prestigious law school.

David P. Schloss, acclaimed author, advisor and friend, for his inspiration, advice and timely intercession in this project. Dave wrote the best-selling book, *If at First You Don't Succeed, Buy This Book,* and he personifies the precepts he shares.

Kathy Clevenger and *Calvary Chapel Bookstore,* for including DANGER ROAD among the books for sale in their wonderful bookstore.

Randy Jordan and *Maribel* at the *Family Christian Bookstore,* for promoting my very first book signing — and for also being the very first store to stock DANGER ROAD for sale.

Lorna Owens, International Speaker, Life Coach and founder of "Women Behind Bars," for inviting me to appear as her guest on "The Lorna Owens Show" on WMBM 1490 AM and for encouraging me to persist in my continued efforts to get DANGER ROAD into the hands of imprisoned inmates all across this nation. Lorna is a life coach, to be sure, and a very good woman, one of His!

Vince Forzano, South Florida boxing official, children's book author and close friend of Gil Fernandez, Jr., for his help and genuine willingness to be transparent, and for allowing us to include his personal photographs in this book.

The Broward County Clerk's Office, for the use of their archived microfilm trial transcripts, which formed the basis of the narrative and dialogue in this book.

And I can never forget the unwavering support, encouragement and friendship from the following people who went out of their way to read and then publicly recommend DANGER ROAD: Magistrate Judges *Debbie McCloskey* and *Mindy Brown;* Chief of Homicide *Brian Cavanagh;* trial lawyers *Howard Finkelstein, Alan Schreiber, H. Dohn Williams, Bob Stone, James Facciolo, Reed Tolber, Chuck Prince, Willie Tucker, Jeffrey Levy, Larry Spark;* forensic psychologist *Dr. Michael Brannon;* and also *Dr. Ed Aqua, Kerry Avila, Minister Gerry James, Anita Mitchell, Stephanie O'Neal, Janice M. Valvano, Nikki Waller* and *Richard R. Blake.*

I would like to also publicly state my sincere appreciation and gratitude to the following business owners who demonstrated a real generosity of spirit in displaying and selling DANGER ROAD from their restaurants and businesses:

Joey Esposito and *Sally Rembisz,* of the ever-popular "Cafe Seville" in Fort Lauderdale; *Tony Cupelli,* of "Cafe Europa," one of our city's favorite eateries on Las Olas Boulevard in Fort Lauderdale; *Robert Garcia,* owner of the upscale "Salon Elegant" in Davie, Florida; *Susie Komolsane* and her son *Eddie,* of popular "Sukhothai" restaurant (best thai food in Broward County!) in the Gateway Plaza in Fort Lauderdale; *John* and *Michel,* of "Tarantella" Italian restaurant in Weston's Town Center; *George Pashalis, Dimitri Maras* and *Michael,* of the renowned and always favorite "84 Diner" in Davie, Florida; and as for courthouse eateries: *Su,* owner of "Jimmy's;" *Johnny,* of "Courtside Cafe;" and *Daniel Carver* and *Brian Saraceno* of Gangster Subs; opposite the Broward County Courthouse in downtown Fort Lauderdale.

Dedication

This book is dedicated to my father, the world's best
'Pop,' for being such an incredible example to emulate, a man of integrity
and truth who personifies decency, work ethic and love of family.

This book is also dedicated to the awesome women in my life.

My grandmother, Mary Power Leahy (who is no relation to crime victim
Walter Leahy discussed in this book), personified her maiden surname in
every respect. She was an author, poet and adventure-lover who inspired
the rest of us to write. Mary had boundless energy and integrity, on a par
with my other grandmother, Victoria Santilli Contini. Victoria was as loving
and kind as she was hardworking and tough. All the men in our family —
my father and I, my son Johnny and my brothers, Don and Anthony — owe
whatever determination and work ethic we have to the phenomenal example
provided by these two dynamic women.

This book also is a tribute to the rest of the wonderful women in my life: my
always encouraging, affectionate and heaven-sent mother, Noreen Patricia
Leahy; my beautiful, sweet-spirited and supportive wife and life partner,
Elizabeth; my saintly and silly sister Kathleen; my precious and adorable
daughters, Kathleen and Mary; and my father's devoted wife, Marta.

Starbucks "Blend"

"Danger Road: A true crime story of murder and redemption," is a special 'blend' with Starbucks coffee — actually Starbucks Coffee Company, insofar as the book was written at Starbucks! To be exact, the T Mobile Hotspot at five different Starbucks stores in Broward allowed me to go wireless on my laptop and write the book whenever I had the right moments or thoughts in whatever part of the county I happened to be at that time. Starbucks was my "third place," as it's affectionately referred to within the company — away from home and the office, proving that anybody can write a book and get away for a cup of coffee at the same time! I will always believe that everyone has a book in them; it's finding the time to write it that's the challenge. *Artie Dohler*, the District Manager of Starbucks, and the following Starbucks store Managers were especially hospitable and inviting, even to the point of extending me the privilege of having some very special and fun book readings and booksignings once DANGER ROAD was published. These wonderful people are now my friends: *Shawn Sturm*, at the Broward and Federal store, *Jeff Neer*, at the Weston Town Center store, and *Vionette Torres*, at the store across from The Galleria.

Table of Contents

Chapter 1

Brain Cells

April Fools Day 1983 I was in a bar on Fort Lauderdale beach getting half drunk and hustling some nameless girl. Poor thing, she was as lost as I was — only neither of us knew it.

"Can I have another beer?" I asked the bartender.

"I don't know, can you?" the smiling bartender replied facetiously.

Sporting a Hawaiian shirt and a tan, this wannabe comic behind the bar looked like one of the Beach Boys. He provided the perfect visual to blend in with the fragrance of suntan lotion and the sound of the Jimmy Buffet song cranking away in the background. *Wasting away again in Margaritaville...*

He put another bottle of light beer in front of me and asked, "So, do you live here?"

Not sure if he was asking if I lived in Fort Lauderdale or if he was being sarcastic about my recent nightly appearances in the bar, I chose to answer the more straightforward question.

"I just moved down here to stay with my father. I'm waiting for the bar exam results," I said while raising my eyebrows to signal my uncertainty about whether I would ever be a lawyer.

"You keep killing those brain cells and you'll have nothing left by the time they make you an attorney," he quipped, laughing good-naturedly.

"You gonna be a *lawyer*?" asked my potential score on the next barstool, sitting up a little straighter.

"Oh, *now* you're interested," I responded, teasing her. I leaned in a little closer to her, figuring I had nothing to lose. There was that smell again, only this time the sun tan oil was mixed with cheap perfume and Pine-Sol.

Just then, the outside lights went off as the lights in the bar blazed on. Under that kind of wattage, I could see my barstool-mate was no belle of the ball. But she did a double take, too. I didn't exactly look like anyone's Romeo after a hard day of drinking at the beach.

In that bright light, the streaked bar mirror revealed that my hairless baby face looked tired, and my brown hair was sand-matted and sticking up all over the place. And as if that weren't enough to attract the lonely young woman, my tanned face had white rings in the shape of my cheap sunglasses. They made the perfect frame for my tired, bloodshot eyes. I was just the kind of guy you'd want to take home to mom.

"Last dance, last chance for romance," crooned the DJ, as the bar-back did his cleaning thing, with the Pine-Sol, all around us. "You don't have to go home, but you can't stay here," the DJ sang. Aside from the weight-challenged co-ed in the Ohio State T-shirt and the old guy flashing her his Rolex knock-off, everyone else in the bar emptied onto the sandy and slippery wooden dance floor.

"Can my future ex-wife and I have one more for the road?" I slurred, figuring I needed it now more than ever.

"Oh, great," she complained playfully, "we haven't even started yet and I'm *already* your ex?"

———————

Little did I know that while we were flirting and drinking, three men were being murdered in Miami. I also was clueless that seven years later I would be retained to defend the ex-cop accused of being their cold-blooded killer.

The jury was out on whether I had killed too many brain cells that night. With any luck, I had at least a few left. That bartender was right; I was going to need them.

Chapter 2

Birth and Death

It was now July 4, 1990, three days after my first child, a beautiful little girl named Kathleen, was born. I couldn't have been more proud. I felt like I was the first man ever to become a father. I must have made 50 calls from the pay phone in the lobby of Baptist Hospital in Miami, just before running almost as many laps around the hospital.

When I came back to the room after making the calls, Elizabeth asked me, "Where did you go? When I woke up, you were gone."

"I went for a run after I beat up the payphone downstairs. I called everyone we know to brag about you and the baby!" I said.

"Why didn't you just use the phone in here?"

"I didn't want to wake you, honey."

Elizabeth smiled lovingly at me before gazing down again at the baby. Anyone could see from the look in her big brown eyes that she was overjoyed at having this beautiful baby girl. Baby Kathleen had slight Asian features, clearly favoring her mother. Half-Japanese and half-Irish, Elizabeth was pretty, petite and looked a little like a young Amerasian Sally Field. When we added in *my* half-Italian, half-Irish heritage, I figured we'd have to feed Kathleen baby food made of meatballs, sushi, and corned beef and cabbage.

Elizabeth ordinarily had boundless energy. We knew she was going to need every bit of it when we took the baby home. But that didn't matter now; the image of mommy and daughter together in those first days was the very personification of serenity. As for me, I could barely keep still. Not known for my self-control, I abruptly said, "I'll be right back!" as I bolted out of the room.

"Where are you going now?" Elizabeth called after me as I practically ran through the door.

"I want to get today's newspaper so we can show it to Kathleen when she grows up…" I said, my voice trailing as I jogged the hall toward the elevator.

When I picked up a copy of *The Miami Herald* in the lobby, my eyes went immediately to a photo of a scary-looking, bearded, longhaired guy named Gil Fernandez, Jr. The piercing eyes and chiseled, menacing face depicted in the large front-page photo were enough to make me look away. Above and below the fold on the front page were smaller photos of 11 dead people. The images of them while they were still alive were arranged in a circle around the photo of Fernandez, their alleged killer. Some of these people looked pretty rough, too. Being a former prosecutor, I was a bit desensitized to violence. This kind of thing typically wouldn't have bothered me. But in this case, I was hoping to save the paper for posterity, a commemorative keepsake of sorts. All I could think was that this thug had desecrated baby Kathleen's paper with all his carnage.

"So much for the presumption of innocence," I said under my breath, chastising myself. I knew I should think a little more like the defense attorney I was but I didn't care. I didn't like that this guy had ruined my newspaper.

When I got back to the room, I slapped the front page of the paper with the back of my hand and complained to Elizabeth, "Look at this idiot's mug on the front page. The article says he's an ex-cop and mob enforcer, and that he killed 11 people. Look how he ruined our baby's newspaper!"

As I said this, I had no idea that only a few days later I'd meet Gil Fernandez face to face.

Money, money, money

Kathleen had been born via cesarean section. How could she know we didn't have health insurance and couldn't afford an operation? The $14,000 surgery was about $14,000 more than we had in the bank. I'd been self-employed for less than four years and was clueless about where my next check would come from. I've always said there's a fine line between self-employment and unemployment. If I didn't get a case or a check that week, I figured I was pretty much unemployed.

Financially, I had a major gun to my head. Elizabeth was now going to be a stay-at-home mom who would be preoccupied with nursing and diaper changing, among other things. She was the quintessential new mom, even insisting on using a service that would deliver clean cloth diapers to the apartment every few days. Disposable diapers weren't good enough to grace the soft and supple skin of our precious little Kathleenchan.

My financial pressure cooker also was boiling over with the added responsibility of providing for Elizabeth's dependent mother. Yoshikosan, a sweet little Japanese woman, had lived with us from the moment we got married. We had to have a slightly bigger place to accommodate her, which meant there was always a bigger nut for which I was responsible. And now with Kathleen's arrival, the challenge was especially acute. I would continue to be the sole breadwinner, only now the need for winning bread was greater than ever.

"How am I going to provide for everyone when there's nothing coming in the door some weeks?" I worried aloud to Elizabeth in a weak moment.

"Now who's the idiot, John?" I thought. "Your wife is laid up with stitches in a hospital bed after just giving birth to your baby girl and you're making her worry about money. God should just zap you right here from on high and get it over with."

Elizabeth interrupted my self-deprecating thoughts and said sweetly, "God's not going to bless us with this baby and then stop providing for us."

She was right. At least I hoped she was. But I couldn't help from thinking it was all on me. Whenever I heard sayings like "let go and let God," it sounded *way* too convenient. That always seemed like some sort of an excuse for not busting my hump to look for the next case. Elizabeth could tell by my blank stare that I was still worried. "We've always been fine, haven't we? Please quit worrying, OK?" she said, holding my hand.

"You're right, sweetheart," I said, knowing it was my job to pretend everything was cool and convince her my fears were only fleeting. "Maybe it was that newspaper and all the murders and negativity. But I'm going to forget about all that. I'm psyched now, I really am. You should have heard me on the phone. I couldn't stop running my gums, waking up everyone to tell them about Kathleen." I did a good job of convincing her. But in the back of my mind, I wasn't convinced myself.

When we left the hospital that afternoon, I was the caricature of a new father, doing my Cecil B. DeMille thing: I walked backwards, videotaping mommy and baby as a nurse wheeled Elizabeth out of the hospital in the mandatory wheelchair. Elizabeth, radiating like never before, sat holding our baby girl. Both were wearing matching flowery Laura Ashley dresses we bought in preparation for this day. We also had a matching outfit for a baby boy, since we didn't know the gender in advance. The camera was rolling right along with the wheelchair, capturing priceless footage that hasn't been viewed since.

As we drove home, my grinding fear about how to pay for all this had reached fever pitch. It was Independence Day but I felt anything *but* independent. Miraculously, just a few minutes after we got home, I received a call from the father of the scary guy in the newspaper. Apparently, Gil Fernandez had become a born-again Christian sometime after the killings and wanted me to represent him because of what he thought was our shared faith.

"God must have a great sense of humor," I thought.

The family

Gil's dad, Gil Sr., called me after being recommended by friends from my church. He asked me if I would meet with him, his wife Emma and Gil's wife Marianela. My investigator Cary Kultau accompanied me to the parents' home where we camped out for most of the evening.

Mr. and Mrs. Fernandez had a small and simple home that was neatly kept and warmly decorated. One of the first things I saw when I came into the living room was a picture of a handsome-looking Gil Jr. as a teenager. The bright smile on his face only enhanced his chiseled, Latin good looks. Gil Sr. had the same ruggedly handsome features as his son, only he was about half the size. Emma Fernandez was as pretty as her husband was handsome. She smiled sweetly at me as she invited me to sit on their comfortable couch.

Gil's wife, Marianela or "Neli," as everyone called her, was pregnant with Gil's second child. She was pretty and had long, curly black hair draped over her tall, athletic frame. She looked like a dead ringer for Cher — the Cher *after* the nose job. And she was even prettier than the singer when she smiled. Neli graciously served us iced tea as her six-year-old son Gillie played in the other room. The entire family struck me as being especially polite and respectful. I was having a hard time imagining that the guy in the *Herald* photo had anything to do with them. "There must be a mistake. That guy couldn't have come from this family," I thought as Mr. Fernandez interrupted me.

"We heard you were a Christian, Mr. Contini. That's what we want for Gil, a Christian lawyer," said the patriarch. "Gil had another very good lawyer, Mr. Howes. He's won some big cases, too. But being a good lawyer isn't enough, not to my son. This other guy, he's not a Christian, at least as far as we can tell."

Mr. Fernandez explained that Howes was the veteran defense lawyer who had been representing Gil throughout the lengthy investigative phase that lasted up until his arrest. Gil knew that law enforcement had been targeting him as the chief suspect in at least eight homicides, so he retained counsel to advocate for his interests and run interference if the police crowded him too much.

But Howes just might not have been the right choice in this case, as he had earned a reputation for representing South Florida mob figures. Or at least that's what the Fernandez family thought. Gil's family felt that sticking with John Howes would send the wrong message. Their concern was that John's formidable presence would only fuel the public perception that Gil Fernandez was in fact an enforcer for the local mob.

Coming to Howes' defense while distracting the family from the issue of needing a Christian attorney, I said, "Even though having a Christian lawyer is nice, it's not good enough if the lawyer doesn't know how to handle murder cases like this. Your son needs someone who also knows what he's doing in criminal defense, someone who has tried these types of cases all the way to verdict and achieved acquittals in first-degree murder cases. I've done that, as you'll see from my brochure here…"

"Mr. Contini, we know all about your reputation in the courtroom. We know about that I-95 murder case."

I didn't have to finish my spiel. The Fernandez family had already learned from friends that I had recently won a first-degree murder acquittal in the I-95 shooting case of accused killer, Humberto Gallo.

"We checked you out on all that, Mr. Contini. Your winning other murder cases and knowing how to handle this kind of case is good, of course, but it's actually more important to us that you be a man of faith like my son.

"And you are, *right*?" he persisted.

There it was, the subject I preferred to avoid. These people wanted a Christian lawyer above all and here I was, selling my secular wares.

"God's going to zap me, I just know it," I said to myself.

"Yes, of course," I lied; knowing that phoning in my faith from a pew on Sundays wasn't going to cut it with these people. Seeking to cover myself, I quickly added, "I'm always humbled by men like you and your son, who put God first before everything else. I wish I could say I always do that. I guess I use the excuse that my line of work is pretty stressful and it's easy to forget."

"Why don't you just tell him you have your doubts about the whole born-again thing? John, be straight with these people!" I screamed inside my head. "Because you're worshipping the six-figure fee and the press coverage you're expecting. That's why, you phony," I continued to myself, feeling like the poster child for the imposter syndrome.

"We understand, Mr. Contini," said Neli, Gil's very sweet wife. "It happens to all of us, especially at stressful times like these." She then poured me another glass of iced tea, reassuring me with her kind, accepting eyes. Neli had a real sensitivity and a sweet spirit. To me, she seemed rather saintly.

The Apollo

Apparently, I did a good job convincing the Fernandez family about my faith because I got the job. Now it was time to get down to business. I kicked things off by saying, "I know Gil owned the Apollo Gym. What can you tell me about it?"

I had learned from the July 4 article that Gil had become the owner of the Apollo Gym just a few months before his arrest. This haven for hard-core, steroid-shooting bodybuilders was located in a strip shopping center near the Seminole Indian Reservation, north of Hollywood, Florida. Unfortunately for Gil, the article also mentioned that police alleged it to be the home of a ring of bodybuilder mob enforcers.

Gil Sr. said, "I wasn't surprised when Gil bought the gym. The police gym used to be his second home when he was on the force. He even competed in the 1978 Police Olympics." Mr. Fernandez beamed as his wife brought coffee to Cary and me. Then his mood changed quickly and he said with a combination of sadness and anger, "But the police say a lot of bad stuff goes on there."

I could tell from the look on Neli's face that she wanted to protect her father-in-law from as much of this as she could. She waited a beat before she changed the subject. As she looked over at Gil Sr., she asked tentatively, "Mr. Contini?"

When she received a nod of approval from Mr. Fernandez, she said, "I think you need to know this: We knew for months that Gil was going to be arrested. If he were going to run or be a flight risk, as I think you called it, he would have done it already."

"How did you know he'd be arrested?" I asked. "The answer to that might be helpful at the bond hearing."

"Two pastors from our church — Pastor Dwight Evans and Youth Pastor Harry Keith — told us he was going to be arrested. Detectives from the Broward Sheriff's Office came to see them. The detective's names are Kallman and Damiano. They asked a lot of questions, wanting to know if my husband confessed things in church. The detectives told the pastors my husband was going to be arrested. So, he had plenty of chance to run if he wanted to."

"Will the pastors testify to this at a bond hearing?" I asked, quite curious. My concern was that they wouldn't, given that they could be charged with obstruction of justice if they admitted to giving Gil a heads-up that he was going to be arrested. I thought they might have been specifically asked by the Broward Sheriff's Office, or BSO, as everyone called it, to refrain from saying anything to Fernandez to tip him off.

"You would have to ask them, Mr. Contini..." Neli said.

"Mrs. Fernandez, please call me John. OK?"

"Yes, I'd like that" she responded. "And please, call me Neli."

The oldest trick in the book

Before I could say anything else, Neli, who was anxious to tell her story, said, "We were home on the morning he was arrested; it was July 3. The phone rang at six o'clock and the person hung up when Gil answered. My husband said that's the oldest trick in the book. He told me the police always call to make sure the person is at home before coming to arrest him. I think that's why Gil left the house right after he got the call. He didn't want little Gillie and me to see the police take him away…"

Gil's father finished the story, as Neli was visibly upset. Emma comforted her with a hug, while I leaned in closer to focus on what the father was saying. "My son told me that Pat Diaz, a homicide detective, used to work with Gil when he was with Metro-Dade. He's the one who took my son into custody. And he was all business, like he didn't even know Gil."

"What did Gil tell you about their conversation?" I asked, as Cary carefully took down every word.

"He just said things like, 'Gil, the game's up. You're looking at three murders,' or something like that." Then Mr. Fernandez thought of something else. He reached for a copy of *The Miami Herald* that was on the coffee table. Pulling his reading glasses from his shirt pocket, he focused in on the front page, running his finger over the words, trying to find something.

"Wait a minute, it's not in this article. Yeah, now I remember, Gil told me this himself. He said he told this Diaz guy that the only thing he ever wanted to be was a good cop. Gil got mad at Diaz and said, 'I never took a dime from anyone while on the police force. The only thing I was guilty of is doing my job. Those people you work with drove me out of police work. I hope they're happy now.'"

Gil Sr. threw the newspaper on the coffee table and sighed. I could tell his mind was racing and he was having a hard time focusing. His eyes wandered for just a second during a moment of introspection, and then he pointed to the paper and said, "There are so many bad things being said about Gil in the paper. I don't believe any of it."

"All this has to be very hard on you and your family, Mr. Fernandez. I can promise you we'll find out what's going on here. OK?"

"I know you will. But everyone has already seen the things printed in the newspaper." Not able to let the subject go, he picked up the paper again and searched for a specific paragraph. He pushed his glasses up on the bridge of his nose, pointed and continued, "I don't know if I like this part. The guy wrote that Gil calmed down and got a peace about him."

"But I don't understand. That's a *good* thing," I said, interrupting him.

"Yeah, *that's* good, but wait. Then they say he told this Diaz character, 'I'm in God's hands. He'll forgive me for everything I have done.'"

"I don't like that part about 'He'll forgive me for everything I have done.' That doesn't sound good. Emma and Neli agree with me. They're making it seem like he was talking about these murders."

As he spoke, I noticed his eyes were becoming red-rimmed. I tried to distract him, so he could stay composed in front of his wife and daughter-in-law. "I can tell you're proud of your son," I said, diverting his attention. "You remind me of my dad, except you're Latin and he's Italian. He's strong like you. My dad always said I should be a lawyer because I talked myself out of a lot of jams growing up. He always said, 'they're either gonna make you president or they're gonna hang you.'"

Gil's father was laughing now. Little Gillie sat in his mother's lap, hugging her and focusing his big, brown eyes on his grandpa. Emma and Neli were smiling now, too, allowing me to continue the diversion. "Suffice it to say, I'd get in trouble from time to time. Nothing too big, though. Otherwise, they'd have never hired me as a prosecutor back in '83. There's enough to make the presidential thing a real stretch, though. But don't worry; I haven't done anything worth hanging. Not yet, anyway," I teased.

"I ain't worried," he said, smiling. "Just get my son out of this mess, will you?"

Ink

As I drove home reflecting on how nice these people were, my thoughts turned quite selfishly to myself. This big-money case would cause my financial life to change and solve a lot of my problems. I knew everyone who read a newspaper or watched TV in South Florida would know about the case because it already was an overnight hit on the evening television news. And then there was that infamous July 4 article trumpeting the ex-cop, born-again Christian who allegedly killed a bunch of people. That article also mentioned that Gil was a Mr. Florida bodybuilding champion and an organized-crime enforcer. I knew these sensationalized aspects of the case would be printed ad nauseum in the daily papers, giving everyone plenty to talk about around the water cooler at work. Frankly, this appealed to me, too, as my ego was jonesing for its next fix. I knew I was only as good as my last case; or more accurately, as good as the *press coverage* of my last case. Even though the Gallo case was big, the headlines of the acquittal were doing nothing for me now. I had to admit, I was getting addicted to the ink. Now that I had another big case, my passion for justice wasn't driving me at all, not even down the block. It was all about me. Suddenly, the front cover of Kathleen's newspaper didn't bother me at all.

I met the Fernandez family again the next day, only this time on my turf. My office was located on the 15th floor of the 110 Tower, across the street from the Broward County courthouse. My official digs were located just above my favorite satellite office: the sidewalk coffee shop.

I showed deference to Gil's father by letting him have my burgundy tufted-leather desk chair. He liked that. As the family patriarch, I knew he would appreciate the gesture of respect. Neli told me he had felt disrespected by Gil's former counsel, John Howes, who had a tendency to interrupt him. There was no way I was going to make the same mistake. Howes and I were more alike than we were dissimilar in that regard, though. Right or wrong, it also was my style to control the conversations with a client's family. But not this time, not after what I had heard.

I wanted to visit with Gil at the jail that morning, but visitations were disallowed due to an unrelated security lockdown. It would have been nice to give the Fernandez family a good report about how he was doing but now that would have to wait. When I told them Gil's new home in the jail could be viewed from my 15th-floor office window, Gil Sr., Emma and Neli just stared down at it for a long moment. Then silently they held hands, put their heads together and whispered a prayer.

After they finished, we spent several hours going over every little nuance they could tell me about the allegations against Gil. I prodded them for any information they might have forgotten the day before. Then Gil Sr. sat in the big swivel chair at my desk and signed the retainer agreement. He also provided me with a significant down stroke, most of which went straight to Baptist Hospital to pay off Elizabeth's operation.

Chapter 3

Operation Muscle

Before I met Gil in the jail, I wanted to get a more objective look at the Fernandez case. Although his family was helpful, they were anything but objective. The jail lockdown actually helped me because it gave me time before I met with Gil to meet with Billy Venturi, the investigator hired by John Howes. Venturi was a tall, bearded swashbuckling private investigator who had achieved the rank of homicide investigator by the time he retired from the Metro-Dade Police. He seemed perfect for this Metro-Dade triple-murder case, except that his fees were enormous.

One thousand dollars of my initial fee went to Venturi in exchange for just a few hours of his time and complete copies of his files. At that rate, I'd have gone back to the poor house if he stayed on the case. But his files were important. They were extensive and therefore extremely helpful in providing the backdrop for why BSO thought they had their guy.

My new investigator Cary Kultau also was a veteran detective, and was formerly with the Pompano Beach Police Department. Cary and I soon discovered that the Apollo Gym was once a hangout for police officers who liked to pump iron. Over time, however, the gym picked up a more sinister reputation. It also was rumored to be a front for drug deals, extortion and small-time gambling operations.

Hubert "Bert" Christie, a bodybuilder 20 years Gil's senior, owned the gym on and off over the years. It didn't take long after Gil met Bert for the senior bodybuilder to become Gil's mentor. Gil saw Bert as a father figure in the netherworld of bodybuilding. Some say Bert introduced Gil to the steroids that helped him achieve the massive 275-pound body he had when he was arrested.

According to police reports we obtained, Bert also had a reputation for consorting with organized crime figures. He was alleged to be the boss of a ring of violent bodybuilders who collected from loan sharking and gambling deadbeats. Supposedly, the ring eventually branched out into a new business. Police reports stated that ring members shot up the homes of drug dealers and then tried to sell them protection. Detectives said these bodybuilder enforcers also deceived smugglers into phony buys, stole their cocaine and threatened them with machine guns if they complained.

Supposedly, Christie's ties to organized crime ran deep. He was suspected of carrying out three contract killings for the Mafia between 1980 and 1982. This information came from a federally protected witness who told police he worked for the Colombo crime family. Christie also had a reputation as a debt collector for Joseph "Joey Flowers" Rotunno, a supposed Colombo crime family associate who allegedly ran a gambling ring from Al's Florist, his flower shop in Hollywood.

According to law enforcement, Christie hired the muscle for his collections business directly from the gym. Police say Christie first signed up Gil and then recruited Tommy Felts, a bodybuilding champion and hot-tempered cocaine dealer from Hollywood. Felts drove a flashy red Porsche, which made him conspicuous around town. He also had a catchy nickname: He was known as "No Fingers" due to the loss of a few fingers in an accident.

No Fingers, who was murdered in 1985, had been a fixture at the Apollo Gym and was reputed to have participated in the crimes for which Gil was just arrested. Police obviously couldn't arrest a dead man, but they *could* arrest Bert Christie, whom they believed masterminded the murders. By all accounts, the case against Christie was razor thin. But it didn't stop his indictment.

Rumors and innuendo

From our research, we could see that law enforcement had been slowly, quietly building a case against Gil and Bert for the 1983 murder of three people. By 1987, word got around the police community that Gil was a suspect in these multiple murders. As a reference to the fact that Gil, Bert Christie and Tommy Felts were all connected to the Apollo Gym, the police called the investigation "Operation Muscle."

The pressure on Gil mounted as local newspapers quoted law enforcement personnel saying damaging things about him. Gil's former work buddy and arresting officer, Miami-Dade homicide detective Pat Diaz, was quoted in the South Florida *Sun-Sentinel* newspaper, saying, "I would classify him as one of the most dangerous individuals we've had to deal with."

Eventually, Gil's reputation became so bad that Hollywood Police Chief Richard Witt told his officers to find another gym. Gil was so angry when he found out; he called Witt and asked why he ordered the officers to stop working out there.

"Because you have a bad reputation," was Witt's blunt reply.

Cops weren't the only ones who steered clear of the gym. In 1987, defensive end John Bosa wanted to keep his 265-pound body in shape while waiting to sign a $225,000 contract to play with the Miami Dolphins. Bosa shopped around Broward County for a serious bodybuilding gym and decided on the Apollo. Dolphin team management, including Coach Don

Shula, found out about it and warned the 23-year-old to stay away from the gym. Bosa followed their orders and never went back.

Bosa wasn't the gym's only brush with a famous person. On one of its walls was a picture of Reve Walsh, the wife of John Walsh, who later became the host of *America's Most Wanted*. Reve placed third in the 1981 Mrs. Florida body sculpting competition and had formerly been a fixture at the Apollo. Her husband sometimes accompanied her during her workouts.

Reve never returned to the gym after the disappearance of her son in 1981 and the subsequent discovery of his head in a South Florida canal. Although the sensationalized, nationally covered Walsh case had nothing to do with the allegations against Gil and Bert, it was ironic that a photo of the wife of one of the country's foremost crime hunters hung in the same place where so much illegal activity was alleged to have originated.

Relentless pursuit

Eventually, the allegations swirling around Gil were enough to unnerve him. Especially when BSO detectives Joe Damiano and Sergeant Tom Carney confronted him at another gym where he taught aerobics. One of the police reports detailed the conversation in which Gil gave the detectives a piece of his mind: "I don't like what I'm hearing from my friends," Fernandez said angrily. "How could you tell people I'm responsible for these murders? Why weren't you men enough to come and see me in person when this first happened? Do you think I would be speaking to you if I did these crimes? Look at me. I drive a '76 piece of junk. I'm an aerobics instructor and have bills coming out my a**."

"Why don't you come down to the station and talk with us then, Gil? Give us a statement and clear this whole thing up," replied Sergeant Carney. "Here's my card and phone number. You going to call?"

"Yeah, I'll call you next week and we'll sit down," Gil responded.

Damiano looked surprised. But Carney wasn't. He knew Gil wouldn't call.

Damiano and Carney were convinced of his guilt, and the investigation reached fever pitch as Damiano and fellow detective Mike Kallman teamed up to openly approach anyone who ever had dealings with Gil. They asked gym members what they knew about Gil and how they knew him, along with a lot of other questions that made the target of their investigation obvious.

The detectives also asked everyone they questioned whether they knew Walter "Wally" Leahy, Jr., age 25; Richard "Dickie" Robertson, age 26; and Alfred "Al" Tringali, age 31, who were the murder victims named in the current indictment. The inquiries, however, didn't stop at the door of this indictment. The detectives also did everything they could to elicit details about the murders of at least eight other victims — men and women they suspected were dead because they had crossed the paths of Gil Fernandez and Bert Christie.

Carney, Damiano and Kallman, who by now were hip-deep in the investigation, originally came to the case after being hand-picked to work for the sheriff's pet project: the BSO Organized Crime Division, known as OCD. Although seven years had elapsed since the murders, the sheriff directed Carney, Damiano, Kallman and a host of other detectives to do everything they could to indict and arrest Fernandez and Christie. In spite of this aggressive pursuit, the list of murder victims kept growing at an unprecedented pace. With each new victim, the level of frustration felt by this elite group of law enforcement guys increased. That frustration was only exacerbated by the fact that some of the victims had been eliminated right after detectives came around asking questions about them.

That would have been enough to turn even the most well-intentioned, veteran detective into a rogue and anything-goes Robocop overnight. They could hardly keep up with these new unsolved homicides and the unrelenting pressure it created within the BSO. Since the detectives and the sheriff were convinced that Gil Fernandez was the common denominator in this homicidal quagmire, they weren't about to stop until he was indicted. Obviously, they weren't impressed with the "Free Gil Fernandez" T-shirts sold at the gym to raise funds for the Gil Fernandez defense fund. And they certainly didn't buy any.

Miami's meanest cop

According to police and the press, this black-belt karate instructor, kick-boxer, and former Mr. Florida and Mr. Gold Coast bodybuilding champion was more than qualified to be a skilled murderer. Unfortunately, he also looked every bit the part of a hit man and mob enforcer. He stood over six feet and weighed 275 pounds, a virtual wall of solid muscle. In case anyone doubted his dominance, he had the boastful words "Incredible Hulk" tattooed on his left upper arm.

Mitch Palermo, a young BSO jail guard who coincidentally worked out at the Apollo Gym, also could vouch that Gil had an attitude. "The first time I saw a bodybuilding contest, Gil was competing," Palermo said. "I thought Gil was a jerk, because he wouldn't get off the stage when he lost. But then I looked at someone like that and saw how gutsy he was, and being a kid, I actually looked up to him."

And Palermo wasn't the only one who admired him. Gil had a high opinion of himself, too. According to Palermo, "Gil would show off to us in the gym. He'd flex in the mirror. He'd look at himself and smile, saying, 'It's good to be God.'"

Adding fuel to this fire of infamy, Gil also was a notorious former Metro-Dade police officer and firearms expert. A 1979 article from the now-defunct *Miami News* called him "Miami's meanest cop." The title was well deserved, according to most who knew him.

It was alleged that Gil actually bragged to his friends about forcing handcuffed detainees to eat cigarette butts that had been left in the cruiser ashtray by cops on previous shifts. One of his friends even told us that Gil occasionally forced prisoners to do unspeakable things to each other at gunpoint. These stories were repeated among all his friends, apparently for their comic value.

By Gil's own admission, he was intolerant of criminals and had a mean streak in those days. He admitted to sitting on the hood of a moving police vehicle during the 1980 McDuffie riots in Miami as he threw gasoline grenades at people in the crowd. He also acknowledged that if someone ran from him on the job, he got a beating when Gil caught up to him.

Several complaints were on file with Internal Affairs because he beat people after handcuffing them. A high school student alleged that Gil "charged and cursed at him" for jaywalking. Not surprisingly, personnel reports described him as having "an aggressive personality." Sergeant Chester Butler wrote, "Officer Fernandez is without a doubt the most aggressive officer on his squad."

Eventually, the brutality complaints caught up with Gil. He was taken off the street and moved to the complaint desk. Later, he was relegated to working the property room. Both of these positions were considered bottom-of-the-barrel assignments for a cop.

Law enforcement also had gathered evidence of Gil's steroid use. In fact, this is the only crime Gil ever admitted committing while being an officer. We obtained a police report in which Gil was quoted, saying, "The only thing I was guilty of doing when I was a cop was steroids. When you're in a bodybuilding competition, the judges want you to be freaks and have incredible bodies. In order to win, you had to use steroids."

Most observers wouldn't have had difficulty guessing this from looking at his Herculean physique at the time of his championship bodybuilding victories. Steroids are known to cause aggressive and violent behavior, and Gil's behavior was no exception to that rule. As just one example of this, two people said they saw Gil knock the teeth out of the winner of the 1983 Mr. Florida contest.

Had Gil combined cocaine with those steroids, it would have been a powerful mix. One and one don't equal two when simultaneously ingesting narcotics; there was the potential for them to equal 10. The potential for disaster — perhaps even murder — could be increased exponentially with the ingestion of these synergistic drugs.

Another perspective

It seemed like everything we read or heard about Fernandez from police or the media was negative. Of course, his family said nice things about him, but that was to be expected. Seeking another perspective on this guy, I called Vince Forzano, a friend of Gil's that Neli recommended. I was going to see Gil that afternoon and I wanted to squeeze in the visit with Vince first. "It would be great if he had anything to say that would actually help the defense," I thought as I dialed the phone. Vince answered and said he had some time in about an hour, so I arranged to meet him at the coffee shop below my office. When I got downstairs, I saw Vince drinking a tall glass of iced tea at a table on the sidewalk. After exchanging the usual pleasantries, I got right to the point.

"What can you tell me about Gil or the case?" I asked him.

"I love him. That's the most important thing. I want you to know the *real* Gil. You can't believe everything the papers are printing," Forzano replied.

"OK," I responded, disappointed that he didn't have some smoking gun to help with the facts of the case. He went into a narrative and it was immediately obvious that he loved Gil like a brother. I just let him go as I ordered my usual from the waitress: a big cup of black coffee.

"I remember the first day I met Gil at Tracy's Karate Studio. He was 19 years old and around 225 pounds. He was tall and powerful. It was obvious that he was an athlete. He signed up for karate because he wanted the discipline that comes from the martial arts. He noticed me one day when I was cleaning the studio and asked what I was doing. I told him I was working in exchange for lessons. I'll never forget what he said: 'You'll appreciate them more if you earn each lesson through hard work.'

"You OK about me telling you all this?" he asked politely.

"Sure, go ahead," I said, not realizing how much longer he'd go on.

"Each day after that I saw Gil working diligently on his techniques in the studio. He never tired of his practice. He would often encourage me to train with him. Within a short period, he became a big brother to me, the best friend I had ever had.

"I was small and in my teens. I only weighed 145 pounds, so bullies in the karate studio often confronted me. But Gil protected me. He eventually trained me until I won tournament after tournament. He was winning, too, so the front of the karate studio was soon filled with our trophies. Eventually we both became full-contact karate fighters. Gil was always there to cheer me on. He never let me down or disappointed me when I needed him. He always encouraged me to be the best at what I did, no matter what I chose to do."

"I'm glad you're telling me all this Vince, because you're right, the newspapers would probably never print that nice stuff. It doesn't sell newspapers."

"Oh, and let me tell you this," he said quickly, noticing I was looking at my watch. "Gil's family and mine were one and the same. My mother and father loved him like a son. My parents felt he was a good role model for me and never questioned when I was with him. When my father needed help around the house and I would complain about doing it, Gil would *make* me do it. And then he would help me. He said that working around the house was a good way to pay my parents back for the sacrifices they made for me. He helped me paint my house one day and made me laugh the whole time we did it."

"Thanks for telling me all this, Vince…" I said, not knowing he wasn't done.

"When Gil's son was born, that was one of the greatest days of Gil's life. To watch him play with little Gillie brought tears to my eyes. He never once yelled at him and always took him wherever he went. I asked him why he would take an infant to a movie and he said, 'because time with my baby is so precious and I don't want to miss a minute of it.' Gillie never cried at the movie or anywhere else, as I remember. He just loved being with his dad."

In a way, I wished this guy Forzano wasn't telling me all this good stuff about my new client. I was about to meet Gil for the first time in the jail. The last thing I needed was more pressure on me. I was hoping that all this thinking about what a good daddy he was and all that other great stuff wouldn't affect me or make me feel too much for the guy. Maybe that's why Forzano wanted to talk to me, to get me hooked emotionally. If that was his motive, it was working.

"Thanks again, Vince for…" I said before he interrupted me.

"Then in 1980, I left Florida to train in classical dance at the New York Conservatory. I had gone to the top of my game in karate and found that ballet lessons would help me become a better fighter. I fell in love with ballet and gave my best effort to learn this beautiful art form. I thought for sure that Gil would laugh at me but once again he encouraged me to do it."

"I've got to go see Gil, Vince," I said while getting up. I had already finished my coffee.

"Just let me tell you about the last time I saw him and I'll be done, really. I was in New York for two years. When I got back, Gil welcomed me home. While I was gone, Gil became involved with bodybuilding. When I saw him again, he resembled Michelangelo's *David*, as his first wife Pam used to say. The transformation was amazing. He had developed every muscle in his body to perfection. He was now winning bodybuilding tournaments and making a name for himself in a new profession."

"I've got to go see Gil in the jail now, Vince. I *have* to go; I really do. Otherwise, I'll run into the shift change and won't be able to see him for a couple more hours. But if it's OK with you, I'd like to tell him about our meeting and about all the nice things you've said about him, OK?"

"Yes, please tell him I love him and I'm praying for him, OK?"

"I promise I will. Gil is blessed to have a friend like you."

"I'm the one who's blessed, John, just to call him my friend. He's more than a friend — he's my brother."

Chapter 4

Armed and Dangerous

I met the notorious Gil Fernandez for the first time at the main jail in downtown Fort Lauderdale. Since Vince had just finished singing his praises, I was primed to meet an altogether different guy than the killer in the newspapers. Plus, his family had already humanized him quite a bit in my mind. If he was anything like his family, I knew I'd like him.

The jail was built after I left my job as a prosecutor in the State Attorney's Office in 1986. The same developer that built the Marriott at Harbor Beach built the Broward County jail — for a mere $47 million. But there were a lot less amenities than at the Marriott. From the beginning, there were complaints about it being noisy and cold. I could attest to both. The pervasive cold cut like a knife and damn near froze everything you touched, despite whatever sunshine managed to sneak through the thin-stripe windows that lined the jail's facade. The windows also doubled as a tortured reminder to inmates of just how much they were missing.

Escape from this jail was made nearly impossible because the windows were only six inches wide and several feet long. John Fogelman, a convicted rapist, was the only person who ever tried to escape by way of one of these windows. This sickie was alleged to have been released from an earlier rape sentence, only to get out and rape the same woman again. When he was returned to the jail, he managed to starve himself, allowing his body to become so emaciated that he was able to contort it through one of the vertical openings. But as justice would have it, a knot in his tied-together bed sheets had come undone and he plummeted to his richly deserved death. No one had to worry about Gil escaping by one of these windows. He would have been lucky to get just one arm through.

To get into the jail, I had to go through the usual variety of elaborate security checks and procedures. As I waited, I set a gift for Gil on the counter of the guard's desk. Neli had told me that at the time he was arrested, "The Hulk," as Gil was nicknamed, had a maroon leather briefcase in his car that contained his Bible, his last will and testament and a letter he wrote about his conversion to Christianity. These items were confiscated by the police, which left Gil without a Bible. From what I had heard about him, I knew it would be important for him to have one. So, I bought a nice one and wrote a personal message in it.

I scribbled answers to the almost illegible questions typed by BSO on several 10th-generation photocopies of forms that visiting attorneys were obligated to complete. When I was through, I grabbed my accordion file and the Bible, and stepped back from the desk.

"Sir, you can't bring that in."

"Why not?" I asked the jail deputy. "It's just a Bible."

"It's got a hard cover. Hard-covered books can't be brought into the jail. Besides, the chaplain gives 'em Bibles if they ask for 'em."

"But I want to give him *this* Bible because I wrote some stuff in it for him."

"I'm sorry, but I can't let you do that. If I let you, I gotta let everyone," the deputy said, apologetically.

"Even though you can search through all the pages and see that…"

"Look, I ain't losing my job over this," he replied, starting to get irritated.

"I understand." I made a mental note to bring Gil a soft-cover version as soon as I could.

Harry Houdini get-up

Gil was brought out of his cell and placed in a small, drab room with an interior glass window that faced the deputies. I was then led down a long hall illuminated by fluorescent lights. As we walked, a succession of doors were locked and unlocked by a variety of guards.

Finally, I was allowed to join Gil in the room. I couldn't help but notice that he moved slowly, deliberately and with grace as he walked into the room. He was nothing like the scary looking guy I had seen and read about in the Herald and heard about from others. On the contrary, he smiled and looked as if he could be anyone's polite and gentle big brother. The personnel who transported him actually seemed to be more deferential to Gil than to the other inmates. They treated him with a kind of respect I hadn't seen before between guards and a prisoner.

Gil managed to walk with fluidity, even though he had shackles constricting him. His feet were bound with just enough slack in the metal chains to allow for short steps, and his hands were cuffed behind him. Separate chains linked the handcuffs and waist chains with the leg shackles. Chains also extended down the back of his legs from his waist area and made a clinking sound when he walked. Despite this Harry Houdini get-up, Gil still moved like a stallion. He was built like an Arnold Schwarzenegger and yet he moved with the grace of a Mikhail Baryshnikov. And if *that* were not enough to make someone stop and stare, he was also blessed with those ruggedly handsome and chiseled Latin features. There was no disputing that he was an incredible sight.

Although from all appearances Gil seemed to be quite gentle, it was easy to surmise why he was shackled. The jail officials understandably were concerned that it would take more than a few deputies to restrain him if he were ever to attempt an escape. Not that he actually had attempted to escape or been aggressive in any way. They just weren't taking any chances.

When he was safely in the meeting room with me, however, the guard disconnected the handcuffs from the shackles at his waist so he could put his hands in front of him. He was still wearing cuffs, but they were loose enough so that he could move his hands somewhat freely.

"You must be my lawyer, Mr. Contini," Gil said with a smile, as he reached out and shook my hand.

"That's me, my friend."

"My wife and parents said you were tall," he said. "They were right about that. They also said you knew what you were doing. Let's see if they're right about that, too."

"There's the challenge," I thought to myself.

If he were any other inmate or potential client, I might've answered him differently. But with this guy, I simply said, "I know enough to be dangerous. But don't you worry; I plan to be dangerous to the prosecution, not to your cause." It was my turn to smile.

"You'll soon learn that they say *I* was armed and dangerous," he responded. "Whether that used to be true or not, I *am* armed and dangerous now. I'm armed with the word of God and dangerous to the devil."

"Cool, I like that," I said, stroking his ego.

"It's *very* cool. Come over here," he said as he sat down at the table and motioned toward the seat across from him. "Let's pray."

As I sat down, he grabbed my hands and gently pulled me partway across the table so I could be closer to him. Then he lowered his head and began to pray. He held my hands tightly and occasionally pulled me even closer as his voice passionately rose and fell. Eventually, I couldn't get any closer. My mind wandered for a moment as we sat locked together in prayer: "If he's guilty, I'm holding hands with a killer. I wonder what else these hands have done." But those negative thoughts soon went south. Gil's style of praying was so compelling; there was little room for thoughts of anything else. I had never experienced anything like this passionate prayer that must have lasted for 15 minutes. It was a powerful experience — at least for Gil.

While we prayed together, I found myself peeking to see if any of my colleagues in the jail were watching. It was hard to focus on exactly what he was saying to "Father God," as he kept calling Him, because I was too embarrassed and preoccupied with what others were thinking of me. I had only been a Christian for a short while, and unless I was in church on Sunday morning, I was a closet Christian at best.

It was a relief when he finally finished and we could move onto less spiritual — and less embarrassing — matters. By contrast, the discussion of his case was predictably guarded. We both knew he had no shot at a bond. A client almost never does in a murder-one case. Of course, there'd be *no* chance of a bail bond in a case like this with multiple murders and a ton of television and print reporters sniffing around.

After reading the *Herald* article, I knew the arrest had to be a big scene. I wanted to hear Gil's account of it. Not only because it might affect the case but because I knew it would be an interesting story.

"What was the arrest like?" I asked.

"Someone from BSO called and hung up early in the morning on the third. That's an old cop move; they wanted to make sure I was there. I told my wife, 'this is it, baby,' and left the house. I didn't want my family to see what was about to happen, so I got in my car and just started driving.

"As I drove, a helicopter hovered over me. Then a bunch of BSO and Metro-Dade squad cars pulled up behind and all around me. Lights were flashing like crazy, like we were in some kind of parade. I got out of the car and saw the SWAT team, the Organized Crime Division guys, dogs and the whole enchilada. When I stepped out, there were shotguns and machine guns in my face. You would have thought they were arresting John Dillinger. I didn't resist; I just dropped to my knees and surrendered peacefully."

"Wow," was all I could say.

We then talked about using the otherwise unfruitful bond hearing to get some early discovery out of the prosecutors. This conversation was boring compared to the image of Gil's arrest that was still sitting vividly in the forefront of my mind. When we got the case details out of the way, we got down to what Gil really wanted to talk about: his conversion to Christianity. He couldn't wait to tell me just how much he had changed when he became a born-again Christian on August 13, 1989, 11 months before his arrest. "The cops hounding me didn't drive me to Jesus," he said with obvious enthusiasm. "It was that hound of heaven, the Holy Spirit, dogging me relentlessly until I surrendered. Praise God!" he almost shouted.

He then talked lovingly about his pregnant wife Neli and his six-year-old boy, Gillie. He also mentioned his second child, who was going to be born sometime in November. He looked sad as he told me that Neli had told Gillie that his father had taken on a new ministry, working with prison inmates. "He believes his daddy is ministering to people in jail," Gil said to me sadly. And from all accounts he was — although not because it was his choice to be there.

Seeing he needed to be cheered up, I said quickly, "Before I forget, I want to tell you that your friend, Vince Forzano, met with me earlier and said a lot of nice things about you."

"Vince, he's good people. But if you believe what he says about me, you're more gullible than I thought," he joked.

"Seriously, that guy loves you. He wanted me to tell you that. He also wanted me to tell you that he's praying for you."

"Good, I'm gonna need it," Gil said, laughing.

Every crime but murder and pornography
Then we got serious again. He went on to tell me how law enforcement had even been dogging him in church. He said they had him under surveillance as he broke bricks with his bare hands during martial-arts demonstrations for various church youth groups. "After performing these demonstrations to get the attention of the kids, I shared my testimony," he said proudly. But his testimony wasn't of the legal variety; rather, it detailed how his life had been changed by his newfound faith.

"You need to know that more than once I said from the pulpit that I acted like a rabid dog toward people. I also said my previous life of sin was totally horrible and that I used to violently go through people. I'm sure BSO will find a way to use that against me.

"Six weeks ago, I told a youth group at the Miramar Church of God that I had been involved in every crime but murder and pornography. The reason I said it was to let those people know — especially the kids — that God will forgive anything," he said sadly. "But you know the cops don't care about that. They don't believe I've changed. I wouldn't have either when I was a cop. They just want to see me fry."

BSO had tapes of this pulpit testimony, so I made a note to file motions to exclude the tapes from evidence. It would be incredibly damaging to have audio recordings of a defendant publicly admitting to how violent he was in the past.

As Gil and I spoke about the old days — the days before his beliefs and behavior changed — he had to make an effort to hold back some very genuine emotion. Seeing tears in the eyes of a mammoth bodybuilder like this was an incongruous sight, to say the least.

"I'm sorry we have to talk about this, Gil," I said, trying to comfort him.

"No, I understand," he replied. "You gotta do what you gotta do."

It was hard for me to tell whether his tears were caused by sadness for the victims of his "rabid dog" behavior, or if he was just experiencing quite understandable grief over the possibility of being separated forever from his parents, and his wife and young children.

Chapter 5

The Bond Hearing

Gil's bond hearing was held at 8:30 A.M. sharp in room 970 of the Broward County Courthouse and was presided over by Judge Robert W. Tyson, Jr. The hearing for Bert Christie, who was charged with masterminding the three murders, was held separately.

The courtroom was an unremarkable-looking, square-shaped, drab room. The only thing distinguishing it from any other courtroom in the building was the contingent of TV news cameras, reporters and still photographers on the perimeter of the room.

Though a defendant facing first-degree murder charges is not entitled to bail as a matter of right, he does have the right to request an Arthur hearing, pursuant to *State v. Arthur*, a Florida Supreme Court decision. After this evidentiary hearing, bond may be denied if, as the ruling dictates, "proof of the defendant's guilt is evident or the presumption is great."

But Tyson wasn't about to put Gil back out on the street — not with all those TV cameras rolling. There were too many public allegations that Gil was a dirty cop with organized crime connections. Not to mention that almost a dozen dead bodies were at least peripherally connected to the defendants. Under these circumstances, it didn't even matter if Gil was guilty. The *appearance* of guilt was enough to compel Tyson to rule against the bond.

We wanted the hearing, however, to force the prosecution to cough up all kinds of discovery. This was evidence they'd only get around to releasing much later if we didn't force them to do so now. This heads-up on the expected trial testimony and evidence was needed to mount the best possible defense.

The spitfire

The prosecutor assigned to argue the bond hearing was Cora Cisneros, who was one of the assistant statewide prosecutors from the Office of Statewide Prosecution. Cora was a spitfire Latina who couldn't have been more than five feet tall. She didn't like me very much and didn't seem to have a problem if I knew it. The problem was, she was confident, intelligent, assertive and even attractive. Under any other circumstances, the old John would have thought about hitting on her. But the John I was *trying* to be had to settle for hating her.

Days before the bond hearing, she sent a letter threatening me with Florida Bar sanctions for alleged violations of the cannons of ethics. The letter condemned my critical comments in the press about the state's star witness, Michael Carbone. She was right; I wasn't shy about telling the media that this five-time felon who claimed to have been present at the murders had sold his testimony for immunity. The fact that this federally protected guest of the witness protection program was willing to "flip" on Gil to save his own hide made anything he had to say highly suspect to me.

Outside the courtroom just before the hearing was scheduled to begin, Cora accused me yet again. "You violated Florida Bar rules by your comments in the newspapers. We'll be seeking an order from the judge…"

"You seek whatever you want to seek," I said, getting too close to her. She seemed shocked by my aggression, leaning back a bit as she saw the contempt in my face.

"You go ahead and do that, little woman, while I inform the Bar and the judge how you're telling all the witnesses not to speak to the defense."

"Don't you call me little…"

"I'll call you anything I want, since you're about a millisecond away from felony charges yourself. You know damn well if *I* had done what *you* did, I'd be indicted for obstruction of justice or witness tampering. You tell one more witness not to talk to me and I'll drag your sorry little a** before Tyson and the Bar and then we'll see who's sucking wind then."

Pretending to ignore my last remarks, she stomped off into the courtroom as if she were running to tell daddy on me. If she didn't hate me before, she sure did now.

It was true that I had been beating the drum in the newspapers and on TV, ridiculing Carbone and the fact that he was an immunized felon. My comments were disparaging, to say the least, suggesting that the state had purchased his testimony and that he'd sell out his own mother to escape the electric chair. Carbone gave compelling evidence to the police that he had been present at the murders. This was proof enough to me that he would do anything to get out of this triple murder beef.

The ethics rules of the Florida Bar *do* proscribe a trial attorney from disseminating public comment about a prospective witness if he intends to affect the outcome of the trial. To my way of thinking, though, an attorney wouldn't be doing his job if he weren't willing to risk a weekend or two in jail on a contempt beef to keep a client out of the electric chair. The Florida Bar would take exception to that position, I'm sure, but that was my position nonetheless.

Cora was already effectively conducting her own media relations campaign. In an effort to deputize the public into signing on as junior G-men, she publicly asked every John Q. Citizen to come forward with new evidence in the case. She not only trumpeted that my client was essentially guilty, she was scaring the daylights out of the good people of South Florida with her histrionic and non-stop references to multiple murders.

It was then that I decided to go with the old adage, "all's fair in love and war." Two could play that game, I reasoned. So, I began to use the press to my advantage, too. I wasn't about to stand there like a good little lawyer embracing the Florida Bar rules while she poisoned the entire potential jury pool.

The buzz

Days before the hearing began, the entire courthouse was abuzz with stories of the drama that was about to occur in Tyson's courtroom. Almost everyone who worked in the building was acutely aware of the sensationalized triple-murder trial, and they were working every kind of angle to get in the room so they could watch the drama unfold live, up-close and personal.

Those jockeying for position on the benches included other prosecutors and public defenders, clerks and secretaries, police officers and court deputies, a few judges and their assistants, and curious private citizens. The competition was hot for seats on the limited number of benches behind those that held the media representatives and the victims' families. Had the court authorized the sale of tickets, someone would have cleaned up.

The victims' families sat grouped together on the benches nearest the jury, which was a real problem. The hate directed at me from that section was penetrating. The families certainly had a right to their inconsolable grief and venomous anger, but Gil and I were their logical targets and that didn't make my job any easier.

Walter Leahy's sister's hateful stares in particular were unrelenting. She never smiled at anyone, which was understandable under the circumstances. Her pain and rage obviously ran deep. Although I couldn't show it, I really felt for her.

Luana Tringali, the sister of victim Al Tringali, also was there with her family. The shiny dark hair that curled around her pretty face made her actually look quite stunning, though I doubt she felt that way while waiting for the start of the proceedings. I could see and even feel her pain and anger from across the room.

According to police reports, Luana, who once worked for the FBI and later became a paralegal in the county attorney's office, joined the Apollo Gym after the murders to see if she could find out who killed her brother. In a macabre twist of fate, Gil Fernandez became her personal trainer. At that time, she had no idea that Gil was alleged to have been involved with the death of her brother. A gym member said he saw Luana angrily slamming locker doors at the Apollo Gym on the day she learned that Gil was a suspect. And who could blame her.

Adding insult to injury, Luana was later deceived by the state's star witness, Michael Carbone, who claimed to be at the murder site. She met him at the Apollo and dated him, not knowing that he was with her brother at the very moment of his death.

Don Knotts, a small Basset hound and Herman Munster

Just before the bond hearing began, Gil was led into the courtroom, shackles and all. He smiled warmly at me as the bailiffs cuffed him to the arm of one of the chairs in the empty jury box. The bailiff let me know I could join him, so I walked over and shook his hand for the first of our many photo ops. Then he lowered his head and began to pray.

Gil was once again passionately and unflinchingly displaying his faith. I cringed because all I could do was think about the eyes in the courtroom that must have been trained on us. In spite of my embarrassment, I bowed my head along with him and even said a short, whispered prayer. I also said a silent prayer that I wouldn't be so embarrassed by this outward demonstration of faith. But I *was* embarrassed. What made it even worse was my belief that Gil was 100 percent sincere. I felt like such a fraud.

After what seemed like an eternity with our heads bowed, the door from Judge Tyson's chambers opened and he entered the courtroom.

"All rise," said Mike Ruvolo.

Mike was the court deputy, which is the official name for a bailiff. Mike spoke loudly so he could be heard over the undulating wave of noise that rose and fell from the spectators, which accompanied the sound of audience pews creaking and chairs scraping the floor as everyone in the courtroom stood.

"The Honorable Robert W. Tyson, Jr.," continued Mike, as Judge Tyson entered from his chambers.

To me, Tyson looked like an odd three-way mutation of Don Knotts, a small Basset hound and Herman Munster after a night of heavy drinking. I'm sure he looked a lot better to other people, but I had to see him as ugly to better prepare myself for how I suspected he would rule. He was known throughout the courthouse as a prosecution-oriented judge and I knew this zebra wasn't going to change his stripes now.

With a grumpy look, he sat down behind the bench and called the bond hearing to order. "Counsel, are we ready to begin?"

"Yes, Your Honor," we all said in unison.

"Good. Bring in your first witness."

My first order of business during the bond hearing was to elicit the testimony of Pastor Dominic Avello of the Cornerstone Christian Fellowship, and Pastors Dwight Allen and Harry Keith of the Miramar Church of God. These men had all seen Gil's transformation up-close and even figured prominently in the process.

"Pastor Avello," I asked, "Are you convinced, as a pastor and man of God, that Gil's public profession of faith is genuine?"

"I have no reason not to," Pastor Avello replied. "Gil has been attending Cornerstone Christian faithfully for almost a year. He's been very active with our youth group. He often shares his testimony and encourages others."

The courtroom was quiet, except for the rapid clicking sounds made by cameras capturing tomorrow's wannabe newspaper photos. Legions of still photographers were doing their sniper-like, telephoto-shooting thing, while the TV folks were contorting themselves every-which-way to maneuver their oversized shoulder cameras.

"Pastor Avello, did Gil ever get emotional in front of you, or otherwise communicate some sort of sincerity about his faith?"

"More than once," the pastor replied. "Gil is an incredibly charismatic speaker and he appears, by all accounts, to be sincere in his walk with the Lord."

"Can you tell this court about any emotion surrounding Gil's conversion?

I knew most people probably suspected Gil was faking his faith. There had been plenty of prisoners who "found Jesus" at the eleventh hour in jail and left him on the steps on their way out of the courthouse. I felt it was important that everyone know this type of conversion of convenience had nothing to do with Gil and that his professed faith was real, at least as far as I could see.

"Gil's emotion was very real. He appeared to have the degree of brokenness needed to turn his life over to Jesus."

"Did his family join him there at Cornerstone?" I asked, hoping to paint a warm and inviting visual for the not-so-benevolent dictator on the bench.

"Yes, his wife, Marianela, and their little boy, Gillie, joined them at an altar call last summer. They've been faithfully attending and worshipping with us ever since."

Pastor Dominic, as Neli called him, glanced at her in the second row of the spectator gallery. Her eyes moist, she smiled back, mouthing the words "thank you." Emma and Gil Sr. held hands as they leaned against Neli, keeping their own constant vigil throughout the proceeding.

"You mentioned an altar call, Pastor. What is that, in case that's an unfamiliar term to some?"

"We invite those in attendance at the conclusion of the worship service to come forward and publicly profess their faith in Christ."

"Is this what Gil did last summer?" I asked.

"Yes, I believe it was in August. He came forward, along with his wife and little boy. I'll never forget, actually, because Gil was on crutches and all three of them were lying prostrate on the altar, crying. We laid hands on them and prayed with them. It was a very special time."

Neli was emotional now and was being comforted by a hug from Emma. She looked over at Gil and tried to smile. Gil gave her a strong thumbs-up and smiled back. His emotional strength at that moment equaled his physical strength, or else he'd have lost it, too.

Pastors Dwight Allen and Harry Keith of the Miramar Church of God testified next. They backed up Pastor Avello's assertion that Gil had become a Christian before his arrest. They both stated that as far as they could see, he had truly changed. Gil would not let me elicit the pastors' testimony that BSO had informed them months earlier of the fact that he would be arrested for murder. This would have proven the point that he wasn't a flight risk, but Gil declined to use that chip. He was too concerned for the pastors, believing that BSO might entertain the thought of arresting them for obstruction of justice.

Toward the end of the three-and-one-half-hour hearing, I placed Gil on the stand. The courtroom fell silent.

"How are you doing?" I asked.

"All right, praise the Lord," he said.

"Gil, you were aware for over a year that law enforcement had targeted you as their number one suspect, right?"

"Yes, I was."

"But you never ran from the area when you had plenty of opportunity; isn't that right?"

"I'm not running from this," he said adamantly.

"Can you assure Judge Tyson that you will be present for any and all court proceedings, if he allows you to have a bond in this case?"

"I'm not guilty," Gil said as he kept his eyes on Neli. "Hey, they've been trying to get me for years. They ruined my reputation so I couldn't get a job anywhere. I dug ditches for months — and I have a college education!" he said. "But I never ran. I want to be vindicated."

Gil paused for a moment and then said quietly, "Let's get this over with."

Ordinarily, an attorney would never put the defendant on the stand during a bond hearing because it would expose him to potentially damaging cross-examination. I saw no danger, however, in allowing Gil to testify. I knew it would reinforce what the pastors had said about his strong ties to the community. And besides, Cora would never be able to hurt him on cross. Gil was too smart — and as an ex-cop, too experienced — to give up any information the other side could use.

But Gil's testimony and the pastors' passionate endorsements did nothing to penetrate Cora's resolve. She asked Gil in a sneering tone, "So you found God, Mr. Fernandez?"

Within a millisecond he replied, "No ma'am. He was always out there. He found me."

"Good one, Gil," I thought.

Fortunately, Gil's response cut short Cora's attempt to make fun of his faith. I'm sure she would have loved to score points on that remark in front of the TV cameras, but it didn't work. That didn't stop her from continually trying, however, to work the media to her advantage. Especially if it meant she could potentially embarrass me in front of the cameras. In one of her attempts to do so, she complained to Judge Tyson, "Mr. Contini doesn't stand up when he objects."

Shamefully, I retorted by mocking her diminutive stature, responding, "Your Honor, I just wanted to be eye level with the prosecutor."

The laughter in the courtroom was immediate and explosive. Cora blushed and shot me a nasty look. She was acutely aware that the TV cameras were recording the interchange. I could see in her eyes that the embarrassment this caused her made her hate me even more.

As the hearing droned on, I got down to the business of doing my best to persuade Tyson to release Gil. I reinforced Gil's testimony by repeatedly echoing that he never fled — even though he knew he was being targeted for eventual arrest by BSO in connection with the murders. Just as he wasn't a flight risk then, he wasn't a flight risk now. Of course, that argument would have been even stronger if Gil had allowed me to disclose that the Miramar pastors told him of BSO's intent to arrest him for the murders. But Gil wasn't willing to trade the pastors' safety for his own, so I backed off.

After Gil was done testifying, I made my final statement.

"Your Honor, the prosecutors can present no physical or forensic evidence whatsoever, and they have no other competent witnesses to back up their unsubstantiated allegations. If the prosecution had *anything* else, this case would have been made seven years ago!"

Tyson was expressionless as I spoke, despite the passion in my voice. After a pause, he decreed that Gil would be held without bond. Neli and Gil's parents appeared visibly defeated, even though I had prepared them for this moment. I told them several times that Tyson wasn't going to grant us a bond. But I suppose they deluded themselves into believing that the facts and the law would actually carry some weight in this case.

As the bailiffs escorted Gil in shackles out of the courtroom, the TV camera operators shifted into high gear and followed him. The still photographers also went nuts once again, clicking away like a zillion crickets after dark. Gil comforted his family as he moved through the low, swinging doors along the railing that separated the trial participants from the crowd. He was all smiles and twice mouthed the words, "I love you," first to Neli and then to his parents.

Then he said, "Praise God." I struggled with that one. But I was far from discouraged. The prosecution's case was nothing but a bag of excrement, in my opinion. It was my job to do whatever I could to eventually make everyone else share my opinion.

I wasn't done fighting yet — not by a long shot.

Chapter 6

*Speedy Trial, My A***

As soon as Tyson denied bond, I filed a slew of pretrial motions on Gil's behalf. We knew in advance Tyson wouldn't grant most of them, but the CYA thing had to be done. And besides, it was a death case, which meant I'd better file everything but the kitchen sink. The gang of prosecutors, however, acted as if I had filed all the motions just to torture them. That wasn't beyond me, but that wasn't the case this time. This time, a man's life was at stake. I'd have been a moron not to file them.

Denise Hughes, Tyson's judicial assistant, called me a few days later. She gave us a court date for a hearing on the first of many of these other motions. The first available date was two weeks away. "How much time are you going to need, John?" Denise asked.

"Does he have anything else that day?" I facetiously replied, implying I would need a lot of time.

"Come on John, we still have to go to lunch and we want to get out of there by five. You know we still have our regular docket, so try not to be long-winded. OK?"

"Ouch! Denise, when have I ever been long-winded?" I teased. "Don't answer that! Seriously, we'll need most of the afternoon, for sure."

"He can only give you an hour that day, unless you want me to delay it a couple more weeks," she replied.

"No, we'll take what we can get for now. Thanks, Denise." The show was set to start again two weeks later, though the commercial break in between was anything but a reprieve. The press wouldn't let the fire die down, not even for a day. They even invented a few new ways to fan the flames.

Coffee and vitamins

"Have another cup of coffee," Elizabeth suggested.

My wife and I hadn't slept much since baby Kathleen was born. As new parents, we got up with every sound she made, picking her up and rocking her back and forth like we were rides at a carnival. But we eventually smelled the coffee. A crying fit was just that — a crying fit. We learned to just change the diaper, do the milk thing, sing the song, kiss her little head and love her a bit, and then go back to bed. Crying would be good for the baby's lungs, right? Besides, she would want us to hold her all day, every day, if we gave in every time she cried. It was her job to test us. My wife finally taught me how to say enough's enough.

Truth be told, Elizabeth did most of the comforting, though I liked the singing and kissing part. After all, the milk thing was Elizabeth's territory. She was the one nursing the baby at all hours. But as I told her once, "that wasn't my fault; it was God's." I expected a laugh. After a night of trying to get Kathleen to calm down, however, she wasn't much in the mood for my comic relief.

"It'll take more than an extra cup of coffee to wake up today," I replied. "I've got to argue a bunch of motions in front of Tyson today on Gil's case."

"Then here, take these vitamins, too."

I wished it were as simple as a few vitamins and a little more coffee. "Let's give *him* some pills. Maybe *then* he'll rule my way." I muttered.

She was too tired to laugh. "God bless her, she's been putting up with this case since right after Kathleen was born," I thought. And I wasn't making our downtime any easier, either. All she wanted was a nice weekend away on Captiva Island. A few shade trees, a cute little cottage with its own kitchen and AC in the rooms, a large umbrella for shade on the beach, a picnic lunch and her favorite magazines. But then she screwed it all up by inviting me.

"Honey, I was thinking about this wallpaper…" she said, showing me a sample in a magazine, "…and maybe a chair rail. We could paint Kathleen's room pink, to blend with this border, the one in the picture here." Elizabeth tried to get my attention on that beach the weekend before the motions, but I didn't respond.

"What did you say, sweetheart?" I asked, feigning interest.

"Forget it. Which motion were you just arguing?" she perceptively asked. "Give yourself a break, John. We're on the beach for you to relax. So, 'be here now,' as you're always saying."

She was right but what she was asking me to do was apparently impossible. I'd try to divorce myself from the case, but like a six-headed monster rearing one of its ugly heads again, the thoughts would resurrect and I'd be off to the races for more self-inflicted torture.

Not emotional, just upset

Finally, Monday rolled around and Elizabeth was spared of my company. But I wasn't. Wherever I went, there I was.

"Mr. Contini, you've filed numerous motions here," Judge Tyson said. I could have sworn he then asked, "Which one would you like me to deny first?" My vivid imagination substituted the word "deny" for "hear," because I suspected these two words often meant the same thing to prosecution-biased Oliver Wendell Tyson — at least in this case.

Despite the predictability of his otherwise imminent rulings, I argued every one of the motions like I had a chance of winning it. And arguing the motions helped to wake me up, so at least they served some purpose.

I almost succeeded in getting the case dismissed at this pretrial phase, based on the premise that Gil's right to a speedy trial had been violated. Under Florida's rules of criminal procedure, a defendant can file a demand for speedy trial and force the court to begin his trial within 60 days. He also had the separate right to be tried within 175 days of his arrest, unless he asked for a continuance or otherwise waived it.

But this wasn't Disney World. Tyson's response was quite predictable: "Denied."

Neli and Gil's parents were more prepared for reality this time. They weren't emotional, just upset. They knew the cameras, reporters and victims' families had a lot to do with determining the outcome of these motions. That didn't make their reality check any less painful, however, as they just gathered themselves for the long ride home.

Gil made them feel a little better when he gave them another "I love you," along with a confident smile. But that acting gig had to have been wearing on him. He praised God again as he shuffled his shackled feet alongside the bailiffs through the door exiting courtroom 970. His strength was enormous — and I don't mean his strength as a power-lifting bodybuilder.

Not to be deterred by common sense or political correctness, I immediately appealed Tyson's curious denial of our "Speedy Trial Motion for Discharge" by filing a "Petition for a Writ of Prohibition" with the Fourth District Court of Appeal in Palm Beach County. The mere filing of this petition essentially silenced Judge Tyson. It temporarily stripped him of any jurisdiction over the case and prevented him from commencing with the trial.

The appellate court had stopped the train, albeit temporarily, announcing it wanted to examine whether the right to a speedy trial had been violated. As part of its review, the Court of Appeal ordered Judge Tyson to "show cause" why the case should not be tossed out. The press went wild trumpeting this new development, causing the prosecutors and the public to fear that this sensationalized triple murder case might actually be dismissed. I'm sure it did nothing to further endear me to Judge Tyson.

After the state's response, the Fourth District Court of Appeal shut us down. Now I knew how Tyson felt. When the next guaranteed milestone for a speedy trial came and went at 175 days, I filed yet another writ of prohibition with the same Court of Appeal — netting the same results.

"Speedy trial, my a**," I thought to myself, as I flirted with the idea of tearing that page out of my Florida Rules of Criminal Procedure book.

Instead, I just inked a few black lines through Rule 3.191, defacing the apparently defunct speedy trial rule.

"What are you going to do now?" a reporter asked me as I stood in the hallway outside Tyson's courtroom after this second denial by the Fourth District Court of Appeal.

"The fat lady hasn't sung yet. The Florida Supreme Court is right up the road. We'll continue to appeal until we get an intellectually honest decision." As I spoke, telephoto lenses were jammed in my face as cameras clicked away. It felt like an assault, like Thompson submachine guns aimed right at me.

Almost obsessive in my relentless — and fruitless — pursuit of a dismissal, I filed yet another petition. Only this time we went further north — to the Florida Supreme Court in Tallahassee. My threats in the press would have sounded lame if they hadn't been backed up with an actual filing.

"I've finally arrived," I bragged to myself, impressed that we were "at the Supremes." But I only got to bask in the glow of that self-absorption for a few hours before Tyson summoned us back to courtroom 970. Predictably, the Florida Supreme Court wasn't about to let a notorious, accused triple-murderer get off on the technicality of a speedy trial violation. In my opinion, if an appellate judge thinks a defendant has killed people, he or she will look the other way — even on an otherwise obvious rule of law. This was evidenced by the fact that we had Tyson and the state dead-to-rights but were overruled anyway.

"So much for intellectual honesty," I moaned to Cary, as I ducked into the restroom to get away from the press.

Neli and Gil's parents were getting used to it by now, so the denials were expected. They were quite desensitized to all the pretrial madness at this point. They were looking forward to the trial and the day when they might actually get a fair shake. Each of them hugged me and thanked me for working so hard. Their hugs and kind words helped lift my spirits. Instead of focusing on themselves, as they had every right to do, they were concerned about my feelings. They had to be the sweetest family on the planet.

Myriad motions

After fighting these speedy-trial battles, I then argued a myriad of other motions. One of my greatest concerns was that BSO had the surreptitious recordings of Gil's sermons at the Miramar Church of God and the Cornerstone Christian Church. Although Gil never mentioned any specifics from the pulpit, his references to his "rabid dog" behavior and his proclivity to "go through people" could certainly be construed as admissions of violence, and perhaps even murder.

The prosecutors publicly stated their intentions to admit these tapes into evidence, forcing us to argue a motion "in limine," which is a request for an advance court order disallowing the admissibility of certain evidence. Quoting verbatim from the Florida Evidence Code, as well as Rule 403 of the Federal Rules of Evidence, I argued against the admissibility of the tapes, repeatedly citing the operative language of the rules.

"Gentlemen and madam, please state your appearances for the record," ordered Judge Tyson to the defense and prosecution lawyers. We all weighed in before the game began.

"These tapes can't come in, Judge, because as the rule states in regard to relevancy, something is not relevant and therefore not admissible, "if its probative value is substantially outweighed by its prejudicial effect.""

The prosecutors and I went back and forth about the fact that the "probative value," meaning the value the information would provide when trying to expose the truth, would be far outweighed by the way it would cause a jury to view Gil. We went for a few rounds before the bell sounded and Tyson announced he would take it under advisement and give us a ruling soon.

Nervous as a whore in church, I resorted to biting my nails like I did when I was a kid. Thankfully, Tyson grew a conscience and ruled in our favor. My ego wanted to high-five itself, but I knew the real reason we won had more to do with the fact that the violence referred to in Gil's testimonials was simply way too vague. Tyson had little choice but to concede that these "admissions" were not specific enough to refer to these murders, or even murder at all.

Although the ruling went in our favor, it could have easily gone the other way. Watching Tyson struggle over this decision was a frightening preview of events ahead. I felt like I had dodged a Peterbilt truck coming at me at 100 miles an hour, only to see a fleet of Kenworth 18-wheelers bearing down right behind it.

Chapter 7

More Victims

After the victory to keep Gil's statements in church out of evidence, it was on to other hemorrhoids. Our next major gig was to literally stop the presses to halt the daily barrage of damaging coverage. Bert Christie's lawyer, Louis "Louie" Vernell, and I made a motion for the judge to issue a limited gag order on everyone connected to the case, including the news media.

Big mistake, but who knew.

From Jump Street, Gil and Bert were represented in the media as the only suspects in a string of horrific murders — and not just those for which they were on trial. Gruesome details were never spared in news accounts. In fact, they were splashed across newspapers and TV screens so often, people were starting to think they knew the murder victims. Reporters also hammered on Bert's alleged organized crime connections, which caused a prejudicial spillover effect onto Gil. Once people thought Bert and Gil were mob guys, there went the presumption of innocence.

In a June 2, 1991 article, *The Miami Herald* printed a list of eight victims and the circumstances surrounding each of their deaths. These eight victims were *in addition* to the three victims named in our indictment. Their pictures were the ones I saw splashed across the front page on the day I became aware of the case. But that didn't stop the other news outlets from running with this supposedly "new" story, turning the people on the list into household names in South Florida.

The coverage kept coming like waves on the shore, echoing the law enforcement allegations that Gil and Bert were responsible for the murders. The media hacks were slick about it, though; I'll give them credit for that. They never blamed the guys directly, so the papers were safeguarded from liability. News accounts would simply quote verbatim from the voluminous police reports, repeating the allegations that "known associates" of Fernandez and Christie had killed some of the victims — at the defendants' behest.

Gil was never charged with any of these other murders. But he and Bert were the only ones who remained alive from the crowd of people allegedly linked to a variety of related crimes. To some, this lent credibility to the theory that the additional murders were committed out of necessity, to get rid of witnesses. According to the law enforcement agents interviewed in the article, Gil's background as a police officer would have taught him how to leave a crime scene free of fingerprints. But you didn't have to be Sherlock

Holmes to figure that out. It was Murder 101. Even bad guys know how to wear gloves to avoid leaving prints.

Police and prosecutors repeatedly asserted that Gil and Bert had the motive, means and ability to carry out these execution-style murders. These accusations were not much more than Dick Tracy-like gumshoe suppositions, but that didn't make them any less credible to the larger and more important jury: the public. Gil and Bert had to read about their alleged responsibility for all the other murders almost every day in the media.

Louie and I fought to get Tyson to muzzle the television and print media guys. Even if what they were saying were true, Gil and Bert hadn't been indicted for the additional murders, so information about them was immaterial in *this* case. We had to do whatever we could to stop the coverage, despite the otherwise coveted First Amendment's freedom of the press. We knew that lots of people believed everything they saw, heard or read. Most people — including me when I first saw the paper at Baptist hospital — too often thought that where there's smoke, there's fire.

We soon learned an unfortunate truth. When you attempt to gag the press, the media circus only gets exponentially worse. The irony of holding hearings over whether the trial judge should issue a gag order to silence the media is that the hearings themselves only engender *more* print and television coverage. When the members of the media feel threatened, they circle the wagons. Suddenly, reporters came out of the woodwork, pointing accusatory fingers at the lawyers who according to them wanted to limit the public's sacrosanct right to know. Posturing like peacocks, they strutted about as selfless protectors of the poor unsuspecting citizens who would otherwise be censored by draconian, first-amendment-hating defense lawyers.

My perception, right or wrong, was that Tyson wouldn't be concerned at all about the chilling effect that a gag order might have had on the First Amendment right to freedom of the press. Like most judges, he enjoyed the press as much as anybody else did. In real life, a gag order only meant less sensationalism, meaning less press for the judge, too. It seemed to me that he was more concerned with the media's lead lawyer, Ray Ferrero, Jr.

When the heavyweights in the press worried about getting muzzled, they spared no expense in bringing in the big guns and all the suits. Ray was the biggest gun of all; he was the perfect person to lead the pack of attorneys that each media outlet had hired. Ferrero was not only powerful in the political arena; but his booming voice, confident demeanor and six-feet-five frame made everyone pay attention.

The hearing hadn't even begun when Ferrero and I had a run-in. "Print whatever you want — as long as it comes from the witness stand," I said to

Ferrero. We were both within view and earshot of the lenses and microphones aimed at us outside the courtroom before the hearing.

"Are you telling us how to run our newspapers?" asked Ferrero, who was standing among his media brethren. He stepped toward me, spoiling for a fight. "Are we supposed to print only what *you* think we ought to print?"

As lead counsel for one of South Florida's most influential newspapers, the Chicago Tribune-owned *Sun-Sentinel*, Ferrero spoke as the advocate for a consortium of powerful attorneys. This consortium consisted of *Miami Herald* attorney Jerry Budney and a cadre of other lawyers representing four local television stations. Naturally, everyone on the media side was opposed to the gag order.

"Just imagine for a moment that the defendant is someone in *your* family, Mr. Ferrero," I implored. "And while you think about that, how about remembering the whole notion of the defendant's right to a fair trial?"

"The public has a right to know, Mr. Contini," responded Ferrero, "...and not just what *you* want them to know. But the judge will let us *all* know. So, respectfully, save your arguments for the courtroom."

Ray Ferrero knew something I didn't: Not many judges would have the courage to stand up against the media, Tyson included. Tyson was a little guy, but he seemed to get larger every time his name appeared in print. Though he was physically small, his ego was as big as mine. It's a wonder that both of us could squeeze into the same courtroom every day.

Although we had little chance of winning this media beef, I had no choice but to make an attempt. After all, Gil and I were living in the shadow of the electric chair. Try as I might to block it out of my mind, the reality of the death penalty wasn't going anywhere.

"Denied," Tyson chirped.

When the hearing for the gag order was over, I was the only one left gagging. I could no longer be deluded into thinking that a guaranteed fair trial was as important as a guaranteed free press.

Molloy and I just looked at each other, as we often did after rulings. "I wonder who has the better poker face between Doug and me," I thought, before being interrupted by Tyson's admonishments to the press. The judge was lecturing the media-consortium lawyers, telling them they should *voluntarily* stop publishing stories related to all murders for which the defendants were under investigation but not indicted. But there were no threatened sanctions included in Tyson's toothless admonishments. Asking these media vultures to make nice and limit what they cover was like asking the Arabs to quit making oil. What kind of admonishment was that? The ruling surprised no one in the Fernandez family.

"That and a dollar and change will buy you a cup of coffee, Judge," I almost smart-mouthed. Instead, I muttered under my breath, "They weren't even listening to you, Judge."

Finally, when the judge's remarks were over and he was done playing to the camera, Ferrero and company left the courtroom. I would have given big bucks to see one of Ray Ferrero's invoices after a lengthy hearing like that. And to think, each of the other media lawyers were billing around $300 bucks an hour, too.

Neli and Gil's parents left just ahead of the Ferrero group, after exchanging smiles, hugs and a few encouraging words with Gil. After they left, I took the opportunity to steal a moment with Doug. Controlling the press wasn't my only problem. Now it was time to address the use of the information that had already been printed, most of which came from police reports. The prosecution — the same guys who leaked the reports to the press, I figured — were doing everything they could to enter this highly prejudicial information into evidence.

The poisoned well

"Why in the world are you including these police reports on this other guy, "John Joseph Matera"; this "Johnnie Irish" character?" I asked Molloy.

"You insisted on *complete* discovery; you got it," Doug responded.

"But what does a 'reputed captain in the Colombo organized crime family,' have to do with us?" I asked insistently.

"Read the report." Molloy replied. "A Mafia guy who's a federally protected witness told detectives that Johnny Irish disappeared in 1980 and that Bert Christie killed him. He said Bert cut him into pieces and disposed of the body in the ocean."

"Yeah, so what's that got to do with Gil? What does it have to do with the indictment for these three murders?" I pressed.

"Bert's on trial, too, John. These reports were in Bert's file from the BSO Organized Crime Division. It might not be *admissible*, but it *is* discoverable."

"John, it's usually the other way around: you guys complain if you don't get everything. You argue you're entitled to anything discoverable — not just things that are admissible, but anything that *leads* to admissible evidence. If we didn't produce the reports, you'd be arguing that we're withholding discovery from you." Molloy was as slick as they come.

"Don't hide behind that! You're poisoning the well, Doug. You know it and I know it. It's not about you giving us all the discoverable reports we need; it's about you guys throwing in everything but the kitchen sink. You're infecting the court file with these other organized crime investigations and murder allegations," I whined. "Furthermore, I know you're doing it so the press can run with it," I said, hurling the accusation at him.

"I can't win with you. Either you get the reports and then complain that they've got nothing to do with your guy, or you don't get the reports and complain that we're withholding them from you. John, let me ask you something: Are you ever *not* getting a raw deal?"

Molloy was too damn smart to spar with for very long. We were still gathering our files and briefcases when I suddenly remembered the name Johnnie Irish. Louie had shown me the diamond pinkie ring he wore and said it once belonged to Irish. He must have thought I'd heard of the guy when he was alive. Of course, I had since learned who he was in death.

"That's great," I thought disgustedly. "If the allegations about this dead guy and Bert are even *remotely* true, and Louie's prancing around sporting the dead guy's ring... This is *not* good."

Not really done yet with Molloy, I asked him, "Are you also saying the report you gave us on George Gold, the Miami lawyer who was murdered, *also* is just discovery?"

"Same response, Mr. Contini," Molloy replied, a bit arrogant this time. He was ready to leave.

"Doug, seriously," I continued, "can you give me a second? This report speaks to a murder three years *before* the murders in our case. It says right here, 'Gold was shot in his office on June 17, 1980, in a possible case of mistaken identity. His partner allegedly was the target of the contract hit because he owed New York mobsters $1 million. A federal witness said in his statement that he helped Bert stalk Gold's partner shortly before Gold's murder.'

"Why would you include this in discovery, when it speaks to a murder that predated these murders by three years? Even the report states it was a case of mistaken identity."

Doug replied, "My answer is the same. It's obviously of more interest to Bert and his lawyer than to you and Fernandez, but it's still arguably discoverable."

"Sure. But as long as Gil's denied a separate trial, it's spilling over to us," I repeated.

"Can I go now?" Molloy asked, half-smiling as he walked toward the door.

Louie on Las Olas

This was bad. The murders that prosecutors were trying to link to Gil and Bert seemed to be almost without end, so I knew I had to go over the rest of the police reports with Louie. Discussing them also gave me an excuse to have a few glasses of wine with him at Il Giardino's, a local gin mill on Las Olas Boulevard.

"Louie, what's this police report about Caesar and Patricia Vitale? It says here that Caesar was a driver for former crime boss Joe Colombo, Sr. Listen to this: 'The couple was shot in their Plantation, Florida home on Feb. 15, 1982. The same federal witness who talked about Gold said in his statement that Bert was the triggerman in this Mafia killing.' What's up with this?"

"How do I know?" Louie quipped. "There's probably another report in there that says we know where Hoffa's buried."

He had me laughing again. Louie was good at that. He was twice my age but acted more like my little brother. The waitresses found him charming, too. They probably thought this small, funny guy was cuddly-looking as they brought him drinks and laughed at his rapid-fire jokes.

"Let's hope you can charm the jury, too," I told him as I watched him make eyes at the waitress.

"What's not to love?" he asked, smiling ear to ear.

He was convincing. And with his smiling eyes and contagious laugh, he was even loveable. I thought, "I wish we could try the case in this bar. It would be a lock."

Hung over
The next morning was a bit rough. I had stayed out late with Louie, drinking too much red wine. I had a wife and two babies in diapers. What was the matter with me?

"Do you prefer to hang out and drink with Louie Vernell?" asked Elizabeth later that night, visibly hurt.

"It's just the stress of trial, honey," I told her. "You need to understand that Louie and I have to talk about things that happened in court and plan for the next day. Please understand. OK?"

"I need to *understand*?" she asked, getting more upset. "What I understand is that from the smell of things, you drank a lot last night. I was here alone with our babies. I moved from Miami, away from all my friends. I have nobody else here. I was looking forward to you coming home and talking to me, and to having dinner together."

She was crying now. I felt like pond scum. "I'm so sorry, honey," is all I could say while I hugged her. "When this thing is over, I *promise*, we'll do a lot of things together. OK?" I couldn't blame Elizabeth for her tears. She had sacrificed a lot for our new family. But new family or not, the life and death trial was continuing. Three hours of sleep and three cups of coffee later, I was back in court, ready to fight again.

I wasn't done yet with all the police reports that constituted the prosecution's "discovery." This time I worked on Cindy, who happened to be the first prosecutor to show up. Tyson and the jurors weren't in yet, so it was an opportune moment for me to get in her face.

"Cindy, you guys are speculating big-time on Gil's involvement in the murder of David Theodore Richards. Look, even your own report here states that."

"Don't tell me; tell the judge," Cindy replied.

"Come on Cindy. Talk to me. Look, it says here, 'Richards was a financier for a drug ring run by race boat champion Ben Kramer and Indianapolis 500 driver Randy Lanier, and was shot in his Fort Lauderdale home on Aug. 3, 1984.' Then it says, 'Gil allegedly tried to extort money from Richards' friends after the killing.'

"Cindy, this report has *nothing* to do with this indictment! Why did you guys include this in our discovery, if not just to poison the well?"

"John, if it's *not* admissible, the judge will tell us," she said dismissively, turning away from me to go through a stack of papers on the table.

"It was nice talking to you, too," I said sarcastically.

Even more murders

The reports that bothered me most were the ones that dealt with the murder of Tommy Felts, Gil and Bert's alleged accomplice. One report was paraphrased in *The Miami Herald*, lending it credibility in the public's mind: "Thomas 'Tommy' Felts was a member of a ring of bodybuilders who allegedly worked as mob enforcers. He was shot in his pickup truck on Stirling Road in Hollywood, Florida on Oct. 6, 1985. Minutes earlier, he had picked up the Apollo Gym keys from Bert Christie and asked Gil Fernandez to join him for a brief workout. Felts was reputed to have been present at the murders of Walter Leahy, Dickie Robertson and Al Tringali. He told his wife and brother that he wanted to leave South Florida but he knew that he wouldn't be allowed."

The Felts murder had been trumpeted in the press as yet another crime for which Gil and Bert were responsible. In fact, prosecutors and FBI agents claimed that the Felts murder — and the state's star witness Michael Carbone's belief that Gil and Bert were involved in the murder — was the trigger that ramped up the fear factor inducing Carbone to accept immunity and testify. According to Carbone and his FBI agent friends, Tommy Felts participated in the triple murders and must have been eliminated as a witness. Carbone feared he would be the next victim because he was the only other person involved who wasn't dead or in jail.

The OCD reports on Tommy Felts, Johnny Irish, George Gold, the Vitales and David Theodore "Ted" Richards, were too voluminous to contain. And to make matters worse, there were still even *more* murders being discussed in the press. Reading aloud the list of people who were supposedly dead because of Gil and Bert would almost be like launching into a filibuster on the floor of the Senate.

It was time to take this to our "neutral and detached" magistrate. Tyson was about as neutral and detached as I was humble and serene.

"Proceed, Mr. Contini," ordered Tyson, "with your motion to exclude evidence of collateral crimes."

"Your Honor, the statewide prosecutors have totally poisoned the well in this case. They've infected the court file with naked allegations of organized crime ties. They have dozens of police reports alleging our clients are guilty of more than a half-dozen *uncharged* murders."

Louie Vernell then weighed in with his own little sarcastic remark. "Your Honor, these defendants have been accused in the press with everything but the Lindbergh kidnapping." Even though the interruption was an irritant, I couldn't help but laugh, along with Gil and Bert. I turned and noticed that Neli, Gil's parents, and Bert's daughters and ex-wife were laughing, too. But not everyone thought it was funny. The victims' families looked at us with the usual hate in their eyes. And, of course, Tyson wasn't laughing. "We discussed this last week and I've ruled on that issue," Tyson retorted dryly.

Then I grabbed the ball back from Louie. I winked at him and raised my index finger, silently asking him to let me finish uninterrupted. He nodded in agreement. "I know it sounds like I'm raising the same concerns we discussed last week in the gag order motion that Your Honor denied. This time, however, I'm saying the defendants' right to a fair trial is being denied for a *different* reason, Judge. It's not about pretrial publicity. I'm talking about something that's interfering with our fundamental ability to defend against the three murder charges contained within the current indictment."

Molloy started to get up to say something. I decided to be polite for a change. I smiled, cocked my head slightly, raised the same index finger and silently urged Doug solicitously. To his credit, he remained seated and let me finish.

"Judge, the state has intimated that it might seek to introduce into evidence or somehow refer to these *other* murder allegations. We're talking about uncharged murders here, Your Honor. To permit the prosecutors to even *refer* to evidence of collateral crimes for which the defendants are not indicted would be extremely prejudicial and illegal. And just as obviously, it would be grounds for a mistrial.

"Any possible relevance of this sort of evidence — and there is none by the way — would be substantially outweighed by its prejudicial effect, according to Rule 403 that we discussed earlier when Your Honor disallowed those church tapes. As you know, that's the rule regarding admissibility of *any* evidence the state claims is relevant, including for these uncharged crimes.

"Just as we argued before, if the probative value or relevance of any evidence is substantially outweighed by its prejudicial effect, then it's *not* admissible. And I can't think of anything more prejudicial than additional murder allegations. The bottom line is, Your Honor, you know that evidence of collateral crimes is not admissible in the case in chief, to show somehow that the defendant acted in conformity therewith…"

As Doug stood to respond, Tyson put his hand up like a traffic cop. As if he had just suddenly woken up and heard what I had been saying, he asked, "Wait a minute. What other murder allegations?"

"Yeah, like you don't read the same newspapers everyone else reads," I thought.

I replied, "The newspapers have been quoting allegations like those in this report, the one the prosecutors provided us in discovery. Here's an example of the type of stuff the discovery material contains. Please allow me to read it to you: "William Halpern was a firefighter and cocaine dealer who had his throat slashed in Miramar, Florida on Oct. 21, 1986. Harry Van Collier is suspected of this killing. He is reputed to be a member of Bert Christie's bodybuilding and mob-enforcement ring. According to Collier's wife, he came home on the 21st with red stains on his pants. She said he hid knives and cash around the house and barricaded the doors. He was alleged to have told her, 'We finally got the man we've been watching.'

"The inference, Judge, is that there's a mob ring run by Bert, and that they had been watching Halpern before they killed him. This is precisely the sort of prejudicial and inflammatory material that should *never* be permissible."

"I will not permit any reference to these other murders, if that's your motion," Tyson ruled.

"I could kiss you, Judge," I almost said. Looking back at a very relieved and happy Neli, I saw her smother Emma with her embrace. Gil's dad was grinning from ear to ear and I could have sworn I saw him wiping away happy tears.

I knew that never should have been a close call in the first place and that it was time to go for broke. Something told me I'd better keep riding the judicial wave while I was still on the board. I didn't know when I would be beached on the shore with a mouthful of sand.

"Your Honor, there are actually more murders we need to address. This report provided by the prosecution alleges that Harry Van Collier was a member of the mob bodybuilding ring. Police say that he and James Hinote,

Jr., who was a cocaine dealer, were both shot in the head in Pembroke Pines on May 14, 1987.

"The report goes on to state that before the murders Mr. Fernandez had been asking about Hinote's drug business. Van Collier supposedly informed Fernandez and Christie that he planned to leave South Florida and join his wife in New Jersey on the night of his death.

"Tests showed that the bullet that hit Harry Van Collier exploded. Supposedly, Mr. Fernandez showed up at the hospital the next day to have lead removed from his eye. My client is alleged to have given the police a statement that the metal was lodged there during an accident in the gym. The report goes on to say that a machine gun and a shotgun were seized in Van Collier's house, both of which belonged to Mr. Fernandez and were linked to…"

"That will not be referenced in this trial, if these victims are not the same ones named in this indictment," ruled Tyson, as he held up the indictment contained in the court file.

Gil and Bert, who were sitting at opposite ends of the defense table, reached around Louie and me to briefly clasp one another's hands. The Fernandez family was in a group embrace by this time. It was the same with the Christie family. Then the two families were hugging each other, smearing their happy tears all over one another's cheeks. I would have loved to have that moment on film. But the cameras were focused instead on the victims' families' faces, which were filled with painful despair. Apparently, that made for better theater.

Molloy was now standing but said nothing. The photographers clicked away while some of the spectators on the prosecution side wept and shook their heads, clearly disappointed with Tyson's ruling. There was no doubt whose side they were on. Doug remained quiet because he knew the admission into evidence of any of these other murder investigations would constitute reversible error. If the case were reversed, it would have to be tried all over again, even if the state were to prevail. There was no way Doug wanted that either.

Being street-savvy, Molloy no doubt realized that his office had just been handed a very convenient ruling from Tyson. It enabled him to explain to all the other grieving families why their loved ones' murders wouldn't be discussed during the Fernandez/Christie trial. You could almost hear the prosecutors telling the other families, "because the judge ruled that he won't allow it."

"Your Honor," I continued, "we're also seeking the same ruling for the same reasons, with regard to the murder investigations we haven't discussed yet. The police reports on these also were provided as part of our discovery."

"Who are the victims?" Tyson asked.

"Charles Mitchell Hall and Charlinda Draudt. Draudt was Hall's girlfriend. The couple had their throats slashed in Tamarac, Florida on May 6, 1987. There were fingerprints found on the duct tape at the scene that the police say belonged to Harry Van Collier, who I mentioned earlier. Shortly before he was killed, Hall told friends he knew who killed Halpern. He was alleged to have been killed to prevent him from revealing this information."

"Same ruling," Tyson replied. "Are there any other motions?"

"Just a few dozen, Judge," I joked.

No one laughed.

Chapter 8

Motion Sickness

The list of other motions that needed to be filed was seemingly endless. Among them was the motion to have the Statewide Grand Jury indictment dismissed, based on the lack of jurisdiction. In layman's terms, I was trying to get the case thrown out because there was confusion about which state entity actually had the right to bring the case to trial.

"Counsel, let's proceed with the defense motion to dismiss the Statewide Grand Jury indictment," Tyson beckoned. "Mr. Contini, proceed with your argument."

"Thank you, Your Honor," I began. "The defense moves to dismiss the indictment because from the very inception of this case the Statewide Grand Jury lacked the requisite jurisdiction to indict. This is based on information we received from reliable sources in the homicide unit of the Broward State Attorney's Office. We were told this case was rejected by both the Dade and Broward State Attorneys' Office homicide units."

Although one of the counties in question was officially named "Miami-Dade," everyone around the courthouse just called it "Dade." This was how you could tell the insiders from the outsiders.

"But did they let it go, Your Honor? No. BSO shopped it to statewide prosecutors, who accepted this wannabe case and presented it to their very own *Statewide* Grand Jury because no one else wanted it. That's why we're here.

"This is the ultimate case of forum shopping, Judge. It's not unlike selling door-to-door until someone buys. You know the old saying, 'You can indict a ham sandwich'? You can indict anybody for anything. Judge, you know more than anyone that just because an indictment can be issued, doesn't mean it should be."

"Your Honor," Molloy interrupted, "Mr. Contini is simply speculating, based on what he thinks he heard. Prosecutors always have had the discretion to present evidence of crimes to a Grand Jury. In this case, it was the Statewide Grand Jury. If the Grand Jury determines there's probable cause to believe these murders occurred, and that these men probably committed them, then the Grand Jury is charged with the responsibility to indict. That's exactly what happened here."

Doug then said with emphasis, "*That's* why we're here. And that's the only reason we're here, contrary to what Mr. Contini suggests."

Square peg, round hole

"Your Honor," I retorted, looking over at Molloy. "Mr. Molloy knows that murder always has been a local crime handled by the State Attorney's Office in the county where the murder occurred! And in this case, it was Dade County. According to the medical examiner, the victims were alive and present in Dade County before their murders. That makes it a local and not a statewide homicide.

"The Dade County State Attorney's Office has jurisdiction over local homicides in their county. Since the murders were committed in Dade, only a circuit court in Dade County would have jurisdiction, assuming a Dade County Grand Jury were even to indict. That never happened. So, now they're trying to force a square peg into a round hole, Your Honor, forcing jurisdiction…"

"What square peg?" Doug asked, ridicule apparent in his face. Even though he was the consummate gentleman, Doug apparently had reached the end of his patience with me.

"Judge, Mr. Contini is imagining things…"

"Imagining things?" I repeated, only louder. "Am I *imagining* that the applicable statute states unequivocally, under Statewide Grand Jury jurisdiction, that the crime must, and I repeat *must*, 'affect two or more judicial circuits'?"

Molloy jumped back into the pool. "No, *now* you're not imagining. Your Honor, that's precisely the way the statute reads, and that's precisely why there *is* jurisdiction in this case. Two or more circuits *were* affected by the crimes committed by these defendants. The victims were kidnapped in Broward County, which is one judicial circuit. And in one continuous criminal episode, they were murdered in Dade County, another judicial circuit. Under the felony murder rule, if men die during the commission of a felony, whether armed trafficking, kidnapping or whichever felony, then…"

I just had to interrupt him. I couldn't take it any longer. "Judge, these defendants were never indicted for armed trafficking or kidnapping in Broward County, or anywhere else for that matter. We're not talking about the felony murder rule here. The indictment charges them with murder, period. Mr. Molloy is trying to distract you from the only fundamental issue, which is the condition precedent for Statewide Grand Jury jurisdiction in this case.

Molloy tried to interrupt right back, but I kept muscling out the rhetoric by raising my voice and moving closer to Tyson, completely ignoring Doug.

Voice rising, I exclaimed, "The real issue is, how does a murder in Dade County's 13th judicial circuit affect Broward County's 17th judicial circuit? It *doesn't*, which is why they fail to meet that necessary condition precedent for Statewide Grand Jury jurisdiction. Without that requisite Statewide

Grand Jury jurisdiction, the resultant Statewide Grand Jury indictment is no good and *must* be dismissed. It was literally returned by a body of folks with no jurisdiction to indict! And the prosecutors don't have the right to proceed if their Grand Jury had no jurisdiction to indict.

"How does a local Dade County homicide, which can be likened to that square peg, fit into the round hole of two or more judicial circuits? It doesn't. I know it, he knows it and respectfully, I would submit that Your Honor now knows it."

We ran our mouths for a while longer before Tyson finally shut us down. "Gentlemen, I've heard enough. I will defer ruling and take it under advisement. You will receive my ruling in due order. Until then,we're adjourned."

Although the relatively new Office of Statewide Prosecution appeared similar in name and purpose to each county's State Attorney's Office, it was an altogether different animal. Originally established to prosecute complex, statewide white-collar and organized crime activities affecting multiple counties, the focus of the Office of Statewide Prosecution had been adulterated over time by aggressive law enforcement folks who forum-shopped their cases in pursuit of an agency willing to indict.

The jurisdictional goal posts defining the turf of the Office of Statewide Prosecution were moved significantly during this case. The office accepted the case not only to appease the victims' families in Broward but also to advance the agenda of an agency run by competitive people who wanted to get ahead.

There was another important factor in play, too. Broward Sheriff Nick Navarro was under tremendous pressure to wrap up all unsolved Broward homicides. Even though the triple-murder case involved Dade homicides, it was alleged that the victims were kidnapped in Broward — by people accused of being responsible for the supposedly related, unsolved homicides in Broward.

The statewide die was cast on the heels of these Machiavellian inter-agency political machinations. The indictment, by all rights, should have been dismissed. But Judge Tyson wasn't about to invite that level of public wrath, for the same reasons he denied the speedy trial motions for discharge.

"Motion denied," was the way his order read when he returned it a few days later. I'll always believe Tyson knew he was wrong to deny the motion, but the political realities were just too obvious. How many judges would have had the courage to stand up to the pressure, especially with all those Broward victims' families in his face every day. "Let an appellate court deal with it later," I imagined him saying.

Gil and his family didn't even need me to confirm what they already knew in their hearts: that Tyson would rule against us. Gil's family members were strong people, every one of them. The emotional battle scars were almost visible, though, as they tried in vain to encourage one another. That's why it was easier for me to tell them the latest ruling over the phone instead of in person.

Other motions

Before and after these larger battles over the issues of jurisdiction, speedy trial and gag orders, and in between the evidentiary hearings over the church tapes, collateral crimes and other murder investigations, I also set hearings to argue for the removal of Gil's shackles while in court. These heavy chains could be seen and heard everywhere Gil went, promoting the perception of guilt and impending danger. When that motion was denied, I argued it again a bit differently.

This time, I argued that Gil's shackles should be removed for slightly similar but more indirect reasons. The defense table was skirted with wood for the very purpose of hiding the shackles. The prosecution table wasn't skirted, I argued, which would only cause the jury to draw the impermissible inference that the defendants must be shackled, and therefore dangerous. Otherwise, why would there be a need for the massive wall of wood around our table? The jury had to be smart enough to figure something was up.

Tyson got to use his favorite word, yet again: "Denied."

Along with all these other motions, I argued that Gil should be allowed to attend his own depositions. My disingenuous reason for requesting his presence was that I needed Gil to assist me with details and help me to frame additional questions for each deponent.

"Your Honor, he has an absolute right under his Sixth Amendment right to counsel, and that means he ought to be able to assist his counsel at the depositions. The law is clear, as Your Honor knows, that he should have the assistance of counsel, which means I ought to get his assistance, just as he gets mine. Otherwise, how's he going to aid in his own defense?"

Tyson got to do his Pavlovian thing once again that day. "Denied," he said without emotion.

But everyone knew the real reason for the request: Giving testimony in front of Gil would have caused the deponents to clam up. It would be very difficult for someone to say anything incriminating about Gil while sitting in the same room with him.

In truth, what I was trying to do was shameful. Any defense lawyer who didn't just fall off the turnip truck would know that I was complicit in playing a very inappropriate game of intimidation. On this motion, I really couldn't argue with Tyson's denial.

There seemed to be no end to the motions. Louie and I filed several related to "severance," in an effort to separate Gil's trial from Bert's. Deserved or not, Bert Christie had a reputation as a mobster and I didn't want Gil to be tarred with that same broad brush. Besides, Bert's lawyer Louie not only had a reputation for being a mob lawyer; he was driving us nuts. I knew it wouldn't do our case any good to have to sit there next to Louie for the entire trial. Louie was loveable at times. Other times, however, I'd get so frustrated and angry with him that I worried about becoming a defendant myself.

"Denied," was Tyson's predictable response to our severance requests.

"Gee, something different for a change," I thought sarcastically.

Now Gil and his family were still stuck with Bert and Louie — and so was I. You could almost hear the Christie family thinking the same thing about us. The denial of our respective severance motions made the road ahead that much rockier for all of us.

Chapter 9

Let the Games Begin

Feigning confidence and pretending to read my notes, I sat at the defense table, waiting for the teeming crowd of victims' families, courthouse personnel and other onlookers to flood into courtroom 970 for the first day of jury selection. The fact that a lot was riding on my lawyering wasn't lost on me.

The two rectangular brown tables in front of the judge's bench were for lawyers and defendants only. The prosecutors' table faced the judge and was at a right angle to the jury box. The defense table was perpendicular to the judge's bench, facing the jury. This layout ensured that Gil would quite literally face a jury of his peers.

Our table remained skirted by the discolored wooden shield, which was designed to hide the shackles Gil and Bert were forced to wear. Judge Tyson continued to allow this skirting over my repeated objections, despite the obvious inference that the defendants must be dangerous.

A pair of swinging doors and a low railing in the same 1970s brown as the tables — along with about 15 deputies — were all that kept the trial spectators separate from the players. Lined up on matching brown pews behind the railing was the anxious crowd. The trial was open to the public, so there was no admission charge. You needed only to be curious. But for those with a dog in the fight, like the Fernandez and Christie families on one side of the room, and the victims' families on the other, it wasn't curiosity that brought them in; it was a potent mix of fear, love and hate.

I sat alone at the defense table, sandwiched between empty chairs. It was enough to make *me* feel like the defendant. Louie Vernell was predictably late again; and the marquee players, Gil and Bert, were still in transport from the jail.

Then the defendants arrived and everyone knew it. The lights from the television cameras illuminated the entrance to the courtroom. The cadre of camera-wielding photographers, who had been crouching down between the railing and the first row of spectators, suddenly stood up and turned in unison toward the door, contorting their bodies to angle for the best possible photos of the alleged killer.

In shuffled a very chiseled Mr. Florida, shackled and caged in by deputies. Madly clicking their shutters, the sniper-team of photographers had him in their crosshairs. Despite the handcuffs and leg irons, Fernandez moved with confidence and grace. His piercing eyes were alert as he scanned the crowd. He held his head high as he finessed the gauntlet of deputies and tripod-mounted television cameras.

Bailiff Mike walked in front of Gil, who was followed by Bob Behan, the other bailiff assigned to Tyson. Behind them a few paces was Bert, whose entrance was less interesting to the media. After all, he wasn't a former cop accused of being a killer.

Bringing up the rear was Sergeant Jim Stockdale, the supervisor in charge of inmate transport. Behan and Stockdale, who were big guys, stood tall over Bert Christie but appeared small next to Gil.

The courtroom crowd was hushed. All you could hear was the machine-gun-like clicking of the cameras, along with the tinny sound of the shackles. Most of the faces in the courtroom followed Gil's every movement. Undaunted by all the attention, he casually nodded his head and smiled at Neli and his parents.

As Mike Ruvolo escorted Gil to the defense table, I whined, "Why do you have to put that Houdini contraption on him, Mike? He's not going anywhere." I wasn't annoyed at Mike, I was just ticked that my motions to remove the shackles had been denied.

"Sheriff's orders, John. You know that." Mike replied. "Besides, look at this guy," he said, smiling at Gil. "He's a black belt, and into kick-boxing and everything else. What am I gonna do with this guy? The shackles just make it a fair fight."

Gil smiled back. You could see these two already liked each other. I'm sure seeing a smiling Gil made the families hate him even more. Whenever Gil smiled, the clicking of the cameras accelerated to warp speed. This had to add to the families' discomfort.

"What are they looking at?" Gil asked rhetorically.

"They hate you, Gil; like they hate me, only maybe worse. We have to expect that from the victims' families. Try not to let it bother you."

Those who hated Gil before the trial hated him even more now. It was a close-up kind of hate, cooked to a boil from being only several feet away from the man they believed to have murdered their brothers, sons, friends, or in the case of Linda Allard, her future husband. The murders were not confined to just the decedents; the surviving family members suffered a different sort of death. They had to have felt their own spirits and even their futures had been murdered that night, right along with their loved ones.

The prosecution

"Gil, they're offering you a life sentence, a pass on the chair, in exchange for your testimony against Bert," I informed him. My obligation under the law was to communicate every plea offer, however repugnant or unacceptable it might be.

"It's fly or fry, right?" was his shocking yet poetic reply.

Gil rejected this last-ditch offer to snitch on Bert to avoid the death penalty and secure a life prison term. Although he could have ensured his life would be spared, he chose to roll the dice instead. I heard later that the prosecution had extended the same offer to Bert first, receiving the same sort of response. I found it interesting that the prosecutors — who perceived themselves to be on the side of righteousness and truth — would cozy up to whomever was willing to get on the bus first, and then fry the guy who had the temerity to reject their olive branch.

I felt significantly outnumbered by the prosecution team that included three prosecutors: Doug Molloy, who was originally the chief prosecutor; his fellow assistant statewide prosecutor Cynthia Imperato; and Jim Lewis, who was spirited-in at the last minute to act as lead prosecutor for the state. Cora Cisneros was now nowhere to be found.

Doug Molloy was a true gentleman and a worthy opponent. He was sharp, and to his credit, he made juries feel comfortable. Doug had that professorial, Robert Redford look that made people automatically like him. He was just a little under six feet tall, and his hair was dirty blond and longer than Redford's. He wore an earring in one ear — except during court. He was handsome, for sure.

Doug was a smooth trial lawyer who knew how to make things look easy. Everything he did in court seemed to flow like water off a duck's back. In spite of his obvious ability, he almost didn't get to work on the case. His new boss at the Office of Statewide Prosecution, Melanie Hines, had been in head-to-head competition with Doug and another prosecutor, Tony Johnson, for the top job when former Statewide Prosecutor Pete Antonacci was promoted. When she finally got Antonacci's job, Melanie Hines wanted to put as much distance as possible between Doug and her perceived fiefdom. Citing "reorganization" and "administrative changes" to reporters as reasons for his departure, Hines publicly asked Doug to resign his post.

But the victims' families made a stink when they found out that Doug, who had been their champion since the beginning, was not going to try the case. They made enough noise to cause Hines to set aside her political machinations and request that Doug stay on for the duration of the trial.

Doug had nothing but contempt for me in the beginning. Things started out ugly because I had made life difficult during the bond hearing for Cora Cisneros, whom Doug had married right before the trial. He was her immediate supervisor, which I'm sure made their relationship interesting. It was no secret that Cisneros and I had an acrimonious relationship. It had to be a distraction from what Molloy was trying to accomplish, so he chose to rearrange the prosecutors' roles. This meant Cora would no longer be in the courtroom with us.

My relationship with assistant statewide prosecutor Cynthia Imperato was a different matter entirely. She had a contagious laugh and a good sense of humor, which were attributes she probably honed during her days as a police officer in Tallahassee. "Cindy," as she was usually called, also was compassionate. Of all the prosecutors, she was the one who spent the most time with the victims' families, showing obvious sensitivity to their needs.

In addition to these qualities, Cindy also was attractive. She resembled a brunette Cindy Crawford or Kathy Ireland. Whether she knew it or not, she was somewhat provocative looking, in a classy, professional sort of way. To her credit, however, she always relied more on her intellect than her looks.

Initially, my least favorite member of the prosecution team was Jim Lewis. He didn't seem like a team player, and he came off as arrogant and cocky. Assigned to the case only three weeks before the trial, I discovered later he had his own disdain for the head of the Office of Statewide Prosecution. This gave me some insight into why he came onto the case so late.

Jim had supported Doug for the statewide prosecutor position, so Melanie Hines wasn't one of his fans. In fact, she had previously tried to get rid of him. But she was forced to change her tune when she realized he was the only attorney in the office who had ever tried a murder case. As a result, Hines requested that Jim take control of the trial. Lewis said he would take the helm — but only if Hines agreed that Doug Molloy could stay on the case. This provided further pressure for her to do the right thing by Doug.

In spite of this, I felt Jim Lewis couldn't be trusted because he surfaced at the last minute with a toolbox full of "new evidence," which was coincidentally disclosed after he came on the case. This new evidence — or fecal matter as I preferred to call it — was questionable at best. It centered on the curious testimony of drug dealer Paul Combs.

Combs, who was supposedly a friend of the victims, was scheduled to testify about his role in providing eight kilos of cocaine for a drug rip-off that was an integral part of the murders. Instead of being charged for drug trafficking, which would have been punishable by a 15-year mandatory prison sentence, Combs got the gift of complete immunity. His purchased testimony was just as suspect as Michael Carbone's, maybe even more so.

Combs planned to testify that the victims implicated Fernandez before they were murdered. The defense had been informed through the state's amended discovery response, which coincidentally had been amended *after* Jim Lewis came onboard, that Paul Combs would testify that the victims told him they were "going to meet two bodybuilders from Hollywood, named Gil and Tommy." The Tommy to whom he referred was murder victim Tommy "No Fingers" Felts, who was no longer alive to refute Combs' assertions. And since we already made the decision that Gil wasn't going to testify for tactical reasons, he couldn't refute it either.

None of this passed the sniff test, not by a long shot. Legally, it was considered rank hearsay because there were no witnesses to confirm it. Hearsay is defined as "an out-of-court statement made by a declarant offered to prove the truth of the matter asserted." In this case, the "declarants" were dead, and their "statement" — "going to meet two bodybuilders from Hollywood, named Gil and Tommy" — was obviously made "out of court." And, of course, they were offering the "out-of-court statement" for no other reason but "to prove the truth of the matter asserted."

The use of this sort of dead man's hearsay talk would make it easy for anyone like Paul Combs to conveniently invent a story that would simultaneously save his hide and be impossible to refute on cross-examination. I often wondered, "Why would Paul Combs admit to being a serious drug trafficker like this?" At times, I was convinced that Lewis had purchased Combs' testimony by granting him complete immunity and extending him other benefits. Then there were other times I was just as convinced that Combs was actually making up this drug trafficking story without Lewis' help, just to advance his own agenda and get Gil convicted.

Paul believed — along with a lot of other people — that Gil was the killer. So, it wasn't much of a stretch for me to think he made up the story about being the victims' cocaine source. It would have been the perfect retaliation for the murder of his friends. But then again, if he really had been the cocaine source as he was prepared to testify, his desire for retaliation may have actually derived not only from losing his friend, but also from being out over a half-million dollars, which was the street value of the eight kilos of cocaine he claimed to have lost.

Lewis swore to me he would never be complicit in any subornation of perjury, which is the felony he could have been charged with if he had had anything to do with Combs lying on the stand. Later, Lewis told me that Combs originally told his story to Cindy and Doug, *before* Jim was even on the case. And, of course, Combs had never wavered from swearing that his story was the unadulterated truth.

This so-called evidence — if Tyson were moronic enough to allow it — would be incredibly damaging to the defense because I didn't have anyone who could prove that Combs was lying. I obviously couldn't control how the judge was going to rule. Without witnesses to refute Combs' story, all I could do was my level best to convince the jury that he was just another felon bartering his soul in exchange for freedom from federal indictment.

This damning and poisonous dead men's testimony implicating "two bodybuilders from Hollywood, named Gil and Tommy," would absolutely stack the deck against us, leaving less chance for acquittal. If allowed, it would make the mountainous road ahead of us even more insurmountable. And it didn't do much to make me like Jim Lewis. In spite of what he had said about Cindy and Doug having heard Combs' story *before* he arrived on the scene, I couldn't shake the feeling that Lewis was the one who had brought this excrement into the trial. This caused me to doubt Jim's integrity and professionalism before I even got a chance to know him.

Chapter 10

Battle Royale

As we waited for the defendants and the judge to arrive, the prosecutors looked calm, drawing on their strength in numbers. They had an advantage over the defense because they had nearly unlimited funding and ample time to prepare. They were armed and ready for what we all knew would be a war. And they weren't the only ones. There were indications of battle-readiness everywhere, as evidenced by the paramilitary atmosphere inside and immediately surrounding the courtroom. An abundance of police officers swarmed the courtroom and halls, dressed like paratroopers. These gun-toting members of the SWAT team wore black fatigues, jackboots and cargo pants. And although the spectators didn't know it, there also were two plain-clothes officers planted in the courtroom. They — and the big guns hidden under their suit coats — were there to ensure that neither defendant escaped.

This increase in law enforcement presence, from the usual two officers to 15, suggested to everyone that the defendants were dangerous. The additional police coverage was just as inappropriate as it was impermissible, creating the presumption that the killers were definitely in the courtroom, hulking beside their lawyers. Somehow, Tyson allowed it anyway.

The spectators had to wonder if they were in danger because of all the security precautions. Then again, maybe that was part of the whole prurient appeal. In my opinion, this drama and show of strength was just another by-product of the prosecutors' desire to fry Gil and Bert. But some said it was Sheriff Nick Navarro and BSO behind all this bravado. That was a reasonable assumption because the SWAT team and the army of other deputies who filled the courtroom worked for Navarro's BSO, which had control of courthouse security. Maybe the extra security wasn't at the request of the statewide prosecutors after all.

Navarro, the media-savvy sheriff of Cuban descent, was renowned for his reputation as a hard-hitting, organized-crime busting cop. In fact, he actually started the nationally syndicated television show, *Cops*. "Sheriff Nick," as some called him, was said to have never met a television camera he didn't like.

Regardless of who was behind the extra security — even if BSO and the prosecutors were somehow complicit in its orchestration — its effect was to almost mock the whole presumption of innocence thing. The climate of fear was doing a lot to drive public perception toward guilt. It was obvious that the Office of Statewide Prosecution didn't just want convictions; they wanted

Gil and Bert dead. You didn't need to be a jurisprudential scholar to figure that out. Even the most mentally challenged juror or spectator could recognize that some very important people thought the defendants were guilty.

Death threats

While law enforcement personnel were doing their best to promote the perception of danger, I was in the unfortunate position of having real concern for my own safety. It was hard for me to know which source of hate I should worry about most.

There were rumors of retribution for the victims' murders from a variety of quarters. Some of this hatred was directed at me personally, simply because I was representing the man whom the public had come to believe had committed these heinous, premeditated murders.

Then there were those who subscribed to the drug dealers' code of justice and its sanction to obtain vengeance for fallen comrades. I had little choice but to subpoena some of these outstanding citizens to testify in pretrial depositions. Not only was I calling attention to their lives of crime, but my subpoenas were also forcing them to spend money on attorneys. This naturally made me quite unpopular with them.

Rumors also abounded about potential reactions from organized crime figures allegedly connected to the case. Like the drug dealers whose activities suddenly came under scrutiny, these wise guys were furious at the media exposure that brought them out from under their collective rocks. These goodfellas probably feared I'd lay off some of the blame on them. Prosecutors often accuse defense lawyers of playing this blame game to deflect the jury's attention away from their own clients.

When I was a prosecutor just several years before, I sometimes likened the defense lawyer to an octopus that would spray an ink-like substance in the face of its prey. In the case of a trial, the prey was the jury. If the jury's attention was diverted to *other* bad guys, a courtroom version of a smoke screen was created and the jury couldn't see the truth. The real wise guys out there knew I'd be tempted to do this sort of thing as Gil's defense lawyer. Now that Gil was facing the chair, I figured they would hunker down and prepare for the blame game. My concern was, would they try to do something to me to stop the game?

In addition to the reaction from the criminal element, there was also the understandable righteous anger and hate coming from the victims' families. Though my focus had to stay fixated on doing whatever I could to keep Gil alive so he could be with *his* family, it was easy to imagine the families' pain and anguish. It must have been overwhelming. Unfortunately, I didn't have the luxury of expressing my sympathy to them. Truth be told, they wouldn't have accepted my condolences anyway. My status as their adversary was sealed as soon as I chose to represent Gil.

There was no way for me to keep from feeling the collective rage and emotion that was silently — and sometimes audibly — fired at me from the audience as I sat captive at the defense table. And just in case I had somehow missed the message, I received several telephone death threats from people who might have been happy to see me go from counsel for the defense to violent-crime victim.

Perhaps I took these death threats too seriously, but fear will do that to you. Thankfully, two of my loyal friends, Dave Blood and Bill Kelly, agreed that I needed to be careful and insisted on acting as my impromptu security team. The Marlboro man on the billboard down the street from the courthouse was not much more than a Dave Blood wannabe. Dave was a ruggedly handsome guy who stood six-feet-four when slumping. He tipped the scales at 230 pounds. If you look up the word "bodyguard" in the dictionary, you would see Dave's picture, right alongside the photo of my other buddy, Bill Kelly. He was no slouch either. At six-feet-five, he weighed in somewhere over 235 pounds.

Tossing down a few cold ones at Il Giardino's, Dave and Bill unveiled their counter-surveillance plans. Maybe it was the alcohol, but I felt warm all over while listening to them concoct their scheme. They sounded like the real deal if you didn't know any better. These two guys had it all figured out, so it was safe for me to order another cold one.

"We'll take turns driving him to the courthouse. I'll drive him tomorrow and you can take him the next day. That way, those mental giants will never see him in his own car," laughed Bill.

"We'll take the elevator only if we have to. Let's use that set of stairs over on the other side of the building. We have to be sure we never take the same way out of the courthouse," said Big Dave.

"I suppose this means I have to join you two over here every day and toss down a few Coronas after you rescue me?" I teased, nursing my beer.

"Yeah, that's all part of the plan. And by the way, you're buying." Bill Kelly howled at his own joke.

These precautions felt a bit melodramatic to me, so I was a little embarrassed to be going along with the plan. I felt as though we were overreacting. But the phone calls were real, so I suppose we had to take some sort of precautions. For all I knew, one of the people staring at me hatefully in the courtroom had actually made the calls.

All of this made me a little paranoid for my family's safety, so I set about to ensure that my home couldn't be located using conventional search measures. I made sure my name disappeared from my home property tax records, as well as from records associated with the Florida Division of Drivers Licenses. My house was purchased under a corporate name, reflecting the corporation as the owner and registered agent in the property appraiser's office. The name of the corporation was innocuous sounding, so it never provided a clue as to its connection with my wife or me. My water and cable bills were listed under my mother-in-law's and maternal grandfather's names. This actually cost me extra money for new security deposits, but I felt it was worth it. My investigators quite easily found people via these utility company databases, so it only made sense that bad guys could hire private investigators to do the same thing. With all these measures in place, I knew if folks wanted to find me, they'd have to physically follow me home.

But I wasn't the only one who was nervous. The police presence, in tandem with the extraordinary grief and anxiety emanating from the victims' families in the audience, made the courtroom air thick with nervous tension — as thick as the stench I knew would soon be coming from the witness stand. So, the stage was set for real drama when the courtroom doors opened and deputies escorted Gil and Bert into the room.

They walked slowly because their feet were still shackled. My repeated motions to remove the modern-day leg irons had been just as repeatedly denied. The odd gait that's necessary when one's feet are bound together made Gil, who could have doubled for The Incredible Hulk anyway, seem like some sort of monster. His hands were also shackled, creating the image of a dangerous animal that had to be restrained. Bert, who was shackled, too, had noticeably dark circles around his sunken, steely eyes. He looked sick, and the shackles did nothing to give him a warmer, friendlier appearance.

Gil smiled at me as he approached the defense table. Mike Ruvolo removed the handcuffs in preparation for the jury's entry and I hugged Gil before he sat down. In spite of being bound in chains, a peaceful glow emanated from him. Though he had to have felt uncomfortable, self-conscious and sad to be caged up like this, he managed to radiate a dignity of sorts. He was literally fighting for his life, and yet he nonetheless seemed to have a real serenity or peace about him.

Bert Christie

Bert Christie then approached the defense table, led by Bob Behan, who had escorted him from the jail. Seeing how sick Bert was, I had to wonder if his physical condition wasn't punishment enough for his alleged crimes. It wasn't a stretch to assume that many members of the victims' families would have loved it if he were to suffer a slow, agonizing death. And it looked like that was already happening. Bert had his colon removed in 1979. Additionally, he suffered from acute asthma and hepatitis, which was reflected in his cold eyes and jaundiced complexion. Months before the trial began, he was bleeding internally and it was feared he wouldn't be alive to appear in court. Just glancing at him, you could see the cumulative effects of his various illnesses.

As Bert got closer to the defense table, he gestured weakly at Vernell's empty seat as if to say, "where's Vernell?" I could only shrug my shoulders because I had no idea where he was. Bert then looked into the audience and spotted his two daughters, Tara and Dana, who were 19 and 21. You wouldn't say his daughters had that girl-next-door look, unless you happened to live next door to a hot nightclub. Sporting all the latest fashion, they looked provocative without even trying. Suffice it to say, the eyes of most of the men in the courtroom were on the girls when they walked into the proceedings.

Bert had a tendency to look right through people, managing a smile on occasion, but only when it suited him. Unless, of course, he was looking at his pretty, young daughters, with whom he shared mutual adoration. The slightly darkened skin around the girls' eyes let you know they were their father's daughters. Other than that distinguishing characteristic, they looked just like their very attractive mother, who was sitting next to them. Technically, Theresa was Bert's ex-wife, but she apparently still provided emotional support for her ex-husband. She also had to be a breadwinner, as she was forced to raise his two daughters as a single mom with her own income, given Bert's no-bond status.

The girls and their mother sat in the second row on the defense side of the courtroom, right alongside the Fernandez family. As the day progressed, I often saw them gesture lovingly at Bert with supportive little smiles and heart-tugging, doe-eyed looks.

Christie's family stuck together like Gil's, which I admired. To quell my nerves, I tried to distract myself by watching all of them greet each other and pray together. My voyeur thing was interrupted when the judge's private door to the right of his bench abruptly opened, followed by bailiff Mike's announcement of Tyson's arrival. I quickly swiveled around in my chair and faced forward, just as the judge entered the courtroom and ascended his bench. As soon as he perched himself on his seat, he looked squarely at the defense table.

Perhaps because of our fights over pretrial motions and writs of prohibition filed with the Fourth District Court of Appeal and the Florida Supreme Court, the judge didn't care much for the defense. On most days, I didn't think his rancor was directed at me personally. He might just have been tired of my incessant attempts to win any kind of advantage for my client. But he definitely disliked Louie Vernell. He was visibly frustrated over the many times Vernell had been late, causing repeated delays in the pretrial proceedings.

"Where is Mr. Vernell?" he asked, sounding annoyed.

Molloy, Cindy and Lewis just shrugged their shoulders, raised their palms and shook their heads, frowning. They must've taught that at the latest seminar for prosecutors who want to throw salt on the wound. It worked flawlessly, as they telegraphed in unison to Tyson that Louie wasn't anywhere to be found.

Denise Hughes, Tyson's judicial assistant responded, "This session was moved up by one hour. Mr. Vernell didn't know it was…"

I interrupted her to say, "I sent Mr. Vernell a copy of all notices of hearing, including the notice about the time change. Let me be very candid; we've had no response."

Louie Vernell

Vernell was torturing me because he was forever weakening the defense position by all his stunts. Since neither Louie nor I could get Tyson to agree to our motion for severance, I took every opportunity to separate myself from him in the judge's eyes.

Aside from all the chaos he caused, I wasn't even sure if he would stay on as Bert's attorney. None of us could know if he was in for the long haul, or whether he would skate before the trial. He was always crying poor mouth, whining that he wasn't being paid for this case, so he had to commit to obligations elsewhere — presumably those for which he was paid.

Directing his comments to Denise, Tyson said, "Let me go another way. Have you had contact with Mr. Vernell?"

She replied, "I called Mr. Contini and Mr. Vernell."

"When?" Tyson barked.

"Yesterday. When I finally spoke to Mr. Vernell, he said he didn't know that the time had been changed to 1:30 and that he hadn't received any notification. He said he would try to make it but he didn't know if he would be on time."

Because of Vernell's lateness, we were forced to have a seemingly endless discussion about the number of times he had been contacted and the methods that were used. As we wasted the court's time discussing this madness for the record, you could hear Louie coming. Louie dragged behind him his squeaky cart carrying his trial briefcases wherever he went. The screeching sounds of the wheels on that antique of a cart could be heard getting closer and louder out in the hall. It was almost haunting. His cart had the kind of wheels you see on the luggage that pilots and flight attendants carry through airports. The problem was, these wheels probably hadn't been oiled since he bought his old, worn-out briefcases. From the look of them, that had to be sometime during the Truman administration.

Louie's screeching luggage cart created a comical scene, which was enhanced by a certain lack of style on his part. He had gray hair dyed a reddish-brown. Depending on how good his most recent dye job was, the red color was sometimes only on the top, giving him the look of someone who had an oddly colored toupee dropped on his head from a fourth-story window. To make matters worse, he had the strange habit of twirling his hair with his fingers. This nervous tick was often hard for me to watch. But the prosecutors seemed to get a kick out of it; I would sometimes catch them looking amused as he wound his hair-wrapped finger in a fast circle.

Bert looked pissed as he watched Louie's undignified entrance. He shot me a look and shook his head, as if to say, "Can you believe this guy?"

Then Gil muttered, "Louie, Louie, Louie. What's up witchu, Louie?"

Despite Louie's unsophisticated look and major quirkiness, he could shoot from the hip with the best of them. He had already been a lawyer for 38 years, longer than the 33 years I had been alive. Truth be told, I hoped I would look as good in my late sixties.

Louie became a lawyer at a time when it wasn't necessary to go to law school. If someone worked for a judge for 10 years or more as a law clerk or in another function, he could become an attorney without going through the bar exam. He was one of the last people who became a lawyer in this way.

Over the years, Louie developed a reputation for representing some of South Florida's mob figures. These wise guys once respected him. Over time, however, they tried their best to use him as their flunky. They paid him short money and presumed he'd be there to represent the mob's assorted low-level dirt bags whenever they got caught. In fairness to Louie, he might have considered these guys to be his friends, not knowing they were using him.

They should have shown him more respect. Louie was actually a very good and charming lawyer who had the ability to flip a switch within milliseconds, fighting with ferocity when necessary. But he was obviously stretched too thin on this case. He had taken on way too much to keep up his lifestyle. Half of that was the fault of those cheap and disrespectful wise guys. The other half was Louie's for allowing it.

The prosecutors and homicide detectives openly speculated that the wise guys probably had serious dirt on Louie, which they surmised was enough to force him to retain a certain loyalty. They spread rumors that the mob might have helped him to get away with a few curious things of his own, but they never advanced any proof.

Surprisingly, Louie wasn't very circumspect about his alleged organized crime connections. Or maybe it was just that he didn't go out of his way to change the perception — warranted or not — that he was somehow in bed with these guys. Even while he was in court, he wore a diamond pinkie ring that he claimed was given to him by mobster Johnny Irish. And according to a police report released as part of the state's discovery response, the phone number for an organized crime-owned business called Million Dollar Bingo rang into Louie's office. Police alleged that Joseph "Joey Flowers" Rotunno was the mobster who ran this bingo junket. Again, in fairness to Louie, he might not have known the business was even considered suspect by law enforcement.

Along with everyone else in three adjacent courtrooms, Tyson heard Louie's squeaking arrival and it annoyed him to no end. By the time Louie and his beat-up cart squealed their way past the swinging railing doors to the front of the courtroom, Tyson's rage was boiling over. Everyone could feel the tension rising as the screeching noise of Louie's wheels got louder.

"Mr. Vernell. You're *late!*" Tyson boomed, blowing a gasket.

"Judge, I… I… I beg your pardon," Louie stammered, trying to catch his breath. "I stopped at the mall… the mall in Hollywood to get a hotdog because… because my blood sugar was dropping. When I came back outside, I couldn't remember where I parked my car."

Louie held up his hand, as if to say, "wait a second" and stopped talking. He then wiped his mouth with the back of his hand, leaned forward on the defense table and tried to catch his breath. The Christie family looked horrified, fearing this would only hurt Bert's cause. Neli reached over and silently comforted Bert's daughters as the horror unfolded.

After Louie's breathing became more normal, he continued by saying, "Then the security guy in one of those little carts let me ride with him up and down all the aisles until I found it."

Louie's story was like something out of a *Saturday Night Live* skit, only made funnier and more bizarre due to the spit that sprayed toward Tyson as Louie ran his mouth.

I felt like shouting, "Quit while you're behind, Louie!" But then I saw an opportunity for comic relief. Cupping my hands around my mouth to amplify the sound, I said loudly, "Look at his tie, Judge. That mustard is evidence he's telling you the truth!"

The trial observers and media personnel doubled over laughing in response to my outburst. I knew I had thrown Louie under the bus, but I did it to help him out of an even tighter jam. Besides, it was in my best interest to distract Tyson and keep him from getting too maniacal.

I was laughing so hard at my own joke I literally had to hold my stomach. Thankfully, everyone was laughing with me, even the Christie family. Everyone but Tyson, that is.

Even Louie thought it was hilarious. Seizing the moment, he picked up his tie, lifted it to his nose and sniffed it. The laughter in the room was now out of control. As the noise got louder, Tyson gave me the evil eye. Without a word, he communicated a message with his eyes: "Sit there and shut your mouth!"

Because of the crowd reaction, Tyson had to double his usual decibel level to be heard. He'd been putting up with Louie's crazy excuses throughout the pretrial hearings and had pretty much had it with him.

"Mr. Vernell, please sit down and don't *ever* be late to this courtroom again!" Tyson said, almost shouting to be heard over the laughter. You could almost see his blood pressure rising. The crowd, which only a few seconds before had been howling with laughter, abruptly quieted when they saw the look on Tyson's mug. All that was left of the light mood was one lone cameraman at the back of the room. Though he covered his mouth and pressed his head into his chest, his body shook as he tried in vain to suppress his laughter.

Louie knew Tyson meant business. So, he smiled charmingly and said, "My apologies, Your Honor. It won't happen again."

It took a few minutes for Vernell to rearrange his many trial briefcases around the defense table and sit down. At length he did. *Finally*, we were ready for jury selection to begin.

Chapter 11

Voir Dire

Jury selection also is known as "voir dire." Roughly translated, these words are French for "to speak the truth." The voir dire is arguably one of the most important phases of any trial because if it works according to design, in the end you'll have an unbiased jury. In real life, neither side actually wants an unbiased jury. They each want a jury that thinks like they do.

During voir dire, the lawyers for each side actually "pre-try" their cases under the pretext of picking a fair and impartial jury. Lawyers typically ask self-serving hypothetical questions designed to elicit sort-of commitments from the jurors as to how they might vote in certain scenarios. Lo and behold, these hypothetical questions coincidentally mirror the real-life facts and testimony involved in the case the jury is about to hear.

Some judges — especially the more controlling ones — attempt to limit lawyers from pre-trying cases in this way. But an aggressive trial lawyer will nonetheless keep trying every-which-way to get the jury thinking about real-life scenarios, even though the jurors haven't even reviewed any evidence in the case or heard any testimony. If a trial lawyer does his or her job, the jurors will indicate in advance how they think and even how they'd vote regarding certain scenarios. So, in truth, each side really wants a biased jury — contrary to whatever disingenuous arguments they make to the judge.

In the case of *State of Florida v. Gilbert Fernandez, Jr.*, it was doubtful that we could ever find an impartial panel. By the time we got to this phase, there already had been an enormous amount of inflammatory and prejudicial pretrial publicity. I wondered whether there was anybody left in Broward County who didn't think Gil was a serial murderer, a cold-blooded hit man for the mob, and an extremely violent and dangerous person. Even I was guilty of thinking this after my initial reading of the sensationalized article on the cover of *The Miami Herald*. That chilling article, with all the photos of the victims and gruesome murder details, essentially was an indictment in itself.

To add insult to injury, the trial was to be held in Broward County, which was the home field for the murder victims' families. Broward had been blanketed with daily news articles and TV coverage for what seemed like forever. There was no getting past that fact. Dade County hadn't been as poisoned by the daily press about the murders, which meant the entire pool of jury candidates would have been less informed about the case. Had the proceedings been held in Dade County, which is the largely Latino county where the men had actually been murdered, there was the possibility that we'd have a lot more Latinos on the jury. Had that happened, at least an argument could be made with a straight face that Gil had a jury of his peers. And truth be told, drug-related murders were more commonplace in Miami. This had the effect of desensitizing the entire county population, and therefore the potential venire, or panels of prospective jurors. Right or wrong, for all these reasons a trial based in Dade County would have been better for Gil.

Another problem of tremendous concern to me was the prejudicial effect the paramilitary atmosphere in the courtroom would have on the potential jurors. We filed additional motions to limit the number of law enforcement personnel in the courtroom, but with Tyson, that was an exercise in futility. I also filed yet another motion to have Gil's shackles removed, again to no avail. These motions ended up on the front pages of the local newspapers and the hearings were televised on the nightly news, but none of that moved Tyson to do anything but summarily deny the requests. Finding impartial people who were not intimidated to be in the courtroom, which had the vibe of a set for an episode of *The Sopranos*, was going to be an uphill battle, to say the least.

Mental gymnastics

As important as these other issues were, my main responsibility was to find jurors who wouldn't push for the death penalty. Of course, I wanted to expose or even create reasonable doubt and pull off a not guilty verdict. But first things first. It was most critical that I hedge against the possibility of Gil being sent to the electric chair in the event he was convicted.

Reluctantly, I was forced to question the juror candidates about their feelings on the applicability of the death penalty in certain situations. It would be a delicate dance. I didn't want them thinking that I might be conceding some degree of culpability. Like every other defense lawyer on the planet, I wanted the potential jurors to remain totally open to the possibility that my guy was falsely accused. Yet, I knew if I even talked about the death penalty, it could suggest that this option would be very much germane and in play. If I didn't guard against this possibility by pre-trying the death penalty issue, however, I could end up with jurors who were predisposed to think in terms of death if Gil were convicted. It was a real Hobson's choice.

The bottom line was that I really had *no* choice but to question them on their feelings about the death penalty. I had to engage in the artful sport of mental gymnastics. Too many questions stated too aggressively and the jurors would think I knew something about my client's guilt that they didn't. And yet, if I said too little, Gil could fry if convicted.

Naturally, the prosecutors were looking for jurors who favored the death penalty. Though they wouldn't admit it, they didn't care whether a juror was biased by the pervasive and prejudicial media coverage that heralded Gil as a cold-blooded murderer. In fact, if they were brutally honest, they'd concede that they were indeed hopeful that the well had been sufficiently poisoned in Broward to ensure a jury predisposed to vote "guilty" and "death."

There was no doubt in my mind that there had been a concerted effort by law enforcement and the prosecution to leak information about the other eight murders to the press. In spite of the noise I made over the media having access to the information about the other alleged murder victims, once the salacious and gruesome details were recorded in the clerk's office, the files became public record and the press could have a field day. Tyson's request that the media voluntarily monitor their own coverage was as useless as it was ridiculous.

Once the BSO Organized Crime Division produced their complete investigative files, they were essentially saying that the murder investigations into the eight additional murders were no longer "ongoing." Under Florida Statute 119, there's an exception to the Public Records law, which allows the police to refuse to release files of "ongoing investigations." So, through the release of the files they were saying, "We've got our men," despite the lack of indictments for those murders. It certainly was in their best interest to use this technique to influence the court of public opinion, and therefore potential jurors, into believing that Gil was guilty.

The judge's instructions
Bailiffs Mike Ruvolo and Bob Behan brought an initial pool of 60 potential jurors — the usual number for a capital murder case — into the courtroom. After each juror answered the questions on the standard written questionnaire, Tyson gave the group the special instructions that were necessary when the death penalty is one of the possible punishments. He began by instructing the jury that even though they were being given information about the possibility of the death penalty, it didn't mean they should assume in advance that the defendants were guilty.

"That's OK," I thought with a sinking feeling. "The media already took care of that."

Tyson smiled charmingly while educating his students about the kinds of questions they'd be asked by the lawyers. He gave them a heads up that they'd be asked about their feelings on the death penalty and he encouraged them to be entirely candid in their responses.

"The fact that you have reservations or religious beliefs about capital punishment does not disqualify you to sit as a juror. It is entirely possible to have these beliefs while still honoring your juror's oath and the laws of the state. If you feel you would automatically reject or advocate for the death penalty based on your beliefs, however, you're not qualified to sit as a juror on this case."

Juror candidate number 12 was shifting in her seat. I watched her, wondering whether the thought of capital punishment was bothering her or if she was just anxious to get the heck out of the courthouse and go back to work.

Molloy noticed her too, and he let me know that he noticed her. "That guy doesn't miss a beat," I thought. There were times I wanted to tell the jury that Doug wore an earring after work, thinking that might turn them against him. But then I thought, "Wait a minute; that just might endear them to him." But maybe I could tell them, "If he'll hide that earring from you, what *else* is he hiding?"

"Grow up, John," I countered to the guy inside my head. "That would just backfire on you." The silent trial in my head was already beginning. As I babbled inside my brain, Tyson wooed the jurors with a cocked head and a prom-date smile, and said, "If you are chosen as a juror and the jury reaches a guilty verdict, you would be called upon to make a sentencing recommendation. I'll make the final sentencing determination, but the opinion of the jury will carry great weight when I'm making the decision."

"This little sideshow about the possible death penalty is getting really tiresome," I complained to myself. "You can use fancy words and dress up this sow's ear like a silk purse, but we're still talking about frying people."

Gil read my thoughts. He elbowed me and said, "Relax counselor. God's got it."

Then I noticed a few of the jurors staring at him, wondering what he was saying to me.

"Man, these people won't let the guy sneeze without studying his every frickin' move," I thought.

"They're watching you, Gil, so look real nice. OK?"

"Whadaya mean? I don't *always* look nice?" He said sarcastically as he turned and leaned into me a bit, smirking.

"I didn't mean *that*," I whispered.

"Then mean what you say and say what you mean," he whisperingly teased me, whacking my knee with his under the skirted table. As he did, the shackles made a slight rattling sound.

I was in his ear now, whispering.

"Shhhhh!" I implored. "The jurors are going to hear the chains."

"John, they *know* what time it is," he said with cheerful resignation.

The whole death penalty thing was where the rubber hits the road for most people; at least I was hoping that was true. But I knew that unless these folks had a clear predisposition against the death penalty, they could be almost hypnotically desensitized into a cavalier nonchalance about it. With enough sing-songy, matter-of-fact judicial jargon, almost anyone could be lulled into complacency about the whole affair.

The death questions bothered Neli too much to just sit there and pretend she was fine about listening to them. So, she excused herself when we finished with the next juror. Gil just watched her leave before stealing a look at his parents. They'd been holding hands the whole time, but now they were almost sitting in each other's laps. It has to be a parent's worst nightmare to watch his kid face the death penalty. That is unless you compare it to the nightmare being experienced by the victims' families on the other side of the courtroom, which had to be even more horrific.

At that moment I would have rather chewed tin foil than listen to the judge wax poetic about the electric chair. But I had no choice, so I busied myself with studying the jurors and pretending to be interested in the pearls of wisdom coming down from on high. I tried to remember whatever little I ever learned about neurolinguistic programming, body language and all that science junk, hoping to determine which of the candidates would be slick enough to communicate their alleged prejudice about the death penalty one way or the other. If they were like every other panel of prospective jurors, they would be as ingenious — or as disingenuous — as they could to get out of sitting on this jury.

You could almost expect to hear one of the jurors say, "Oh, I *do* believe in justice. A man should be put to death if he killed somebody." I imagined my response to be, "Unless, of course, it's one of your loved ones on trial. Right ma'am? You want justice when it's someone else who stands accused. But justice is the last thing you want when it's your own loved one in the hot seat. *Then* you want mercy."

Chapter 12

Tedium and Excitement

If this was going to be anything like past trials, I knew the questioning of prospective jurors could go on for what would feel like forever. Some of the inquiries would be tedious and routine: "Are you a citizen of the State of Florida? Are you registered to vote? Are you a party to a lawsuit in any way?" Sitting there listening to the same old questions asked repeatedly was like watching paint dry. But the mundane and the profound often take place simultaneously while trying to find 12 impartial jurors and four alternates. I knew there also would be other very important questions. The answers they elicited could possibly even determine the outcome of the trial.

One question I knew the prosecutors would ask was, "Could you vote to convict someone of murder if you know one of the possible sentences is the death penalty?" Naturally, this haunting question forced me to be acutely aware of the nuances contained in every answer that followed. If there were any bias in a prospective juror's viewpoint, this question was one of the tools we used to sniff it out. Just hearing it caused a heightened level of red-alert adrenaline that's part of the twisted excitement of being a criminal defense lawyer on a first-degree murder case. This adrenaline was the drug that wired me up to do my job efficiently.

Even in the jury selection phase, I had to be all things to all people, which was incredibly difficult to pull off. Although I had been blessed with this ability in other trials, there was no guarantee I could make it happen again. It took an incredible amount of energy and focus to remember that I had to speak differently to the jurors than I did to the judge and the prosecutors. It was like spinning a bunch of plates in the air at the same time. I tried not to worry that I might drop one of them. "Gil's life might depend on it," was the thought that kept me up at night.

To make my job easier as the trial went along, it was important to relate in a friendly way with the judge. But at the same time, it was my job to push the envelope as far as I could with Tyson without offending the potential jurors. That was yet another delicate dance. I had to come across as knowledgeable, likeable, funny and aggressive to the prospective jurors, while being cognizant that the prosecution had the focused mission of undermining my efforts and objecting to everything I was trying to accomplish. I had to keep one eye open for the slings and arrows of my opponents, all the while taking my own shots at them.

Excuses

Predictably, when we started questioning the jurors, they all had excuses for not being able to serve on the jury. Some of the reasons were shameless, while others were more legitimate:

"I'm going on vacation to Europe for three weeks."

"Oh, really," I thought. "Not any more pal; not when Tyson gets through with you."

"This guy's going to Europe. Hey, I'd take a vacation to the worst neighborhood in Miami just to get out of here," cracked Gil.

The next young woman was sincere. "I have small children at home and there's no one else to watch them." Her excuse was the best and most legitimate. I nodded my head in agreement that I would have no problem with her being released. But then I couldn't help say to myself, "At least you still *have* children. People's children were murdered in this case. My guy's got small children, too, as do most of the courtroom personnel. You want your kids to grow up to respect their civil liberties, don't you? Then you've occasionally got to do the inconvenient thing: your civic duty. With rights come responsibilities." Just as quickly, however, I hammered myself in my own head, "Enough speeches, John. What if it were Elizabeth? You'd be encouraging her to get off the jury, too, you hypocrite."

Then a guy's excuse hit home. "I have a note from my doctor saying I should avoid stress."

"Give me your doc so I can use him, too," I thought. "I'd like to avoid this whole stress thing. Having to stare down the electric chair is *very* stressful."

One by one, potential jurors were dismissed for cause, meaning either or both sides felt the person was not appropriate for this trial. These challenges for cause had to be approved by Tyson. Lawyers prefer these kinds of "strikes" or dismissals for cause because they get an unlimited number of them. This is in contrast to strikes allowed for "peremptory challenges." There are 10 of these for each side on a murder-one case, with even less for crimes less serious than first-degree murder. No reasons needed to be stated to the judge to get these goodies, which is why they were limited in number.

The death penalty

The relentless questioning droned on and on. All of us — defense, prosecution, prospective jurors and court personnel alike — found it very difficult to stay alert at times. Then one man in particular, Joel Kaplan, said something that got everyone's attention:

"I know Gil Fernandez," he said.

I paid close attention as Judge Tyson asked him about their relationship.

"I know him through the church he attended before he was incarcerated," Joel answered. "I'd seen him many times on Fridays and Sundays at church. And the way I can say I know him, sir, is that he's a man who I believe was broken before God. I've seen him in a bed of tears. I've seen him praying. Quite honestly, I was very shocked when I heard the news. I had no idea of the facts or if they indeed *are* facts. All I know is I was really shocked."

"Do you think you can render a fair an impartial verdict?" Tyson asked.

"Yes, sir."

"All *right*! Bingo." I said quietly to Gil.

"Don't get too excited. You know they'll get rid of him," whispered Gil in return.

The judge turned to Lewis and asked him to question Joel. Lewis looked at Joel and said, "Have you formed an opinion based on what you know about Mr. Fernandez' character or from observing him in church?"

Joel answered, "I don't know whether Gil is guilty, but I do know that he's a born-again man. If indeed he committed those crimes, he's not the same man anymore. That man is dead. He's a new man."

Jim then asked him, "The fact that this man is, in your mind, dead; could that affect the way you would weigh the evidence in regard to what happened in 1983?"

Joel responded, "No, not according to our legal system."

"Could you segregate your personal feelings about his religious conversion or your views about his character and put them aside?" Jim asked. "Could you base the verdict on the facts you see presented and the law the judge would ask you to follow?"

"I believe so."

"Great. Now, what's your personal feeling about the death penalty as an appropriate sanction for any crime?"

"To be quite honest, I'm not clear how I feel about it. In fact, I was in Judge Futch's courtroom yesterday. He had a trial pending that also might involve the death penalty. I had to call my pastor last night and discuss some things with him so I could better understand my thoughts on the subject.

"After that discussion, my personal feeling is that I couldn't condemn a man to death. I base that mainly on a scripture in the Bible in which a man brought a woman to be stoned to death for doing something wrong to Jesus. Jesus said to let those who are without sin cast the first stone. Since I'm not perfect, I can't cast a stone and sentence somebody to death," Kaplan answered.

Gil and I both kneed each other under the table, as Cindy stole a darting glance at us.

"She's getting as quick as Molloy," I thought.

"Do you understand that even though the judge will have the final decision, you would *have* to recommend either life imprisonment or the death penalty?" Jim asked.

"Yes, sir."

"Would your personal views regarding the death penalty affect which recommendation you would make?"

"Yes, I'm sorry, I would probably recommend life imprisonment."

"As opposed to death?"

"Yes."

"Thank you. State moves for cause, based on the death penalty," Lewis said to the judge.

I called for a side bar during which I objected to the strike for cause, arguing that Kaplan said he *probably* would vote life. He didn't say he *definitely* would vote that way.

It was a wasted trip to the bench. Tyson dismissed Joel for cause. From a legal perspective, he might have been right to do so, although I obviously wanted to keep him. He would have been a great asset to our side.

Tyson then called a break. Hanging out in the hallway, Doug and I exchanged a few pleasantries and teasing barbs.

"Doug, do you suppose there's any way you guys could let just one or two jurors stay who aren't hell-bent to vote for the death penalty?"

"Why, because we bounced Kaplan?" Molloy asked. "John, you know there are people who use the Bible to advance their own predisposition for or against the death penalty. It's only right that we find out if these people have the ability to set aside their personal opinions and follow the law."

"But Doug, you guys aren't looking for people to follow the *law*; you're looking for people to follow *you*. You're just death-qualifying this jury and tossing anyone who's not jonesing to pull the switch."

"The death penalty is still the law in Florida, John, regardless of your feelings. Let me tell you now if I haven't told you before; if there's ever been a guy who deserved the death penalty for what he's done — brutally executing these guys for money — it's your guy."

Too spent to get into what could otherwise be a long argument, I just thanked him for his zeal for law and justice and said, "We'd better save it for in there."

Pressure

The gravity of Gil's plight was accentuated daily as I saw Gil's wife and parents faithfully sitting in court every day. It also was underscored by the expansion of my own little family. Our new son, Johnny, had just joined his sister, Kathleen, who now was eleven months old. Judge Tyson, to his credit, allowed us to quit early after I announced that morning, "Judge, I'm a daddy again. We were blessed with a baby boy, a son named Johnny."

"Congratulations," Tyson said with a smile," Mommy's OK, too?" I nodded appreciatively as he continued, "Maybe we can adjourn a little early today. We'll see how much we get done. OK?"

"That would be great, Judge. Thank you," I said, feeling closer to him. Even the prosecutors congratulated me. They almost seemed to like me for a moment there. Bailiffs Mike and Bob backslapped me and said "congratulations!" almost in unison. Their handshakes were followed by big hugs from Tyson's judicial assistant Denise and Beth Kessler, his clerk. I had already been bathed in congratulatory hugs from Neli, Emma and even Bert's daughters. Gil, Bert and Louie also had congratulated me earlier that morning, and when I first showed up, Louie presented me with a fistful of baby-blue bubble gum cigars.

My own sweet babies were constant reminders that I was defending a man who was in danger of forever losing his own family. After Johnny's birth, I looked at Gil's dad with a whole new perspective, just imagining his emotional pain. My little Kathleen changed my life big-time. But Johnny, because he was a boy, brought into sharper focus not only the old man's pain, but also the fear Gil must have felt over possibly losing his own sons.

My family wasn't the only one growing larger. Neli had given birth to David, Gil's second son, months before the trial. Her nurses allowed me to visit her in the room at the hospital in Hollywood. I beat myself up a bit, thinking, "Why are you doing this, John? You're only putting a bigger gun to your own head by getting too close to this family. You're the one piling all this pressure on yourself, all because you know nothing about appropriate boundaries!" Then I thought, "You're already here, she and the baby are healthy. You just might win this thing. Then you'll be glad you went to the hospital. It is what it is." These types of conversations with myself, which I had all too frequently, were absolutely wearing me out.

When the trial began, Mike told Neli she could bring the baby into the courtroom, as long as he didn't cry. Miraculously, he never did. I'll never forget seeing Gil shackled as he left the courtroom every day, leaning over to kiss his newborn's head in the hallway. I truly appreciated that Mike and Bob allowed this otherwise forbidden affection and touching during the prisoner transport process.

The pressure I was under increased exponentially as I felt the weight of what Gil stood to lose. My tendency was to self-medicate with some red wine to take the edge off after fighting in court all day. "Old habits die hard," they've always said — whoever "they" might be. I insisted on keeping up my practice of drinking wine with the boys on Friday nights. That didn't do much to calm Elizabeth's fears as a second-time mother with two babies in diapers.

"Don't mess with my Fridays or you'll lose your Saturdays," I'd threaten when she would question me and I was feeling particularly macho and self-absorbed. Then we'd go to church on Sunday, where I'd repent for being an idiot during the week. Then the next week we'd repeat the cycle all over again.

I don't think much of what I heard in those Sunday sermons was sinking in. Elizabeth wanted me to drop $20 in the church offering one Sunday and I blew a gasket, reminiscent of Tyson flaming out at Louie. "That's the spirit, John; you cheerful giver!" I thought later. Suffice it to say, I was a work in progress. Truth be told, I couldn't handle the hands in the air and the speaking in tongues at her little Charismatic church in Hollywood, so I complained until we moved to the more traditional First Baptist Church in downtown Fort Lauderdale. But unlike my friends in the Catholic faith that I was raised to embrace, these Baptist folks didn't drink red wine with me, at least not openly. So I was left to take the edge off all by myself, or with Louie, and my buddies Dave Blood and Bill Kelly.

But no matter how much I had to drink the night before, there was no getting around that I had to go back to court the next day. I found a few cups of coffee would remove the wine fog and early morning attitude, and I would be good to go. And that was a good thing because the endless jury selection process was nowhere near over.

Back to business

I couldn't control the justice system or the will of most Floridians, a majority of whom had stated their favor of capital punishment at the polls. But I could do everything within my abilities to convince this jury to consider all the factors that go into making such a monumental decision. First, though, I had to do and say whatever I could to get as many like-minded people on the jury as possible.

Give me bull-headed morons. I didn't care, so long as they thought the way I did after hearing everything I had to say about the state's excretion of a case. I would take even *one* person who thought like me, as long as I had eleven sheep that were willing to follow.

This meant that the unrelenting and almost punishing questioning of prospective jurors would go on and on, each person being asked virtually the same tired old questions. It didn't take long for the intelligent candidates to see what caused other potential jurors to be struck for cause. They knew they could get bounced by saying things that one side or the other would hate.

A lot of the jurors were dismissed for cause and still others were eliminated through peremptory strikes. Louie had 10 peremptories that he could exercise for Bert and I had 10 for Gil. This gave us 20 combined strikes, as long as we collaborated and made sure we weren't each striking the same people. That's one area where we worked well together — aside from in the bars along Las Olas Boulevard.

This striking business was a whole other delicate dance. The potential jury members watched while we whispered to each other, wondering what we were saying. Let's face it; we had to have looked conspiratorial with our heads up against one another, whispering and pointing to our individual paper diagrams of who's who on the jury. They knew, of course, that we were talking about them. But I suppose that was OK. Soon, they'd be talking about us.

All of this striking only meant that we had to keep grabbing panels of 60 people to be brought up by even more deputies from the fifth-floor jury room. I knew the media coverage would affect our ability to find impartial jurors, but nobody thought it would take *this* long. Things were moving at a snail's pace, averaging several days of questioning to produce one qualified juror.

Chapter 13

Trial and Tribulation

We'd been picking a jury for close to two weeks when things got even more interesting. It was my buddy Bill's turn to play bodyguard. When he drove me home one day, he stunned me by saying, "Is that media guy supposed to tell the jurors they'll be sequestered for months?"

"You're not serious, are you?" I replied, never knowing when Bill was messing with me.

"Johnny, I kid you not," he responded. "That media relations guy, Craig, was standing there in the hallway outside the courtroom telling all those jurors that they'd be sequestered for six to eight weeks, minimum."

"No frickin' way. Craig Burger did that?" I exclaimed, feeling shocked.

"Oh, yeah, he was teasing them. He told them they wouldn't see their families for six to eight weeks. Let me tell you, they weren't happy. That boy was having a good ol' time."

Bill knew by my reaction that he must've stumbled onto something important, something that definitely shouldn't have happened. Too bad it was a Friday night because I had to stew about it all weekend. By the time Monday morning rolled around, I was ready to ask Tyson to dropkick Craig Berger all the way to the beach.

"Judge," I started, "we have a serious issue. The jury was tampered with on Friday."

"Why didn't you raise this with the court right away? Why am I only hearing about this now?" Tyson moaned accusatorily.

"Dr. Bill Kelly, the tall gentleman standing up in the back row there, informed me after-hours on Friday; otherwise you would have heard about it as soon as I knew," I replied.

Looking at me, Tyson said, "What can you tell me about this tampering business?"

"All I can tell you is what Dr. Kelly told me. He said the media liaison told approximately 42 prospective jurors, with no bailiff present, that they were going to be sequestered for six to eight weeks. He said they weren't going to see their families for that long. The jury candidates were understandably pretty unhappy about it."

"That's unfortunate. Bailiffs, bring in the jury so I can inquire whether they heard this and if it affected their ability to perform their duties."

"Unfortunate?" I muttered in disbelief.

"Do you have anything else you want to say, Mr. Contini?" Tyson scowled.

"Did you say, 'it's unfortunate,' Your Honor?" I asked, incredulously.

Tyson then snapped, "You stood here a moment ago and wrongly told this court that there was jury tampering. What you described is not jury tampering, though I concede it might well have been irresponsible. I intend to inquire as to what they heard and whether it will affect them," he repeated, shrinking a bit in size and volatility.

"Respectfully, Your Honor, I don't see how you can avoid striking this panel of prospective jurors, given what they now believe about sequestration and the inability to see their families," I pressed, while standing to address him.

"Counsel, remain seated!" he snapped. "First you wanted them sequestered, now you don't! Which is it?"

"I want you to make a decision. Then *you* — not your media geek — can explain it to the jurors," I exploded right back.

Then with my voice a little calmer, I said, "I'm sorry about the geek remark, Your Honor."

Tyson ignored me and said, "Bailiff, bring in the jury, please."

As Bob left to get the jury, Tyson conceded, "All right, you made your point. I'm going to issue an order to stop bailiffs, news media and *anyone* connected with the court from discussing this case so people don't casually overhear it."

Although he acted like he was inconvenienced by my request, he obviously knew it needed to be addressed. To his credit, he even admitted he had dragged his feet a bit on this issue, "Frankly, my clerk Beth indicated a week ago that I should order this. I somewhat resisted it. Maybe she was a little more far-sighted than I was."

Beth Kessler was indeed sharp. At least concerning Beth and the need to listen to her more often, Tyson and I finally agreed.

After the order was issued, media liaison Craig Burger probably received a stern warning from Tyson or from his own boss, Court Administrator Carol Ortman. I wasn't privy to the form or content of the reprimand but *something* happened, because his behavior that day went from cocky to low profile faster than Louie could twirl his hair.

Here we go again

In spite of Tyson's admonishment the day before, Vernell was late again. The afternoon session began and Tyson took the bench promptly at the appointed time, 1:15. The first thing he did was look at the defense table.

Not seeing Louie, Tyson asked, "Is Mr. Vernell here?"

Beth responded that Louie had called Denise. He said he was trying to get all his file boxes upstairs. I cringed inside, knowing Louie's cumulative episodes of lateness were reflecting badly on the defense. Being co-counsel with him was like watching myself in a videotaped loop of a car crash. It happened repeatedly and I couldn't do anything about it.

Already angry with Louie from previous episodes, Tyson fumed and said, "I've been having trouble with Mr. Vernell every day. The first thing we will deal with is Mr. Vernell, when he arrives."

Outwardly, I said, "Thank you, Judge." Inwardly, however, I was cursing Vernell's name.

Tyson continued his tirade, his veins bulging in his neck, "Let the record show that counsel and the accused are present, except for Mr. Vernell. He has been consistently late. It saddens this court, but I move to do something about this today. It's 1:25. I came in at 1:15. What time did Mr. Vernell call?"

"1:10," answered Beth.

Just then, Louie's screeching wheels announced his arrival. The squeaking got louder until the doors swung open rather violently to reveal the disheveled Louie, then breathlessly saying, "My apologies… to the court. The elevator… Deputy Roderick was with me… was stuck on the seventh floor… for like nine minutes."

At the defense table, everyone had either covered their ears or were getting ready to cover them. Molloy and Cindy were rolling their eyes. Lewis just stared at the floor, maybe even feeling sorry for Louie. He knew what was about to happen.

Ignoring Louie's excuse, the judge, who was now on the warpath, began by saying "The first thing we're going to address is timeliness during the trial. Yesterday, I reminded Mr. Vernell to be here on time. I told him if it happened again, I would put it in writing and take sanctions. This is the fifth time I'm noting this! Each time I have brought this to his attention, I received a fine apology, saying that he couldn't be here on time. His apologies seem to be empty.

"The court orders Mr. Vernell to be on time at all times during this trial. Failure to be here on time will subject you to criminal contempt. And for failing to abide by an order of this court, you will be subject to up to six months in the Broward County jail and a $1,000 fine."

The Christie girls, along with their father, hated life with Louie at that moment. You would have thought their movements were choreographed if you didn't know better. They were shaking their heads in almost perfect unison, arms folded, eyeballing one another.

"Your Honor, may I respond briefly? Again…"

Once again ignoring Vernell, the judge continued, "The court herein makes this order. It shall be typed up and a copy will be given to Mr. Vernell."

"Your Honor, may I respond briefly?"

"I apologize, but this was necessary."

"Your Honor, my profound apologies to the court and court personnel, and to all others I might have inconvenienced. I called your secretary's office at approximately 1 P.M. I was downstairs, Your Honor, because of my particular habit or practice, I have about eight boxes. It takes me a considerable length of time to get through the guard gates.

"And for about nine minutes, we were stuck on the seventh floor. Deputy Roderick was with me and can confirm it. We all had to leave the elevator. I have always held this court in profound respect and I certainly don't want to offend you in any way…"

"I'm not taking this personally. I've made my observations," Tyson said, matter-of-factly.

"Who are you kidding, Judge, you're not taking this *personally*?" I said to the guy in my head.

Seeing there was nothing left to lose, Louie went for broke — literally.

"Your honor, I have to address the court. I have not received any money on this case since July 1990. I frankly find myself in the position of having to take other cases to survive financially. Without these cases, I can't pay for my office and my telephone. That's why I was late this morning; I had a deposition to attend. I was working so I could make the money to keep my office open during this trial."

Louie had only been paid $5,000 from Bert Christie, so he had previously asked Tyson to approve payment to him as though he were an Assistant Public Defender working in the Public Defender's Office. Tyson initially turned him down because he had already received some private money from Bert. According to law, the Public Defender's Office can only represent those who are truly indigent and unable to pay *any* fee whatsoever. Because of this denial by Tyson, Louie was forced to take whatever work he could get to keep his doors open.

"Your apology is accepted," Tyson said, ignoring Louie's cries of poverty. "From now on, you are to arrive one-and-a-half hours before we begin. You have to do this because you need time to sort out your things. You have constantly used this as an excuse." Then, backing down a bit from his hard-line stance, he said, "Do I need to force you to be here one-and-a-half hours or even 15 minutes ahead of time? Or are you going to be here on time, without complaining about elevators and the large number of cases you have to bring?"

"Today was an unusual circumstance…" Vernell answered quickly.

"Sir, this is the fifth time it has happened," repeated Tyson, this time looking calmer.

"I apologize."

"Then what time do you want to be here if I set a time? Fifteen minutes before?"

"Yes, sir."

"OK. Fifteen minutes before so you can set up. Be available."

Everyone was relieved when Tyson finally got it all out of his system. He became extraordinarily nice, as though he were feeling genuine remorse for spooking everyone like he did. There was a real bipolarity about his mood swings, which I recognized so well from my own behavior. It seemed like for every time he acted up, he'd get convicted in his own heart and then try to make up for it all by reverting to the granddaddy with twinkling and sometimes sad-looking, puppy-dog eyes.

Tyson asked that the next juror be escorted in for questioning. We all felt more relaxed — especially Louie. Everyone quickly settled back into the usual stupor induced by the interminable rounds of questions and answers.

Unbeknownst to everyone in the courtroom, however, this latest round with Louie had forced Tyson to make a decision he otherwise resented: He ignored the applicable law and granted that Louie be paid $25,000 by the Broward County taxpayers as a Special Public Defender, even though he wasn't entitled to it.

If Tyson really had wanted to play by the rules, he would have forced Bert to choose between Vernell and a new attorney from the Public Defender's Office. The defendant and his lawyer weren't supposed to be allowed to have their cake and eat it, too. Tyson's decision essentially allowed Bert to choose his own private attorney and then have the taxpayers pick up the tab. But Tyson was so frustrated and worn down by fighting with Vernell, the $25,000 started to look like a bargain. He must've thought that it was worth the money to purchase freedom from this madness and guarantee that Vernell had no more excuses for being late for trial.

Chapter 14

I'm Not a Witness!

At Tyson's behest, Mike did his bailiff thing and brought in more juror candidates. The last 60 were struck for cause because some twisted sister left hateful notes and inflammatory news articles in the ladies room shared by the prospective female jurors. Tyson and I could finally agree on something else: We would have loved to have tag-teamed that psycho mama and flushed her down the toilet, but we didn't know who she was.

As the 60 new unsuspecting citizens were being seated in preparation for abuse, Tyson shuffled the papers on his desk for no apparent reason. Old dogs can still hunt, so he knew what those photographers wanted. They had film and he had papers to move around. Let's face it, they both wanted footage.

While I waited for the last few juror candidates to find their seats, I checked out the pep rally of reporters and TV cameras. They were a noisy bunch, these media folks. I found it especially interesting that they didn't even try to muffle the sounds they made. It was as though they felt they were too important to be hushed. Maybe they got to be prima donnas because people were often sucking up to them to get on the news, making them feel like rock stars. A pencil-necked geek could carry a camera and all of a sudden become a player. All the women would flirt with him, but if he lost the equipment, they'd walk by him as if he were invisible.

As usual, there in the second row on the defense side was Neli, accompanied by Gil's mom and dad. Gil occasionally smiled and winked toward Neli and his parents, only to turn and work the courtroom again with his eyes. I instructed him to steal a glance now and then at the judge or the prosecutors, which was what I would do if I were the one on trial. And he was good at following my instructions. Hell would freeze over before you could read Gil's poker face.

"Gil," I urged, "look at the jurors for only a few milliseconds, and make sure your eyes look soft and sensitive. Try to appear relaxed, casual and polite. And never stare, OK?"

"You mean, lose 'the look'?" Gil replied, teasing me.

I had to admit, his sense of humor was keeping me relaxed. "You know what I mean."

"What, I don't look soft and sensitive to you?" he said in mock defensiveness, pretending I had hurt his feelings.

"Don't stare at them. But don't look away too quickly, either, as though you'd done something wrong," I continued.

"I got it. Look at 'em but don't look at 'em. Those directions are real clear. I can't screw that up."

He was having fun with me. I was glad one of us was enjoying himself. He was amazingly light-hearted, given the circumstances. Having his family sitting in the second row probably contributed to that. It meant a lot to him, for obvious reasons. He was blessed to have had people there to support him. Then a bomb was dropped:

"Judge," Jim Lewis began, "the state requests that Your Honor order the defendant's wife, Marianela Fernandez, to be removed from the courtroom. She's a potential witness in this case. Pursuant to the rule of witness sequestration, she is not to hear the testimony of the other witnesses and must therefore be excluded from the proceedings."

"Listen to this guy," Gil remarked disdainfully, shooting me a look. "He's getting real cute now." He and Neli exchanged looks of genuine sadness, born of love, frustration and fear.

"That's a bunch of nonsense, Judge. This is Mr. Lewis' own personal pretext to keep her out of the courtroom. He doesn't want the jury to feel for her or see her support her husband. She's not a witness to anything. He knows it and I know it. Besides, Doug Molloy already represented to me that he'd never call her as a witness in this cause."

"There has been no specific agreement..."

Interrupting Lewis, I pointed and angrily replied, "Doug's right there; just ask him. He specifically said, just after he took her deposition, that if he could elicit the same sort of testimony from someone else, he'd excuse her. You're not *that* slippery, Mr. Lewis, so don't play that game."

"I don't play games. I resent your implication, Mr. Contini."

Lewis then ignored me and pitched it again to Tyson by saying, "I believe Mrs. Fernandez is in possession of some material knowledge in this case, including an issue that may or may not come up at the trial — a reference to muddy sneakers that we allege defendant Fernandez gave her on the night of the murders. Inasmuch as these murders were committed in a muddy area, these shoes could be direct evidence in this case."

Tyson then asked Lewis, "Are you requesting that *all* witnesses be removed during jury selection?"

"Yes, Your Honor," replied Lewis, "for the reasons stated."

"Then it will be granted," Tyson decreed.

My reaction was immediate, angry and disrespectful. "It's my statement to Your Honor that Mrs. Fernandez will *not* be a witness. She's indicated that she won't testify, no matter how many subpoenas are thrust upon her. She would sit in jail on her head before she'd help the state convict her husband. She's already said this to me, so I don't think she's going to be a witness.

"If she's willing to do jail time to prevent the state from convicting, then why the heck should she be excluded from supporting her husband in the courtroom? We have victims' families here day after day."

"Is she listed as a possible witness?" Tyson asked.

Lewis responded by saying, "She is and has been from the beginning of this case."

"Then any listed witnesses should be excluded from the selection process," the judge said.

"Your Honor, this doesn't make any sense. She heard about muddy sneakers during pretrial hearings. What difference does it make if she hears about them again?" I asked.

"I'm not going to make an exception," Tyson said. "I'm very sorry. It's been requested by the state and I've granted it. Prospective witnesses will be excluded from the jury selection process."

Just then, Neli stood up and said, "Your Honor, may I say something?"

"Yes, ma'am," Tyson responded.

"Doug Molloy promised that he wasn't going to keep me out of the courtroom and out of my husband's trial. He made this promise in front of other people when he took my deposition. This is my husband on trial!" she said emphatically.

Doug was looking guilty now but I got the distinct impression he couldn't honor the deal even if he wanted to. I think he'd have stood behind his word if it were left up to him. Because Melanie Hines had Lewis calling the shots now and Jim didn't care what promises Molloy made. If he could get rid of the wife and keep her from view of the sympathetic female jurors — especially with Gil's baby in tow — he was going to do it. He wanted to win, period.

"Ma'am, I totally understand why you want to be in the courtroom," said Tyson, getting a bit crabby now. "It's been requested that witnesses be excluded during the selection process. This request is granted for all witnesses. This is a serious case to the state and the defense, and to many, many people. All witnesses — without exception — will be excluded," Tyson said adamantly.

Neli responded with controlled anger, "I'm *not* a witness! I'll leave, but I'm *not* a witness. I *won't* testify in this trial. You're *not* going to make me go against my husband."

"That's up to you," Tyson said. "You are listed as a witness."

"I'm *not* a witness!" Neli said stubbornly.

"If they call her, they'll be surprised at what she has to say," I added.

"The motion is granted," the judge said with finality. "I'm sorry. That's what rulings are about."

I started to say, "I appreciate your ruling, but…" when Tyson interrupted me. "Some people like them, some people don't. If everyone were happy with all rulings, we'd never have any problems in the judicial system. I made the ruling. I'm sorry some people are unhappy with it," Tyson said.

I couldn't let this drop. The ruling made no sense and it was imperative that I got Tyson to see that. Now it was my turn to be slippery. "I'm not going to argue with your ruling, but do I have to list the victims' family members as witnesses to keep them out of the courtroom? That's the logic of the ruling. Anybody on the list is out. I can list whomever I want under that logic. It doesn't matter whether they're called or not, as long as they're on the list."

"Then they're excluded, unless an exception has been made by either side," Tyson said.

This comment made Jim Lewis jump back into the argument. "They can't do that without good faith. If he can proffer to this court any possible testimony that the victims' family might have in this case, I would ask him to do so. To put people on the witness list solely for the purpose of invoking the rule…"

I countered his argument by saying, "But Your Honor, *they're* not moving in good faith here…"

Then Tyson said, "Wait a minute, have *all* the witnesses been excluded?"

"Yes," Jim responded.

Lewis' response apparently settled the matter in Tyson's mind, so he said abruptly, "Thank you. Now the next matter is…"

It was clear the judge was done playing. I was angry as I watched Neli being escorted out of the courtroom by Bob. But there was nothing else we could do, except get back to the game of "make pretend." The jurors were pretending to be honest with us; Tyson was pretending to be objective, neutral and detached; and the prosecutors and I were pretending to want only fair and impartial jurors.

A little levity

Sixty more jurors filed into the courtroom. At times, the monotony of repeatedly asking the same old tired questions, and then listening to people drone on with their guarded answers, made even the most seasoned among us a little punch-drunk. Occasionally, we got some much-needed comic relief.

While questioning what seemed like juror candidate number 3,000, Jim Lewis asked her, "If you could be anyone in the world, past or present, who would that be and why?"

I tried not to look surprised because at first this question seemed bizarre. When I thought about it, though, it was actually a good question, designed to give us a reading on whether this person was a leader or a follower.

The female juror replied, "Cleopatra."

"And why?" Lewis queried.

"Egyptian times, I guess."

"OK. So you could have both power and beauty?"

"Right."

Louie chimed in at this point and pointed out the irrelevance of this line of questioning. Tyson shut him down but then turned to me and asked if I had anything to add.

"Just one thing, Your Honor," I said as I turned to the juror. "Does this have anything to do with Richard Burton?"

In spite of the laughter that came from the prospective jurors, Tyson said with thinly veiled anger, "*Please* gentlemen. It's late in the day."

I thought, "Lighten up, Napoleon. Why do you think those guys on *MASH* are always yucking it up while they cut people open? It's because a little humor goes a long way to maintain sanity. Trial lawyers are no different. We keep from going crazy by finding humor wherever we can. You'd know that Judge, if you weren't such a hemorrhoid."

On a roll, I couldn't help but get one more shot in at Jim's expense.

"OK, I have to ask one more question. Do you have allergies?" I asked the juror candidate.

"Yes, sir," she responded.

"I saw that you started to sneeze. I was wondering if you're as allergic to Mr. Lewis as I am."

Lewis shot me a dirty look, inviting my insincere grin in return. I enjoyed the prospective jury members' laughter at Jim's expense. Then I thought, "That was a cheap shot, John." I felt bad because I was starting to suspect that Jim might not be as bad as I originally made him out to be.

After the snickering by the jury pool and court personnel died down, we got back to the business of pretending to find impartial jurors. The questions and answers went on for a record five weeks as we tried to find a qualified panel. The majority of candidates were dismissed because they had vacation plans, were opposed to the death penalty or because they knew something about the case. This last reason in particular angered me because of the inappropriate leaks and prejudicial comments that kept on coming, in spite of all my attempts to keep them out. Who on earth, after all that media hype, *hadn't* heard about the case?

I couldn't help but think, "We're either going to be left with 12 idiots who never watch the news and want to fry people, or a few who *do* watch the news, and then lie to us and say they don't."

The Fernandez case still holds the record for the longest jury selection proceedings in the history of Broward County. An unbelievable 316 prospective jurors were drilled before we found the 10 women and two men who were chosen to sit on the jury, plus the three women and one man who served as alternates.

For all of us, including these 16 people, the hard work was only about to begin.

Chapter 15

The Carbone Factor

On July 26, 1991, we all gathered together in courtroom 970 to begin the trial. Neli Fernandez was now allowed back into the courtroom, if for no other reason than the prosecutors were tired of seeing jurors walk past her as she sat conspicuously on a bench in the hall. The prosecutors probably surmised that the jurors felt bad for Neli and knew something must have been up to cause her hallway exile.

Though I had gotten cocky after recently walking a guy on a murder-one case, I was as nervous as a rookie. The courtroom was packed not only with media representatives, but also with too many of my peers. I felt self-conscious doing my thing in front of colleagues who would notice if I screwed up. Naturally, the family and friends of the defendants and the victims also were there, all staring at the "presumed innocent."

Gil and I feigned confidence and occasionally stole glances at the jury and the spectators. But we weren't kidding ourselves; we couldn't wait until it was over. Far from it, we hadn't even begun yet.

The framed paintings of dead or retired judges on the sterile, colorless walls of the crowded courtroom provided a solemn atmosphere of respect that was otherwise absent. The lifeless portraits helped balance the seething energy teeming from the rows of spectators, and the prosecution and defense tables. Had this been two centuries earlier, I would have felt like a gladiator in a Roman coliseum, anxiously waiting for Emperor Tyson to begin the games.

Gil and I patted each other on the back, reassuring one another. We weren't the only nervous ones in the room. Cindy Imperato was the youngest and least experienced prosecutor on the team. It was her first murder trial and she looked like she was feeling a little shaky. She had every reason to be because she was chosen to deliver the state's opening remarks in the trial. Anyone in her position would have felt the weight of South Florida on her shoulders.

Cindy got up to speak and Gil whispered the words, "Here we go, Lord." He prompted me to lean against him as he uttered an abbreviated turbo prayer: "Father, we pray your perfect will over these proceedings this day, in Jesus name." He then smiled and punctuated the prayer with an enthusiastic, "Amen!"

Cindy read the prosecutions' prepared opening statement from behind the podium, a move as conservative as her tailored suit. But this was normal for a new lawyer. In contrast, veteran trial lawyers like to get out from behind the podium as they address the jury. I'd been mimicking the vets for years, believing they were right in their habit of walking around the courtroom. I felt it sent the unspoken message that I was in control. The goal was to make the jurors feel just as comfortable as if they were in their own living rooms. As I wandered around, I would speak conversationally to the jurors with the purpose of disarming them. I knew from experience they tended to reward this type of delivery with appreciative nods and undivided attention.

Cindy hadn't had the advantage of spending a lot of time in courtrooms, so her style had yet to emerge. So, she did the best she could, holding onto the podium with both hands as she said nervously, "Your Honor, Mr. Contini, Mr. Vernell, ladies and gentlemen, my name is Cynthia Imperato. I'm one of the assistant statewide prosecutors assigned to prosecute Gilbert Fernandez, Jr. and Hubert Christie..."

As she went on to describe the murders, the jury was spellbound. The victims' families were already starting to sob. Objecting and asking Tyson to remove the crying folks from the victims' side of the courtroom would have made me look like Mr. Insensitivity, so I let it go.

However sincere and effective her delivery, it was obvious to me that Cindy was nervous. I was critical of her in my head until I recognized that she conveyed a kind of humility that endeared her to the jury. She appeared to personify just what they were feeling as first-time jurors on a murder-one case. Perhaps she reminded them of how they'd feel if they were up there, trying to do what she was doing. They might have even projected onto her the image of the girl next door or a little sister. Whatever their perceptions, it was clear their sympathies went with the sweet and nervous young woman representing the good people of the State of Florida.

I could see the jurors were rooting for her to get through what was obviously a very difficult experience. They were quietly encouraging her ever so subtly with their animated attention and wide-eyed interest in whatever she was saying. So much for the veteran lawyer, control-of-the-courtroom thing.

I thought, "This jury consists of ten women and two men. Maybe it was Molloy's idea to put the woman prosecutor up there for the opening, since there are so many women on the jury. Maybe the women jurors have imagined themselves as a lawyer like Cynthia at one time or another." Whether they put themselves in Cynthia's shoes or not, I could tell the women felt nervous for her. Actually, we all were as we watched her standing there, all alone, reading from her prepared statement before a packed courtroom and all the cameras. No pressure there.

At length, her well-written statement ended with a compelling and haunting image put forth to the jurors: "When the state has rested its case, *you* will be the voice of the victims. They will no longer be silenced."

After Cindy finished, Louie and I delivered our opening statements. Mine was the opposite of Cindy's in every way: delivery, content, style, passion and energy. We'll never really know whose remarks the jury appreciated more.

Eat S*** and Die

Michael Carbone was the first witness to testify for the state. At five-feet-eight and 220 pounds, he looked the part of a stocky bodybuilder. Carbone was known for using a variety of drugs. At a minimum, he took steroids to build his body and snorted cocaine for recreational purposes. He never graduated from college, was a divorced father of two and his extensive arrest record dated back to high school.

He came to be the state's star witness when he was arrested for the fifth time on September 15, 1990, this time for a violation of the federal extortion statute known as the Hobbs Act. At the time of his arrest, he had already racked up 30 months in prison for weapons, cocaine and bookmaking convictions.

The September 15 arrest was precipitated when the ruddy-faced bodybuilder found himself in debt to a drug smuggler for $3,000. Unemployed and living off monthly disability payments of only $900, Carbone offered to settle the debt by helping the smuggler collect $56,000 from a 100-pound marijuana deal gone bad. To collect the money, Carbone and two buddies showed up at the Hollywood, Florida home of Robert Vasquez, threatening to murder him and spray his house with gunfire. They demanded the $56,000 back at the exorbitant interest rate of $100 a day. Their tactics worked and they managed to walk out with most of the cash.

Then about a week later, Carbone told Vasquez he wasn't finished with repaying the debt. But Michael didn't anticipate what Vasquez would do next: He went to the police. As a result, Carbone was arrested soon after as he stepped off the golf course at the Arrowhead Country Club in Davie, Florida.

Already a veteran of five other felony convictions, he knew he was going down big time if he didn't do something to save himself. It was a no-brainer. Seven years before the arrest he was there when Wally Leahy, Dickie Robertson and Al Tringali were murdered. So, all he had to do was cut a deal to tell his story about what happened that night. He knew BSO was anxious to nail Fernandez, so he figured the FBI and BSO would jump at the chance to have his testimony. He was right.

Carbone somehow convinced the feds he wasn't the killer, but that he knew who the killer was. His own lawyer, Don Spadaro, was as shocked as the FBI agents over his client's revelations. After seven years without progress on the triple-murder case, the feds knew the local cops were desperate to move forward. The FBI agents reached out to Dade homicide detective Pat Diaz, and BSO detectives Mike Kallman and Joe Damiano, who were already working the joint investigation of all the Broward murders.

A deal was reached and the agencies involved collectively agreed to grant Carbone complete immunity in exchange for his testimony against Gil. As a package deal, he also agreed to testify against Bert, whom Carbone said ordered the murders. Carbone's lawyer Spadaro didn't cut this deal; Carbone did. I originally thought Carbone was a moron. But when I found out he cut the deal himself, I knew I'd at least have to give him credit for being street smart.

Protected by full immunity, Carbone was free to spill his guts. He laid a backdrop by giving details about his association with Gil and Bert. His credibility with authorities was then enhanced when he accurately reported details of the murders that had never been released to the public. The homicide detectives had wisely chosen to hold back on certain details surrounding the crime scene, releasing only enough information to report the crime and solicit help from the public.

In his one-and-a-half hour statement, Carbone gave the salivating BSO deputies and their federal friends all the salacious details. He identified the exact location of the bodies, how they were bound and gagged, the color and texture of the cloth used for the gags, the manner of death for each victim and the colors of their T-shirts. He even gave them the eerily prophetic words printed on the black T-shirt that victim Dickie Robertson wore with his Sergio Valente jeans: "Eat S*** and Die."

Gil had been seen many times by police in the company of Michael and Bert, so this lent additional credibility to Carbone's accusations. BSO officials had no problem believing his story that Bert had hired Gil and Carbone on many occasions as collectors for gambling and bookmaking debts that were ostensibly owed to organized crime.

In addition to immunity from prosecution, Carbone was promised a place in the U.S. Marshal Service's witness protection program. As a condition of his participation, he also was obligated to give the feds information on the gambling, bookmaking, extortion and debt-collecting activities of other local organized crime figures. These dirt bags were essentially his employers. According to Carbone, he was collecting their debts when he was arrested. When he ultimately gave his almost 500-page statement, Carbone confessed to having a long history of working with a variety of low-life types to plan assaults and beat up debtors who fell behind on loan-shark debts.

Along with his many other criminal activities, Carbone sometimes worked for Joseph "Joey Flowers" Rotunno. Rotunno was reputed to be a member of the Columbo organized crime family. Michael's connection to him was evidenced when he was arrested alongside Rotunno during a 1984 BSO undercover investigation into loan sharking and bookmaking, dubbed "Operation Scorpion." From that point on, it was a matter of record that the two did business together.

With his dirty background and his willingness to flip on Gil, I just couldn't help disliking Carbone. I was convinced that he had a larger role in the murders than he let on. It just wasn't credible to me that he stood there while people were murdered and was completely innocent.

Waltzing mannequins

Because of Carbone's status in the federal witness protection program, Tyson issued an order requiring television stations to blur and darken Carbone's face when broadcasting his testimony. Additionally, photographers for the newspapers were forbidden from taking his picture.

Before Carbone was brought into the court, I tried once again to limit the damage being done by the presence of excess law enforcement. "Your Honor," I pleaded in a sidebar away from the jury, "Could you please make sure Carbone doesn't parade in here with those two mannequins they've got waltzing around with him?"

Cindy responded, as though personally offended. "I object to Mr. Contini referring to the deputy U.S. marshals as mannequins, Your Honor. That is inappropriate and unprofessional, at a minimum. As for the need for the marshals' presence, Mr. Carbone is in the federal government's witness protection program. They have their own guidelines, requirements and protocols…"

"Not when those protocols interfere with my client's right to a fair trial, Judge," I interrupted. "If this jury sees Carbone with these G.I. Joes, they're going to draw the inference that my guy must be dangerous, and that they need to be afraid of him, too," I continued.

Now it was Cindy's turn to interrupt. "This jury is bright enough to separate the issues, Judge. They're going to know Carbone has been in custody and that he is in the witness protection program."

"No, they're not, Judge. That's the whole point; it's impermissible for them to know he's in the program. The only purpose that would serve would be to prejudice the jury against Gil and Bert.

"How does the fact that Carbone's in the witness protection program have anything to do with the guilt or innocence of my client regarding this indictment?" I continued. "It's got nothing to do with this case. That kind of testimony would only cause the jury to believe that the federal government must think these are scary guys. This would make it impossible for them to get a fair trial. They'll assume that Your Honor must think he's guilty, too. Come on, Judge, there's no way they should be allowed to see this scary side show," I demanded.

"*Enough!* I've heard enough," the judge interrupted. "There will be no more argument from either side. There will be no marshals and no reference made to the fact that he is in the witness protection program. Is that understood?" Tyson asked Cindy.

"I don't believe the marshals are allowed to leave his side, Your Honor. They are required..."

I couldn't help but interrupt her again. "What do they do, escort him to the bathroom every time he's got to go, too?"

A few people in the spectator gallery started to laugh, but then abruptly stopped when Tyson exploded at me again.

"I said there would be no more argument from either side!" he raged. "I've made my ruling!"

His face was beat red and he was twisting his head side-to-side, almost like Linda Blair in *The Exorcist*. "This guy's a nut case," I thought to myself. I would have loved to blurt out what I really felt like saying, which was, "Judge, have you ever thought about anger management?" But I had no choice except to just watch this freak show, too concerned over Tyson's volatility to say anything.

"Mrs. Imperato, please speak to the marshals and inform them that my deputies will work with them to ensure their requirements are met. Make it clear, though, that Mr. Carbone will *not* testify if they accompany him. They will understand. And unless Mr. Contini opens the door, instruct your witness that there will be no reference to the fact that he is in the witness protection program."

Cindy left the courtroom long enough to inform the deputy U.S. marshals of Tyson's ruling, returning a moment later. "Judge, one of the marshals would like to speak to you," Cindy said.

Tyson called for a break and left the bench momentarily. I was still thinking about his sly little comment, "*If Mr. Contini doesn't open the door...*" This was his way of communicating to the state that he might allow this prejudicial crap into evidence if I gave them any reason whatsoever. Perhaps if I went too far on cross-examination of Carbone, he'd allow the state to mention the witness protection program. "Or maybe he's just trying to appease Cindy," I tried to reassure myself.

In spite of Tyson's comment, I wasn't going to be intimidated into doing the soft shoe with Carbone. It was clear, however, that I'd have to stay away from any information about where he'd been staying and what he'd been doing in the months leading up to the trial.

Call your first witness

During the break, I stepped into the hallway to stretch my legs. Amid the crowd that milled around, I saw that two marshals were about to escort Carbone through the judge's entrance in the hall. Right before he entered, Carbone stopped and we locked eyes. He obviously recognized me from the deposition I had taken of him at Maxwell Air Force Base in Montgomery, Alabama.

It was like the moment when two fighters greet each other in the center of the ring before a big bout. Michael nodded at me as if to say, "I know you gotta do what you gotta do." I nodded back. It really wasn't personal at that point. We each had a job to do. He was going to try to be believable on the stand and I was going to try to make him look like a liar.

We had an entire conversation with our eyes and head nods. We both silently said, "It is what it is." There was a weird kind of mutual respect or at least a mutual understanding about it all. Then the moment was over, and Carbone and the marshals entered the judge's chambers. Five minutes later, Tyson returned to the bench.

"Call in the jury," he said, looking at Mike and Bob.

The jurors filed in slowly from the jury room. I pretended to look respectfully at them but what I was really doing was watching every move they made. The prosecutors were doing the same thing, all of us forcing the same polite and awkward smiles.

Chapter 16

The Dirt Bag

"State, call your first witness," Tyson said, as soon as every member of the jury was seated. In walked Michael Carbone. To my quiet satisfaction, the marshals who had accompanied Carbone in the hall were nowhere in sight. This meant the U.S. Marshals Service was following Tyson's order.

Carbone was at least two inches shorter than the five-feet-ten indicated on his driver's license. He wasn't as hulking as he appeared in his booking photo, yet it was obvious he still worked out. He cavalierly walked to the witness stand and sat down, almost like he was about to get a haircut.

In spite of our little reunion in the hallway, I couldn't help but think as he was being sworn in, "I'm going to hate to have to listen to this dirt bag." I noticed how intently the jurors were studying his every movement and expression, and I was hoping they felt the same.

Prosecutor Jim Lewis sauntered up to the podium and greeted Carbone, who nodded in return. Jim then said, "Mr. Carbone, could you please tell us what you know about the events of April 1st and 2nd, 1983?"

The jury's attention, along with everyone else's in the courtroom, was riveted on him as he began. "Let's hope you have some serious stage fright, Michael," I thought, knowing that life would be a lot harder if he did a good job selling his story.

"It was seven years ago, but I remember it actually started the night before April 1st," Carbone said. "I guess that would have been March 31st," he added gratuitously.

"I met Gil Fernandez through my friend, Tommy Felts, who told me Gil was a cop. On that first night, Tommy wanted me to be the security for a drug deal he and Fernandez were planning, because I owned a Thompson semi-automatic machine gun. Tommy agreed to pay me $75,000."

Jim interrupted and said, "Did you ever receive that money?"

"I got $50,000 of it over the next two months," Carbone replied.

"Thank you. Please continue," Jim said.

"Tommy asked me to wait across the street from his house with my Tommy gun and a .357 Magnum. While I was sitting there waiting in my car, I saw Bert Christie come by. He had a gun. Bert stayed for a while and watched the house and then he left. Tommy told me later that…"

"Objection, Judge," I interrupted, "as to what Tommy told him. It's rank hearsay."

"Overruled," snapped Tyson. "I will allow for some latitude here."

"Of *course* you will," I said, almost out loud. Carbone spoke with renewed vigor once Tyson said he'd allow the free-for-all.

"Tommy said Bert would be getting a piece of the action from the deal." Gil sat looking innocent and unaffected, just as I had instructed him. Bert, however, shook his head with visible disgust on his face.

"The deal didn't go down that night, so Tommy asked me to come to his house again the next day."

"Continuing objection, Your Honor, as to whatever Tommy is alleged to have said," I interrupted again, preserving the record. It was fairly obvious that Tyson was going to deny every one of my objections to this hearsay testimony, so the only solution was to record the continuing objection to be used on appeal in event of a conviction. The only other alternative would have been to annoy the jury with incessant interruptions, objecting repeatedly. I believed that would have only led them to think I was hiding things from them.

"Continuing objection noted," replied the judge.

"The next day would have been April 1, 1983. Is that correct?" Jim asked.

"Yes," Carbone answered. "I went back the next day, which was April 1st. This time, Tommy wanted me to wait in a bedroom closet and come out with my Thompson when he called. I waited for a long time. Finally, the three guys showed up. Tommy called for me and I came running out of the bedroom, carrying the gun.

"When I ran into the Florida room, I saw Gil Fernandez shoving a chrome handgun into the mouth of the guy in the black T-shirt. Gil always carried an extra gun strapped to his ankle, usually a .38. I think that was one of two guns he used that night.

"Gil was yelling at the guy with the gun in his mouth, "You f***ed over the boss!" There was a collective gasp from the audience, followed by the quiet sobbing of several women.

"There were two other guys on the floor next to him. I was nervous, so I pointed the gun at Gil by mistake. He screamed at me, 'Point the gun at those guys, not at *me!*'"

"Then a beeper clipped to one of the guy's pants went off. Gil grabbed it and yelled, 'Who's trying to call you?' Then he threw it to the ground.

"While Gil was messing with the guy, Tommy was pulling kilos of cocaine out of an ice chest and transferring them into a duffel bag. When Tommy was done, he went into the other room to get a rope, towels and some cloth."

"I covered the guys with the Thompson while Gil put on weightlifter's gloves. When Tommy came back, Gil grabbed the rope and tied the guys' hands behind their backs. Then he took the towels and blindfolded them.

Tommy gagged them with the paper towels because he said he didn't want to listen to them beg for their lives. Then he put tape over their mouths to hold in the paper towels."

"*You* gagged them, you lying sack of s✱✱✱," I almost said, recalling his admission to me months ago during his deposition. I distinctly remembered him telling me that *he* didn't want to hear the victims begging for their lives. And now he was saying it was Tommy who gagged them.

"Oh, I'm going to have some fun with you on cross, pal," I told myself, elated that he was going to these lengths to sanitize his image. "Michael," I felt like saying out loud, "you'd better keep track of the few times you tell the truth. Otherwise, you'll lose them in that vast sea of lies you're telling."

The silent cross in my head was just getting good when I heard a woman in the spectator gallery start to cry loudly. I then heard a rustling sound, which was the noise made by the people around her as they shifted in their seats and reached out to comfort her.

"Could you please tell us who these victims were?" Lewis asked.

"I didn't find out their names until later," Carbone replied.

This reference to the victims elicited a collective gasp of suppressed emotional pain from the spectator gallery on the prosecution side of the room. The victims' families and friends were finally hearing the story from someone who was present when their loved ones were murdered, and their pain was palpable.

A man in the gallery uttered venomously under his breath, "You *bastard*!" The woman next to him quickly put her arms around him, pulling him close as he started to sob. Tyson shot them a look to make sure it didn't happen again. Halfway out of my seat on the way to make an objection, the judge's stern look aimed toward the audience members stopped me. The shock of seeing Tyson upset at someone other than the defense was enough to keep me quiet — for the moment.

My back stayed bent as I hung in space, leaning partway over the defense table. I looked over at the jury. They were all looking back at me to see if I'd make a bigger stink out of the outburst. But then we all seemed to silently agree to let it go, dismissing it as a somewhat expected event.

Tyson just nodded at Carbone and said, "Please continue."

As if nothing had happened, Carbone said, "Gil kept telling the drug dealers that they had 'f✱✱✱ed over the boss.'"

"Did you know to whom they were referring?" Lewis asked.

"Bert Christie," Carbone said. "We always took our orders from him."

Bert slowly shook his head, again with disgust. He turned to look at his daughters, seated several feet behind him in the gallery and mouthed, "He's a liar, liar, liar."

"OK, Mr. Carbone, what happened next?" Jim asked.

When I was a prosecutor, we always asked that question whenever we didn't know what else to say. Sometimes we alternated that with the other no-brainer, "And then what happened?"

"Gil and Tommy left the house for a few hours to hide the car the victims came in, a Z-28 Camaro. It was brand new, I think — an '83. I guarded the victims until they got back around 8 o'clock.

"When they returned, Gil told me they had left the car in the nearby woods. Then he told me to give him my .357-Magnum and my Tommy gun. He said to help them get the three guys into my 1980 Grand Prix, which was parked in the carport. I thought we were going to Bert's house. Instead, Gil told me to drive out to Jones Fish Camp on the edge of the Everglades. We got off U.S. 27 and turned down a dirt road. It was pretty dark out there except for some moonlight. The road was deserted and next to a canal. I found out later that the people who live in the trailers out there called it Danger Road.

"Gil told me to pull over. When we got out of the car, each of us was holding one guy. They were still tied and blindfolded. But the smaller guy's gag must've fallen out of his mouth because he asked, 'Why? Why are you doing this?'"

Carbone said this last line in a detached way, like he was repeating something he had seen at the movies. "These poor people," I thought as I imagined the impact this testimony would be having on the families. "I can't even offer them my condolences." They hated me almost as much as they hated Gil. Anything sympathetic I could ever say to them, no matter how sincere, would be immediately rejected as disingenuous.

As I thought this, Carbone looked around, trying to see if the jury was buying his story. Then he continued by saying, "We walked for a while on the road, maybe a half-mile. Then I heard Gil get in the water with the guy he was holding. I couldn't see much because it was almost pitch black out, but I heard Gil tell the guy to drop to his knees.

"I heard two shots and then a splash. I guess the dead guy fell in the water."

Almost all the victims' family members and friends were crying now. The details were just too painful. Their agony was no doubt exacerbated by having to hear the nightmarish details from the unrepentant Michael Carbone, the dirt bag who helped torture their loved ones. His lack of remorse over having held the victims at gunpoint for hours and the way he cavalierly described their cold-blooded murders had to rub salt in their wounds.

Carbone continued, "Gil asked for the next guy and Tommy handed him over. I heard two more shots and then another splash.

Gil's family just looked down. They, like me, were waiting for this terrible part of the case to end.

"I was holding the third guy. Gil told me to bring him toward the water but I didn't want to hand him over. So, Tommy grabbed him from me and pulled him to where Gil was standing. I heard a shot. Then I heard someone splashing around in the water." After a pause, Carbone said, "I guess the guy wasn't dead yet."

In response, loud sobbing came from a woman in the prosecution-side spectator gallery. One of the victim's mothers had been pushed to the brink. Carbone looked at Lewis for direction. Jim then looked to Tyson for guidance as to whether he should continue over the sobbing. Tyson held up his hand to Lewis and looked over at the crying woman, waiting for her to calm down. Nobody dared do anything in that long moment. As we waited, the room was as silent as a tomb. The only sounds to be heard were the anguished cries.

After the woman calmed down, Tyson nodded to Carbone to continue. He said, "I heard another shot and the splashing stopped. I didn't hear anything after that."

I looked over at the jurors. Some of them were crying but they were looking away in an effort to squelch their tears.

"Thank you, Mr. Carbone," Jim Lewis said. "After the murders, what did you do?"

"We heard a helicopter overhead, so we thought we should get out of there. We jumped in the car and drove to a bridge over the intra-coastal. We got out, and Gil took the guns and threw them in the water. I noticed he had blood all over his jeans."

"When we were on the bridge, Gil turned to me and said, 'You'd better vacuum the inside of the car and wash it, including the tires and undercarriage. And burn your clothes.'

"Then he said, 'If you ever open your mouth, Michael, I'll kill your family. Even if you go to China, I will find you. I will kill you and I will kill them.'"

In spite of my earlier admonition that he not show anger, Gil glared at Carbone from his seat at the defense table. I whacked his right knee with my left, letting him know he needed to chill out.

"China? Just listen to this guy," Gil whispered, staring at him.

I leaned toward him and whispered a warning to him, "Shake your head in disgust, kind of like the way Bert did it; but *don't* let them see you angry."

Carbone continued. "After that, we met Christie at a gas station. He came up to the car and asked, 'Was the job done?' We told him it was."

"What did you do then?" Jim asked.

"I drove home and told my wife Rebecca the same story I just told you."

Lewis had the audacity to have Carbone repeat the whole story again, under the pretext of wanting to know exactly what he said to his wife. I had objected earlier to all that self-serving hearsay garbage, but Tyson had ruled that it could be admitted. Surprise, surprise.

After the jury, spectators, media, court personnel, and of course, the defense, were treated to the retelling of the story, the courtroom was finally as quiet as the Everglades. Jim simply looked at our "neutral and detached magistrate" and said, "No more questions for this witness, Your Honor."

I had never heard more pleasant words.

Tyson adjourned the session for the day. After I finished giving a few interviews, I waited for Bill Kelly to work his way through the crowd and take me home.

As I waited, Jim Lewis sauntered over to the elevator and pressed the button. While he waited for the elevator to arrive, he seized the opportunity to speak to me. He leaned forward, cupped his hand over his mouth like he was going to share a secret and said in a taunting stage whisper, "Just so you know, I saw Fernandez following along with the crime details in his mind when Carbone was testifying. It was obvious to me he had been at the scene; I could tell by the look on his face. What's more, he *knew* that I knew he was doing it."

Tired now, I just scowled at him and said lamely, "You've been watching too much TV, Lewis."

The elevator arrived. Jim stepped into it and pushed the button. Right before the doors closed, he said matter-of-factly, "Your client's guilty, Contini."

Chapter 17

Cross

"Mr. Contini, do you have any questions for the witness?" Tyson asked.

"Just a few hundred," is what I wanted to say. Instead, I rose and said, "Yes, Your Honor."

Not able to sleep the night before, I kept getting up to scribble notes on blue three-by-five-inch index cards. It took 11 hours over several days to meticulously record all the inconsistent statements Carbone had previously made under oath. These cards, which had the page and volume numbers from each of Carbone's previous statements and depositions, and from his Grand Jury testimony, would serve as cross-examination tools for quick and easy impeachment and cross-reference purposes. The goal was to blow Carbone's and the jurors' minds, quicker than anyone could say, "Could you please repeat that?"

The stack of cards was in my left hand as I held a five-by-seven-inch photo of Carbone in my right. Before I left the defense table, I heard Gil mutter encouragement: "Go get 'em."

As I approached Carbone, I thought, "How am I going to reconcile my desire to be a good Christian boy with my need to eviscerate this thug who's killing my guy?"

"I'll tear him up and repent later," I said to the guy in my head.

I stood in front of Carbone, holding the photo of him from his bodybuilding heyday, when he was a huge and scary-looking steroid freak.

"This animal depicted in the picture, is that you?"

"That's the biggest I ever was," he responded.

"I certainly hope so," I replied sarcastically. "Isn't it a fact that you were bench pressing 565 pounds at the time?" I asked.

"Yes," he replied.

"Isn't it also true that you had the reputation of muscling people around and not taking no for an answer?" I pressed.

"Yes."

"Is this how you looked when you held the three victims at gunpoint with your Thompson sub-machine gun, while you listened to them beg for their lives?" I asked.

Frowning at me, he reluctantly said, "Yes."

"And this is how you looked when you drove them to their deaths and walked them down Danger Road in the middle of the night?" He didn't answer.

"And this is how you looked when you made them kneel in the water and you shot each of them in the head?" I persisted.

"Gil shot them, not me. I wasn't in the water," he replied coldly.

The deathmobile

Getting closer to him and raising my voice, I asked, "And of course we're supposed to just believe you because you say so. *Right?*"

"It's the truth," Carbone remarked.

Carbone shifted in his seat and coughed, allowing me a millisecond or two to nonchalantly rifle through the systemically arranged index cards. I quickly found the reminder for which I was looking.

"And was it *also* the truth when you stated in your sworn deposition that Mr. Fernandez drove the car to the murder scene? You just stated under oath on direct examination that *you* were the one who drove the car."

"It was a long time ago. I don't remember," Carbone said defensively.

I kept my eyes locked on him as I walked over to the round metal trashcan I'd strategically placed between the witness stand and the podium. I gently flicked the card into the can without skipping a beat. The card made a soft thumping sound as it hit the inside of the empty receptacle.

"Mr. Carbone, are you telling this court that on that night — a night that had to be the most horrific of your life — that you don't remember who drove the car that delivered the victims to their deaths? You don't remember who drove the deathmobile?"

"I don't *remember*," Carbone repeated, sounding annoyed.

"You said it was your white Grand Prix that was used that night. Is that correct?"

"Yes."

"OK, I'm really curious. You said your car was a 1980 Grand Prix, right?"

"That's right."

"That car had bucket seats in the front, according to Pontiac records for the 1980 Grand Prix. So, if that's true, then your car was a five-seater, wasn't it, sir?"

"Yeah."

'Now, sir, you were huge, as we've already seen from this photo. And you said Gil and Tommy were with you — and we know they were huge. And then there were the three victims. They weren't small, either. So then, let me ask you, how on earth did the six of you fit in that five-seater car?"

There was murmuring from the crowd. Carbone made an annoyed face as he looked in the direction of the noise and then said, "We squeezed in."

"Sir, are you telling this jury that you all squeezed into the car when the victims had their hands bound behind their back?"

"That's what I said."

"But isn't it true the victims would take up one-and-a-half times the space with their hands like this?" I said as I put my hands behind me, joining them at the small of my back. I wiggled the stack of blue cards in my hand to make sure I had everyone's attention.

"I don't think there was a problem getting all of us in there but it was tight," Carbone said.

"All right. So you're saying there was no problem with six individuals getting into this two-door, five-seat car? Watch me, sir. You do it," I said adamantly as I faced my back toward him and emphasized the imaginary ties on my hands. "Wouldn't the victims have been bigger from side to side, sir, with their hands bound behind their backs? Is that not true?

"I don't know. I can't answer that," was all he said.

While the jury looked at him, I stole the opportunity to thumb through the index cards for the exact reference and page number I needed.

"Do you remember saying something quite inconsistent — or I should say, completely different — when you testified under oath before the Grand Jury?" I asked, holding up one of the index cards.

"No."

The jury had to be wondering what it said on the card. That's how I wanted it.

The card, which was both theatrical prop and research tool, directed me to an exact location in the stack of Carbone transcripts. Having access to this information allowed me to open the correct transcript to the precise page I needed for impeachment. Then I could approach Carbone, transcript in hand, and confront him with his own words, verbatim.

"In seven sworn statements to the police…"

Carbone interrupted me before I could finish and said, "Nope."

"…two depositions totaling 500 pages…" I waved the cards just far enough from his face to keep me out of trouble with Tyson and still convey my disrespect of Carbone to the jury. He interrupted me again, so I raised my voice to be heard. "And each time…" He tried to speak again but I spoke over him.

"Let him answer!" Judge Tyson said angrily. "You're interrupting each other. Slow it down. Mr. Carbone, please give an opportunity for Mr. Contini to ask the question. And Mr. Contini, let Mr. Carbone answer the question. And keep your voices down. You may proceed, Mr. Contini."

"There are at least seven or eight sworn statements, and yet, never before did you come up with some of this fine detail about the car. Is that true?" I asked.

"Yes, that *is* true. But it's hard to think of everything in one deposition, I'll tell you that right now. Each deposition is going to change a little bit because you remember a little bit more."

"Change a *little* bit?" I asked sarcastically. "No, sir. You're *adding* things!"

Time to drop another card into the trashcan.

"I'm not adding. It's the truth."

"Whatever you say, Mr. Carbone," I said, before adding in my head, "You wouldn't know the truth if it bit you on the a∗∗."

Then the judge gave the jury a 10-minute break.

It was almost fun hammering Carbone on the many discrepancies between his two depositions, his testimony on direct examination, and in the sworn statements to Metro-Dade police, the BSO, the FBI and the Grand Jury. After the break, it was time to beat him up about the "deathmobile."

"Mr. Carbone, neighbors in the area of Jones Fish Camp said they saw a large black car that night. Do you know anything about that?"

"No. We were in a white Grand Prix."

"Are you sure you're not protecting the actual killers — your organized crime buddies who drove that big black car? Aren't you in fact throwing this off onto Gil and Tommy to protect the real killers?"

"I don't know what you're talking about," Carbone responded.

"Of course you don't," I said sarcastically.

Name-calling

Changing my approach to get back to the inconsistencies in his testimony, I then asked him, "So, did you tell the truth to the detectives seven years ago when they first asked you about who drove the car?"

"No."

"You're telling us now that you *lied* to the police at that time, right?"

"That's right," he replied.

"Because you were looking out for your own best interests back then, that first time you lied to them, right?" I continued.

"Yeah."

"And you're *still* looking out for your own best interests even now, Mr. Carbone. Isn't that right?" I accused him.

"No, that's *not* right."

"You convinced the police of your truthfulness the first time they approached you seven years ago. So, how do we know you're not just as convincing today with this new story?"

Carbone just looked at me.

"You're a convincing liar. Aren't you, Mr. Carbone?"

"I'm telling the truth," he replied.

"Well then, I'm curious, Michael. At which time then were you lying to law enforcement? Seven years ago or now?"

"Objection, Your Honor, Mr. Contini is asking him the same question over and over, and he has already testified..." Lewis protested.

"Overruled. You may continue, Mr. Contini," Tyson said.

"Wow, once in a millennium he actually rules for the defense," I thought to myself.

Even the jurors looked puzzled at the judge's surprise ruling. I forgot where I was going for a second, perplexed by the fact that the judge ruled in my favor. Maybe he was throwing me a bone out of guilt for the way he'd been toward the defense, I reasoned. But there was no time to think about it now. I had to get back to business.

"You've always testified to whatever's in your own best interests. Is that true?" I continued.

"No, that's *not* true," replied Carbone.

"Really?" I reacted. "Well, if that's not true, then please tell us, which times were you *not* looking out for your own interests?"

His answer was inaudible, but that was OK. He might as well have grunted.

"This jury is being asked, on the basis of your testimony — the testimony of an immunized five-time convicted felon — to possibly send men to the electric chair! Do you really believe..."

Nobody could hear what I was trying to say because of the loud objections from the prosecutors' table. It seemed whenever I said the words, "electric chair," they started yelling. "Pavlov would've loved these guys," I thought.

"Sustained," Tyson said, proving he could yell, too. "Mr. Contini, you will confine your questions to the facts of this case!"

"Take some meds, Judge," I felt like saying. The jurors were wide-eyed and sitting up in their seats now, apparently enjoying the theater of it all. The trial spectators looked like they were watching a Hitchcock movie. Had it been allowed, they'd have made a few bucks selling popcorn that day.

"I'm sorry, Your Honor. It's just *very* upsetting that we're being asked to believe this killer..."

"Objection!" the three prosecutors yelled again in unison, this time making some of the jurors jump.

"Mr. Contini, I am *not* going to tell you again. You will refrain from any name-calling or other inappropriate cross-examination," Tyson scowled.

"Yes, Your Honor. I understand," I replied, feigning some degree of humility and remorse. This allowed a moment to grab the next index card and spot the reference I needed.

"Mr. Carbone, you've been convicted of five separate and distinct felonies in your life, haven't you?" I asked in a hushed tone. I knew pitching change-ups like this would help me stay in the game.

"Yeah."

"You were arrested by the FBI on a federal extortion, and that's when you first *sold* the story you're *selling* us today, right?"

Before the prosecutors had a chance to jump up and object again, I said, "Let me rephrase that. I mean, *told* the story you're *telling* us today."

He grunted, unwittingly affirming my question.

With all their jumping up and down, the prosecutors really were getting their exercise. They should've been thanking me for the calisthenics.

"You were facing life in prison on that extortion case, when you factor in the federal sentencing guidelines and your prior felony convictions. Isn't that true?" I asked.

"No, that's *not* true," Carbone argued.

"You came up with this whole story about Gil Fernandez and how you didn't know in advance that these men were going to die, just to get out of a lengthy federal sentence. Isn't that true?"

"That's a lie," Carbone insisted, shifting his frame defiantly in his chair.

"Do you even know when you're lying, Michael?" I asked him sarcastically. "How are we supposed to know when you're telling the truth, when you've been lying and committing felonies your whole miserable life?"

It was almost comical how all three prosecutors abruptly rose to their feet. They seemed to forget momentarily that only one of them — the one who conducted the direct examination of the witness — was entitled to object. I threw another index card into the can as the ever-present telephoto-lens cameras clicked away in rapid-fire fashion. Tyson was starting to get red in the face, so I told myself to chill out. Ethics aside, I knew my question was improper. For a change, Tyson had a right to be flaming out along with the rest of them. So, I knew it was time to change the subject and quit throwing curves.

"I noticed, Mr. Carbone, in a few of your earlier statements to the police, that you had sworn that Mr. Fernandez was waist-high in the water with the victims. Is that right?"

"Yeah, so?" he replied, still pissed.

"And yet, on direct, you said he carried a gun on his ankle and always wore an ankle holster. You suggested that maybe *that's* where this other gun came from. Isn't that what you said? If that were the case, wouldn't the holster and the gun have been under water?"

"Whatever," is all he muttered, looking at me contemptuously.

"No, it's not *whatever*, Michael. We don't fry people on *whatever*!"

The objections rained down but it didn't matter. The room was filled with laughter — and not just from the peanut gallery in back. This time, the jurors were laughing. That's what I needed, as I often said that laughing juries don't convict. Some of the jurors even conveyed their disgust at Carbone, shaking their heads and contorting their faces. They were getting the message and that was all that mattered. The cameras clicked away, capturing the juror's laughter at Carbone. With a stern look from Tyson, the noise finally subsided.

"Let's take a break," he said. "Bailiffs, please escort the jury out of the courtroom. We will reconvene in 10 minutes."

Gil, Bert and Louie were smiling at me as I returned to sit at the defense table. And I was smiling, too. I felt good about burying this guy.

Chapter 18

Everyone Lies

When we returned from the break, I was more ready than ever to go after Carbone. I wasted no time getting back in his face.

"You were intimate with the sister of one of the victims, weren't you, sir?" I asked him, making sure the jury saw the total disgust on my face.

"What's that got to do with this?" Carbone asked, not wanting to answer.

"You never told her, did you Mr. Carbone, that you had held her brother at gunpoint for hours as he begged for his life? That you watched him die? Did you tell her any of this before you took her to bed?"

"No, I felt bad about that," he replied.

"Oh, you felt bad? Do you want one of these?" I asked him sarcastically as I grabbed a box of tissues from in front of the judge's bench and gestured toward Carbone, inviting him to take one.

The crowd sitting on the benches on the defense side of the courtroom was now calling out to Carbone, laughing and mocking him. The jury was looking at him sideways, too. During the chaos caused by the taunts and mocking laughter, I stole a look at Gil, Bert and Louie, who were smiling ear-to-ear and nudging each other.

"If you were capable of doing that to a murder victim's sister, what would you be willing to do to this jury to get what you want?"

"This is ridiculous," Carbone complained.

"That's *it*, Your Honor!" Lewis angrily protested, "Mr. Contini is beyond the pale here."

"Move on, Mr. Contini!" Tyson demanded, almost snarling at me.

"Isn't it a fact, Mr. Carbone, that these prosecutors over here gave you complete immunity for your involvement in these murders?" I asked, speaking softer now so I could slow the pace and quiet the rhetoric.

"Yeah, that's right," is all he said, still glaring at me.

"Your testimony has been bought and paid for. It's been literally purchased; hasn't it sir?"

The objections were echoing in stereo now. Tyson admonished me again by barking loudly, "Mr. Contini! Not another word…"

Motion for mistrial

It was now out of control. Tyson was losing this jury to the sideshow that doubled as a trial.

"Bailiffs, take the jury back," Tyson commanded. The silence that followed his order was deafening.

Even some of the media folks and trial spectators looked concerned for me. Especially Elizabeth, who thanks to her mom had a couple of hours between baby-nursing sessions. She came to watch the Carbone cross, knowing it would be the best show in town. She was nervous for me as Tyson said to the jury members, "Ladies and gentlemen, please do not discuss this case with anyone or allow it to be discussed in your presence. We will bring you back in just a moment."

More silence followed. Waiting for the jurors to file out of the room was the quietest moment of the day — or the night for that matter, since my babies had taken turns doing lung exercises almost until dawn.

None of us enjoyed this calm before the storm. My instincts kicked in, reminding me that the best defense is a good offense. As the door to the jury room shut, Tyson turned to look over at me. Before he had a chance to speak, let alone work himself up, I laid into him.

"Judge, you're yelling at me in front of this jury, sending the message that you don't like the defense. This is leading them to believe that the defendant must be guilty. You're treating the prosecutors with every kind of deference and respect, and all the while you're screaming at me.

"I want the record to reflect that we are *not* getting a fair trial and that this jury has most likely already drawn the illegal and impermissible inference that you favor one side over the other. It's obvious to any reasonable observer that the court must know something that the jurors don't; that the defendant *must* be guilty..."

It was working. Lights from the cameras came on, followed by the familiar cacophony of clicking from the photographers. Gil and Bert exchanged looks of curiosity, while Louie and I winked at each other.

Tyson now had to shoot from the hip and configure his own defense. He was all too aware that he had an audience — one that sat riveted, watching him. And he was watching them. This audience was Tyson's own jury of sorts. It was comprised of the families on both sides of the aisle, the ever-present members of the media, and the largest jury: the public. Where there were cameras, he knew there were thousands of other unseen eyes and ears. And he could play to that unseen audience with the best of them.

His voice lowered as he made an effort to control his rage. He calmly, judiciously and self-servingly declared, "The record will reflect that this court is treating both sides with the same accord, deference and respect. There has been *no* disparate treatment by the court. The record will further reflect that the court does *not* prefer one verdict to another, and is possessed of no other facts to suggest either guilt or innocence. Counsel is mistaken. If counsel's remarks constitute a motion for mistrial, that motion is respectfully denied."

"We do in fact make a motion for mistrial at this time," I remarked, still playing the victim.

"I've already ruled. And Mr. Contini, you will treat this witness with respect. You will not engage in any more inappropriate conduct before this court. Should there be any further disregard for this court's rulings, contempt proceedings will follow. Now is *not* the time to start this trial all over again. All of you lawyers know how to conduct yourselves, so I'm admonishing all of you — the defense and the state — to conduct yourselves accordingly."

Molloy looked over at me with eyes that seemed to say, "You dodged a bullet on that one." Then he nodded his head ever so slightly, as if he were tipping his proverbial hat and saying "touché." It was a look that only a veteran trial lawyer would have made, as only a guy like that would've known what really just happened. Like me, he knew I'd pushed the envelope a bit too far and there was only one way out of the jam — and that was to mount an offensive. Going after Tyson when he was about to come down on me, was kind of like swinging for the bleachers when you have a three-and-two count in the bottom of the ninth with the bases loaded. You don't have a lot of choice. Doug knew it, and he let me know he knew it. Moments like that made me like the guy, adversary or not.

"Your Honor, this jury is smart enough to know you're angry with me," I insisted. "That will have a prejudicial spillover effect onto my client. At a minimum, I ask you to instruct the jury that the court does not favor one party over another in these proceedings and that the defendants are presumed innocent. They didn't hear any of that stuff about how you don't have any feelings one way or the other about the guilt or innocence of the defendants. All they know is you are raging at the people sitting at the defense table, while being warm and fuzzy with the state."

"I will not give any sort of curative instruction, as I believe that sends the wrong message — the very message you are trying to avoid. But I will speak to the jury about the court's feelings of respect for *all* counsel. I also will once again give the jury instructions as to the presumption of innocence. Is that agreed?" Tyson inquired, looking at all of us.

Molloy spoke up this time. "I don't believe it's appropriate at this time to give the jury another instruction as to the defendants' presumption of innocence."

"In an abundance of caution I will give the instruction," Tyson ruled. Then, looking at the bailiffs, he continued, "You may bring in the jury."

With that, Doug and I sat down, only to rise again with everyone else once the jury filed back into the courtroom.

One gun, two gun

It was once again time to throw a change-up. Showing Carbone a bound volume of court papers, I remarked, "What I'm holding here is your Grand Jury testimony, Mr. Carbone. This transcript records that you told *that* jury there was only *one* gun at the scene and that Mr. Fernandez was the person who had the gun. Do you recall telling the Grand Jury about the one gun?"

"I don't know. It was a while ago," is all he muttered.

"A while ago, maybe, but closer in time to the murders, when your recollection would have been much better, no?" I asked.

"It was a while ago," he repeated defiantly.

"But now you're telling *this* jury on direct examination that you remember Fernandez carrying two guns at the scene, one of them in a holster at his waistband or ankle. Isn't that what you said?" I asked.

"He had two guns," Carbone replied.

"Of course, you had to think of *some* other story for this particular jury, to get around the fact that the medical examiner found two distinct types of ammunition in the bodies of these victims. Isn't that true?" I added.

"I don't know what you're talking about," he answered.

"But you do know that two distinct types of ammunition could *only* be explained by the fact that *two* distinct firearms were involved. Isn't that true, Mr. Carbone?" I asked, still accusatory.

"All I know is that Gil shot those guys," Carbone retorted.

"Sir, you testified in front of the Grand Jury that you heard six shots. Yet, the medical examiner's report tells us there were eight bullet wounds in the three bodies. So, you do the math. You're saying six, and yet we know we have at least eight bullets."

Gesturing toward the jury, I added, "Do you think these people can't add?"

The jury was sitting up straighter now, starting to smell the coffee. The only things adding up here were impeachment points against Carbone.

"I'm not saying that," was his only reply.

"Mr. Carbone, were you doing some shooting that night that you're not telling us about?"

One of the jurors could no longer contain her disrespect and let out an audible sigh of disgust. Realizing what she had done, she looked horrified and covered her mouth with both hands.

"No," Carbone said, clearly annoyed at my question.

"First I'll tell you what we know and then I'll ask you a question. We know there were two different guns used to kill these people. The reports from Dr. Mittleman, the medical examiner, and Mr. Freeman, the firearms examiner, tell us there were two distinct types of ammunition found in the bodies of the victims. Now, my question: You're aware of that, aren't you?"

"I don't know. That's what they're saying," Carbone replied.

"But that's not what *you're* saying. Is it, sir?"

Before he could respond, I hit him with, "You were one of the shooters, one of the murderers that night. Weren't you Mr. Carbone?"

"No, I wasn't!" he angrily snapped.

"You told the Grand Jury a year ago about *one* gun, and you've told this jury about *two* guns. So, let me ask you sir, to which jury were you lying?"

"Objection! Your Honor, he has already answered the question. Mr. Contini is badgering the witness," Jim Lewis complained.

"Sustained. Move on," ruled Tyson.

"OK, I'll ask it in a nicer way. Mr. Carbone, to which jury did you tell the truth?"

He didn't answer.

"Move on, Mr. Contini," instructed the judge.

"You've *already* admitted earlier that you lied to the police to protect yourself when they first questioned you years earlier; is that correct?" I asked.

"Objection. Asked and answered, Judge," Lewis protested.

"Overruled," replied Tyson, quite surprisingly.

"You lied quite convincingly to those detectives back then. And they believed you, didn't they?" I pressed.

"I don't know. You'll have to ask them," he stated.

"You *lied*," repeating the accusation for effect.

"Everyone lies," Carbone retorted calmly. "You've never lied in your life, Mr. Contini? You've *never* lied?"

"You wanna get in my face, Michael?" I asked, my voice rising. "Let's *go!*"

"Do I have to take this?" Carbone asked, turning to Tyson for help.

"Move on, Mr. Contini," ordered the judge in a stern tone.

"Yes, Your Honor." I continued by turning to Carbone and saying, "Those detectives left you alone for a lot of years, so you must have lied quite convincingly. You're a convincing liar, aren't you, Michael?"

He just looked at me with hate in his eyes.

"Your history shows that you are able to convincingly lie to men with badges, guns and the power to arrest you. You don't seem to have any problem lying to them."

"Is that a question, Judge?" Lewis asked sarcastically.

"We'll never know whether you're telling the truth to this jury, sir, because they don't have badges and guns, and they can't arrest you. In fact, now you can say whatever you want because you've got a complete pass on all this, don't you?"

He wouldn't answer. He just looked over at the prosecution table as if to ask, "Hey, aren't you guys going to object? Help me out here, will ya?"

Before his little messiahs could rescue him with objections, I asked, "You already have complete immunity for these murders. Isn't that true?"

He started to say something but before he could respond I added, "You've lied so often that you're clueless about what the truth is any more. Now, isn't *that* true, Mr. Carbone?

"No, it's not."

"Sir, you've admitted to lying to law enforcement whenever it's to your advantage, for example, to protect yourself from arrest or prosecution, right?"

"That was before," Carbone replied.

"*Before*. But not any more, right?"

Carbone just stared at me.

"That's what I thought," I said sarcastically.

More conflicting stories

Having exhausted the topic of the conflicting number of guns, I went on to address other inconsistencies in Carbone's testimony. I pulled out another index card, looking at it only briefly.

"Sir, are you aware that you told the Grand Jury you took Griffin Road to U.S. 27 to get to the murder scene, while in your statements to the police you said you took Stirling Road to U.S. 27, and *not* Griffin?"

"I'm not sure, it was years ago."

"On the most hellacious night of your life, you don't remember the death route?"

Lewis was getting up and barking again, reminding me of Tyson for a moment. Ignoring him this time, I just tossed the little index card ever so gingerly into the circular trashcan and moved on, knowing we had scored another point for the reasonable doubt team. That gave me the extra seconds I needed to grab the next card for yet another pitch, a curve ball.

"Are you aware that the victims told their loved ones on the night before they were murdered that they had a meeting on March 30 at Tommy Adams' house? Did you know they mentioned the guys who were buying the kilos, and that a woman and a child were there in the house, too, along with a million dollars in cash and a money-counting machine?"

"No," he replied.

Pointing to the victims' families seated on the prosecution side of the courtroom, I repeated, "Are you aware that these folks here, the families of the victims, tell an entirely different story from yours, and that all of them have testified to the same thing in earlier statements to the police?"

"Objection," said Jim Lewis, anxious to derail me.

"You're objecting, even though I'm showing respect for what the victims' loved ones said to the police?" I asked incredulously, mentioning the victims' loved ones again for emphasis.

Lewis clarified, "Objection to the characterization, Your Honor."

"Mr. Carbone can say whether or not he is *aware*, Judge," I countered.

"Overruled," Tyson said. "You may answer the question, Mr. Carbone.

"It was Tommy's house, but it was Tommy *Felts*," Carbone replied.

"But what you're saying is not what the victims told their loved ones before they died. They had no reason to lie to the folks they loved. Isn't that more reliable than your story?" I asked, rhetorically.

"No, because I was there," he said defensively.

"But you were *not* there, sir," I added, "when the victims were telling their loved ones that there was nothing to worry about because it was 'safe' and there was 'a family atmosphere.'"

"Who knows why they told their people that. It wasn't true," Carbone insisted.

"But your story came later, Michael." I explained, "Their story — including the one Al Tringali told his roommate, Mike Nadoka — took place *before* the murders, when there was no reason to lie."

"Objection. That's not a question, Your Honor," Lewis protested.

"I'll ask it this way, Judge," I offered. I didn't want to wait around for him to sustain the objection. That was about as much fun as waiting for a girl to say no at a high school dance.

"Doesn't it make sense, Mr. Carbone, that their accounts are infinitely more believable than your own story, traded many years later in exchange for complete immunity?"

"Like I said, I was there," repeated Carbone, shifting in his seat.

"All right, let's go with your story for now. Let's forget for a moment what the victims told their loved ones," I suggested.

"Yes, let's do that," he said.

Stealing a glance at the jury, I noticed a few of them didn't like his sarcasm.

"Do you recall seeing a million dollars in cash or a money-counting machine at Tommy Felts' house on the night of the drug deal?"

I was having a bit of fun with him now. My repetitive questions must have felt to Michael like the Chinese water torture: drops of water continually falling on his head until he started to go mad.

"No, I don't."

"Was there a woman there?"

My cocking my head to the side and pretending to be genuinely curious must have been unsettling to him. Forget unsettling; it had to have pissed him off.

"No, I told you."

"Any children present?" I asked, still pretending I didn't already have the answer. More water dripping.

"No, like I said before."

"Are you suggesting that the victims were lying to their family members and friends?"

"Objection!" said Lewis, half out of his seat.

Before Tyson could rule, I said, "I'll rephrase it, Judge."

"Were they mistaken when they said the meeting about the drug deal happened at a different house, in the presence of a woman and a child, with a million dollars in cash and a money-counting machine?" I repeated, accentuating all the specifics.

"I don't know, I told you..." he half-responded, hating life at that moment.

"But you'll have to admit, this is quite a different version from your own. Is it not?" Not giving him time to answer, I added, "Do you think all the victims who told the same story to their loved ones were making it up?"

"I don't know," he complained, indicating by his voice that he was over it already. As Lewis started getting up again to object, I threw another unexpected change-up.

"Moving on, Mr. Carbone. Do you want this jury — and all of us, I suppose — to believe that Gil got blood on his clothes?"

"Oh good, blood," he must have thought. Everyone from the judge to the prosecutors to the spectators must have breathed a sigh of relief to be able to think about something else, no matter how gruesome. The Chinese water torture was effecting more than just Michael.

"Uh-huh," he said, too casually.

"I'm sorry, what did you say?" I asked, forcing him to repeat his answer.

He gave me an annoyed look and said, "Yes, he had blood on him."

"And it's your testimony, Mr. Carbone, that this person, who had blood on his clothes, was parading around a public gas station, along with Tommy, talking to his so-called boss, Bert?"

"Nobody was around. I know there wasn't because Gil wouldn't have gotten out of the car if there were. And nobody was parading. "

"And what about *your* clothes? You said in your deposition that you were told by Gil — a seasoned, veteran police officer — to dispose of your clothes. Do you remember that?"

"Yes."

"But according to your story, you were on the embankment somewhere more than 10 feet away, right?"

"Uh-huh," he muttered, his voice barely audible.

"Please speak up, Mr. Carbone."

"Yes!" he snapped. I looked over at the jurors and they looked back at me, acknowledging our shared perception that our felon Michael had a temper.

"Why would a fellow like you, who according to your own story had never been in the water or the mud, and had never been anywhere near blood, need to dispose of your clothes?"

As I asked him this, I looked at the jurors. They were looking back and forth, from me to Michael and then back to me, acknowledging our private, nonverbal conversation. It was as if I were saying, "Please pay attention to this, OK?" And they looked back at me as if to say, "Don't worry, we're catching it." They knew I wanted them to visualize the absurdity of this proposition.

"I was told to by Gil Fernandez."

"Do you do whatever you're told?" I asked.

"I wish I hadn't," he said.

"Are you telling the jury there was no blood on your clothes, but you had to dispose of them anyway?"

"That's what Gil told me to do."

"Mr. Carbone, do you realize your Grand Jury testimony is markedly different than your testimony here…"

"Objection!" said Jim Lewis, visibly fatigued by now.

"Sustained," said Tyson.

"I can't ask him if he knows it's different?" I asked, pretending to be shocked.

"Objection sustained," repeated Tyson. He was tired, like the rest of us.

"Well, Michael, you were saved by that one. Now…"

Tyson was getting really annoyed. "Mr. Contini, *please.*"

I continued to pummel Carbone, only because I could. The beating lasted five hours. Thank God, we were in my arena and not his, because if it were the other way around, I'm sure the beating he would have given me would have been far more severe. Truth be told, I might not have been around to talk about it.

Suffice it to say, when I was done the jury knew Carbone's trial testimony differed in many material respects from his Grand Jury testimony, depositions and sworn statements to the police. You name it and there was a discrepancy: the amount of money he was paid for his part in the drug rip-off and murders, the exact route that took the victims to their deaths, the driver of the deathmobile, how many guns were involved, the person who gagged the victims, and whether the water was ankle- or waistband-deep.

After five hours, the Chinese water torture was over. It was time to sit down and relax.

"Judge, I have no more questions for this witness," I said, feeling satisfied.

The walk back to my table was sweet, almost like being high from a few glasses of fine wine. Looking for encouragement, I found my wife in the second row beside the Fernandez family. Elizabeth smiled and mouthed the words, "Good job," before quietly excusing herself from the courtroom to race back to our babies. Then Neli mouthed her appreciation through happy tears, saying, "Thank you."

Gil leaned into me and said, "You did OK. Maybe I'll keep you," smiling bigger than I'd ever seen him smile. As he did, the jury watched our every move.

Chapter 19

Going South

Red wine and the comedy of Louie Vernell was the order of the night on Las Olas as we celebrated Carbone's evisceration. We were fairly convinced that the state's case had been decimated. The laughter rising from our table at the Café de Paris belied the fact that we were up to our "waistbands" in a first-degree murder trial. Certainly, the wait staff and patrons would never have imagined we'd just come from Tyson's Coliseum.

We formed our own mutual admiration society, howling over self-serving fanfare from the most unreliable of sources: Louie, our drinking buddies and me. But it was a welcome release to finally do something with all that debilitating nervous energy. The replays of the day's events we ran aloud in the bar area of the restaurant were complete with high-fives.

Louie kept feeding me ego-inflating lines I loved, like, "You had those jurors' heads bobbing up and down with you like those little dogs on the dashboard of a '57 Chevy!" He was telling the truth. That's why it felt so good.

"It felt better than sex," I said, invoking another round of laughter. There's no greater feeling for a trial lawyer than when the jury is nodding along with what he's saying and doing, essentially telling him they're with him.

Everyone was echoing the mantra de jour, that Carbone had been destroyed on cross. The prosecutors had to have gone to sleep that night hoping and praying that that the old saying "It's always darkest before the dawn" would come true for them. Unfortunately for us, their prayers were answered the following morning when Louie rose to cross-examine Carbone on behalf of Bert Christie.

Unprepared, confused and disorganized

Louie was once a great trial lawyer. And he still had fleeting moments of brilliance, along with the quick-witted, shoot-from-the-hip ability to provide comic relief. His self-deprecating sense of humor made him likeable. It was hard to stay bitter toward him, even when he was ruining our chances for success.

But the fatigue of the trial had already worn on him. Especially since it was piled on top of the burnout that came from decades of being a paid mouthpiece. He was in his late sixties and had been humping it up and down the courthouse steps for far too many years.

Bert was counting on Louie to continue what I had started. He needed to carve up Michael Carbone and serve him to the jury. What happened instead was that he was unprepared, confused and disorganized. Perhaps it was a blood-sugar thing or some sort of bipolarity. I'm not sure. Whatever it was, it caused him to go south on me that day.

"Where are those transcripts? I had them a moment ago. Your Honor, I just need a moment."

"Yes, Mr. Vernell, you may have a moment," Tyson assured him.

"Mr. Carbone, my client, Bert Christie, was not with you.... Oh here it is, Judge. Thank you. Let me ask you a question, sir... and it concerns your deposition answers... but you'll need to excuse me... I just need another moment, Your Honor, to find the page here in the deposition..."

Carbone pounced on the opportunity to say whatever he wanted in answer to that half-asked question about Bert, while poor Louie stammered and dug through mountains of ever-elusive papers.

"Bert was with Gil, Tommy and me the night before the murders when the three guys came to the house. He also met us at the gas station right after the murders, too, when he asked Gil and Tommy, 'Was the job done?' He was the boss and he ordered it," Carbone offered, comfortable now in facing the jurors.

I thought, "Poor Louie. He's really screwing this up."

"Poor Louie? Did I just think that? What about *us*? This can't continue or we're done!" I said to myself, totally panicking. Carbone was not only getting cozy with the jury, he was damn near camping out with them. He turned the witness chair toward the jury box and spoke uninterrupted for what seemed like minutes at a time. He was as friendly with the jurors as a long-lost relative, explaining away every one of his previous inconsistencies.

This was torture for me. The prey had become the predator. Carbone had been beaten down just a day earlier and left only half as strong as he might have been. But with Louie being only half as strong as *he* might have been, Carbone was strengthened by that weakness. Whatever caused this frightening power shift didn't matter. We all knew Louie tried his level best and never meant to hurt our cause. But unfortunately, that's what happened.

I had no choice but to sit there, muzzled, and watch this self-destruction for several hours. Louie appeared to be barely cognizant of anything except the inescapable fact that he was panicking. He had to have known that his own funk was helping Carbone resurrect himself with the jury. It was too obvious.

"Your Honor, may I have some more time to prepare the questions I would like to ask?" Louie inquired.

"Mr. Vernell, I have given you latitude on this and we have already had a recess. You had all day yesterday when Mr. Contini was cross-examining the same witness. With all due respect, sir, you have your papers there in front of you and we really must proceed. Please continue with your cross-examination," replied the judge.

It had to have felt to Louie like he was behind the wheel of a car skidding out of control. He could spin the wheel all he wanted and press firmly on the brake, but that car was skidding toward the cliff nonetheless.

Bert looked like he was in pain. He was already quite sick, but this new waking nightmare with Louie and Carbone was killing him even faster. His family looked about as ill as him at that miserable moment. Gil's family couldn't even stand to watch.

Though he was once a great lawyer in the old mob days of Miami, Louie didn't seem to have a grip on even the basics of trial law that day. And that wasn't like him. He knew, like the rest of us, that a trial lawyer must control the rhythm of questions and answers, and must *never* ask an open-ended question, such as one beginning with "who," "what," "when," "where" or "why."

"And where was Bert Christie, my client, when these killings were going on?" Louie asked.

"He was waiting at the gas station to see if the job was done. He asked Gil and Tommy about it as soon as we pulled in," Carbone repeated, pouncing all over the "where" question.

"And why would a mob boss, as you refer to him, be meeting in a public gas station," Louie then asked, "where people would see him, and when the killer had blood on him?"

He also had to know that it was critical to *not* ask a "why" question to which he didn't already know the answer. Jumping all over this question, Carbone turned toward the jurors as he answered, "Because he ordered the job and insisted on knowing right away whether it was done."

"Come on, Louie!" I screamed in my head.

"This ain't happening," Gil groaned.

Something terrible was going on. Never before had I experienced something so painfully frustrating in court. I was completely helpless. The co-defendant's counsel can't object under such circumstances. Only the prosecutors could have objected and they weren't about to do that. Molloy, Jim and Cindy took turns looking at me with wide-eyed excitement, like kids in a candy store.

It was almost surreal, a slow-motion kind of trial hell. It was as though a building were demolished one day and then reconstructed the next. By the time Louie sat down, the state was very much back in the game. The building was restored, only stronger than before.

The prosecution team wisely decided not to "re-direct" Carbone, which they knew would have given me another opportunity to destroy him. No re-direct for them meant no re-cross-examination for me. Molloy actually smiled at me when he told Tyson they weren't going to re-direct. He knew this had to be like a knife in my gut. It meant Carbone got to slither out of that witness stand in one piece and I'd never get another shot at him. He postured like a peacock on steroids all the way out of the courtroom and I couldn't do anything about it.

It was unfortunate for Gil and Bert — and for me, too — that Louie picked what felt to me like the worst time in the history of jurisprudence to drop the ball. The only hope left was for me to try to undo the damage and re-create some degree of reasonable doubt over the next several days. Thankfully, in the days to come, there would be other felons to cross-examine. We weren't throwing in the towel. In fact, we weren't even looking for the towel. We were cut up and bleeding, for sure, but we weren't done. There were still more rounds left in this fight.

Chapter 20

Combs

As if Carbone's state-sponsored "testilying" wasn't enough of an injustice, the prosecution bought the testimony of yet another convicted felon, Paul Combs. The purchase of Comb's questionable story told me the state was obsessed with sending Gil to the electric chair and would stop at nothing to get him there.

Paul Combs was an admitted narco-trafficker who intended to testify that he provided eight kilos of cocaine to the three victims before they met their killers on April Fools' Day in 1983. As his payoff in the immunity deal he cut with the state and the feds, he received a complete pass for not only any alleged violations of his federal parole, but also for his admitted drug trafficking on the eight kilos. Had he not cut this deal, he would have been facing a mandatory 15-year minimum state prison sentence — and that would have been for trafficking just one kilo of cocaine. In his case, eight kilos were at issue. Like Carbone, Combs was a clever opportunist, to say the least.

Combs was set to testify that he was a friend of victims Leahy, Tringali and Robertson. He was going to claim that Dickie Robertson told him the day before the murders that they were going to meet "two bodybuilders from Hollywood, named Gil and Tommy." Supposedly, because of their friendship, Combs fronted the kilos and then trusted the victims to pay up after they sold them.

Paul Combs' testimony about what the victims allegedly told him before their deaths would be virtually impossible to confront on cross-examination. This garbage came into evidence despite Gil's guaranteed right to confront witnesses against him under the Sixth Amendment to the U.S. Constitution. Tyson virtually obliterated this guarantee by allowing the testimony.

Combs' three "friends" were already dead and therefore not available for cross-examination. Had their words been uttered spontaneously while they were dying, they would have come under the "dying declaration" hearsay exception. But they weren't, so everyone knew the dying declaration exception wouldn't apply. The prosecutors sought instead to introduce the testimony under the "co-conspirator" hearsay exception, which allows for hearsay statements of co-conspirators to come into evidence against one another. But in this case, for that exception to apply the victims would have had to be co-conspirators with Gil and Tommy, their alleged killers. Since this was a murder case and the conspiracy in question would have been a murder conspiracy, the hearsay statements would have to be made in the furtherance of that same murder conspiracy. In other words, the victims would have had to conspire to commit murder against themselves. Thinking that victims would co-conspire with their own killers to be killed was absurd. Yet, Tyson had already ruled after lengthy pretrial arguments that this testimony from Paul Combs applied under the co-conspirator hearsay exception. The victims, apparently now co-conspirators in their own murders, would now essentially be testifying from the grave through the lips of Paul Combs.

I saw Lewis in the hallway before the trial began that morning and let him know what I thought of the feces he was about to dump on all of us.

"Jim, you're actually bringing in this fecal matter about what the dead guys told Combs? You're calling this evidence?"

"Good morning to you, too, John."

"Come on, Jim, you know damn well those guys never told Combs they were meeting 'two bodybuilders from Hollywood, named Gil and Tommy.' They wouldn't have even known these guys' names at that time!"

"Are you suggesting we made this up?" Lewis asked.

"How could I ever suggest such a thing?" I responded sarcastically. "Rank hearsay from three dead guys, resurrected after seven years and delivered from the truthful lips of the angelic Paul 'I'm-a-good-guy-now' Combs?"

"No, I mean it, John. I want to know. Are you accusing me of subornation of perjury?" Lewis pressed.

"Not yet, because I'm giving you a chance right now to grow a frickin' conscience."

"You want to talk about a conscience, Contini? How do you sleep at night?" he asked, quieting his voice in his best attempt to lay a guilt trip on me.

"Don't you find it just a little interesting, Lewis, that Molloy and the others had this case for a year and never had this smoking-gun evidence? Then you come on the scene right before the trial and this new 'evidence' just magically appears! Combs — the good-Samaritan drug dealer — just *happens* to surface right before trial, coincidentally right after you're given the lead. And then you show your appreciation to him by buying his testimony with complete immunity on eight kilos?"

"I resent what you're suggesting," Lewis said angrily.

"I'm sorry you resent my feelings, Jim," I continued. "You're right, it's all so believable. And, of course, you have every right to elicit this sort of testimony, however perjurious it might sound. Testimony, I might add, that managed to stay hidden for seven years. It was hidden even from the other prosecutors, just up until you came up with it right before the trial."

"I'm not going to listen to this," Lewis grumbled. "Tyson already ruled and it's all coming in. Deal with it."

He then walked over to the drinking fountain several feet away, still within earshot of the obscenities I was mumbling under my breath. My professed faith as a Christian wasn't recognizable to anyone at that moment, including me.

I entered the courtroom and took my place at the defense table next to Louie, Gil and Bert. The jury was brought in, followed by Combs, who took the witness stand and was sworn in. He was 31 years old and looked like a thug pretending to be legitimate. He reminded me of a Marlon Brando-like *On the Waterfront* character, auditioning for the role of Ron Howard's Richie Cunningham on *Happy Days*.

Jim Lewis stepped forward and greeted Combs in a friendly way. "Here we go," I thought, mentally gearing up for a beef. My knee kept a rhythm under the table in a lame attempt to process my frustration. I still couldn't believe this testimony was coming in.

Combs went on to testify that he was involved in cocaine distribution in the early 80s. He said victim Dickie Robertson was involved in many of those transactions with him and that Combs used to supply kilos of cocaine to Robertson. He said that approximately two weeks before April 1, 1983, a conversation took place with Robertson about a 20-kilo deal. He said Robertson was confident the deal was going to go down because he saw a million dollars in cash and a money-counting machine. Combs told the jury that he didn't have access to 20 kilos of cocaine, so he had the cocaine fronted to him by a guy named Pepe in Miami.

He further testified that he gave Robertson three kilos of cocaine five or six days before April 1. They discussed that this initial amount would be used "for show." Then he said Robertson told him that the buyers were "two bodybuilders from Hollywood, named Gil and Tommy." It was in the middle of this testimony about bodybuilders from Hollywood that I made the usual hearsay objections. The objections had to be made contemporaneously, despite advance knowledge of the ruling. This would preserve the record for appeal. Otherwise, the appellate issue would be forever waived.

"Objection, Judge. Who knows what the victims might have told him and his drug cronies. He could've been protecting any of his other druggie friends. This is total rank hearsay, Your Honor!"

Mine was a sleazy "speaking objection," which gave the jury information I wanted them to have but wasn't supposed to give them. Truthfully, it was just as objectionable as the rank hearsay about which I was complaining.

"Overruled. Please, all counsel, refrain from speaking objections. Simply state the grounds for your objection, in this case hearsay. On this basis I've already ruled."

Robertson was alleged to have said this tremendously incriminating stuff about "two bodybuilders from Hollywood, named Gil and Tommy" when

Combs and Robertson last saw each other — the day that Combs fronted the other five kilos that brought the total kilos to eight.

Later, Combs said that when he didn't hear from Dickie, he tried to beep him but there was no response. He then went to see Robertson's girlfriend, Linda Allard. He claimed that he and Linda drove around looking for Robertson while he sent a family member to Robertson's house to retrieve cash and Quaaludes from a safe.

After Combs told his "story," which was the nicest way I could refer to it, Lewis politely thanked him for coming forward. He then sat down, signaling that he was done. Tyson then said, "Mr. Contini, you may cross-examine the witness." Lewis was smiling at me.

"Please, God, let me wipe that smile off his arrogant little puke face," I prayed. Somehow, I don't think God liked that prayer.

"Here we go," I said to myself as I slid out from behind the defense table, approaching Combs.

"Hello, Mr. Combs," I said with feigned politeness.

"Hello," he replied.

"It's true, isn't it, sir, that you're testifying in court today because you have complete immunity from the federal and state governments in connection with these crimes?

"Yeah, that's right," he said, acting aloof.

"In fact, haven't you been cooperating with law-enforcement officers since your 1983 indictment on federal drug charges?"

"Yes."

"So, in effect, your testimony was literally bought and paid for in exchange for your freedom from a lengthy prison sentence. Isn't that true?" I asked.

"What I said today is the truth. It doesn't have anything to do with the deal I made."

"Oh, really. Then why, sir, in all of your discussions with law-enforcement officers over the years, did none of this good stuff ever come out of your mouth until only a few weeks ago?"

"I was concerned. I didn't want to get involved," Combs replied.

"So you just belatedly decided to become a good citizen after seven years, Mr. Combs?"

He said nothing and just looked at Lewis.

I paused a moment for effect and then said sarcastically, "Tell us, how long did you grieve for your friend Dickie before you took all the money out of his safe?"

"Twelve hours," Combs replied.

"That was *very* compassionate of you," I said, communicating my disgust to the jury with the intonation in my voice. Combs looked away again, just as disgusted with me.

"You admit to testifying against others in Ohio and Pennsylvania. Isn't that correct?" I continued.

"Yes," he answered.

"You're what's known as a professional witness, aren't you, sir?" I asked.

"No," he replied.

"Other people are always culpable for what you do. Isn't that right, Mr. Combs?"

He just shook his head while muttering something that sounded like "wrong." Then he looked over again at the prosecutors, as if asking for help.

"You admit to moving hundreds of pounds of marijuana, thousands of Quaaludes and multiple kilos of cocaine, including the eight kilos involved in this murder case. And yet the prosecutors are giving you complete immunity. Instead of doing prison time, you're still on that same old federal probation from yesterday's news. Isn't that right, sir?"

"That's right," he quipped, sounding cocky.

"You, sir, refused to tell these good folks on the jury anything, until you first received complete immunity in connection with these kilos and these murders. Isn't that right?"

The inflection in my voice as I accentuated certain words, and the waving of my arms in step with a singsong and sarcastic approach to these questions, were all designed to convey just how untrustworthy his testimony should be considered.

"Yeah," is all I thought I heard. It was barely audible.

"And you just happened to be reading *The Miami Herald* six weeks ago when you decided to do the right thing and come in here and demand immunity. Is that what you're saying?" I pressed.

"Yeah, I read about this in the paper," he replied.

"Sure you did. And when you read the article, it mentioned two bodybuilders from Hollywood, named Gil and Tommy, didn't it?"

"I don't remember."

Barreling down on him, I said forcefully, "And *that's* where you got that information about bodybuilders from Hollywood. Isn't it sir?

"No."

"It wasn't from the victims, who couldn't have known such things. Isn't that true?"

"No, that's *not* true!" said Combs, only stronger this time, eyeballing me rather severely.

"Sir, if in real life you *had* heard *anything* about two bodybuilders from Hollywood by those names — or any other names for that matter — you wouldn't have put a gun to Linda Allard's head when your friends and your money didn't show the next day! Isn't that right?"

Linda Allard, who was Dickie Robertson's girlfriend, was scheduled to testify the next day. I was confident I'd elicit from her on cross-examination exactly what she told the police years earlier — that Combs had put a gun to her head and forced her to take him to a floor safe in the new house Robertson and Allard had just bought together. Combs did this to her, she told the police, because he feared that Dickie had ripped him off for the kilos he fronted.

"That didn't happen," Combs replied.

Allard was going to hate talking about all this in front of the jury because it certainly didn't help the state's case. If anything, it might benefit Gil and Bert, the men she believed were responsible for Robertson's murder. It would almost be fun using that old police report and going over her quoted remarks to the police back in '83, repeating it verbatim for the jury today.

This was a key point in the impeachment of Paul Combs. If Combs had *truly* heard from Dickie and the others that they were "meeting two bodybuilders from Hollywood, named Gil and Tommy," he would have had no reason to threaten Linda Allard with a gun. Well, there may have been one reason: if he wanted to drill her on the whereabouts of the two bodybuilders. But he never did. The truth was that if Combs assertion were true, he would have been out there with the same firearm looking for two Hollywood bodybuilders, named Gil and Tommy.

"So, if she tells us that you put a gun to her head, then she'd be lying about that. Right?"

"Objection, Your Honor," bellowed Lewis, minus that smug little smile.

"Sustained," ruled Tyson.

Even though there was an objection, the jury still heard Combs deny that he threatened Linda Allard with a gun. This would set the stage for reasonable doubt when the infinitely more believable Allard testified the next day that Combs had, in fact, put a gun to her head.

"No more questions for this witness, Your Honor."

I slowly shook my head in disgust for the jury's benefit before returning to the defense table. Paul Combs should never, ever have been permitted to give this incredibly damaging testimony, given its source. Never has there been a better example of absolute, rank hearsay. To me — and I would think to everyone, especially the prosecution — it was obvious that these poor guys would never have told Combs the names of their purported killers before their deaths. They would have had no way of knowing these names, or at least not Gil's name.

Combs had never dealt with these guys before, even according to the state's theory and the statements of the victims. And of course, the victims never had access to the widely publicized details about this case, which hadn't even existed yet! It made me lose whatever remaining faith I might have had that lady justice could somehow remain blind to the pressures of the police, the prosecutors, the public and the media.

The rain

My stomach was in a knot about all this as Tyson's clerk Beth conferred with the judge on a matter of procedure. Suddenly, I was distracted from my misery by a crunching noise. I turned and saw a juror looking with disbelief at Louie. "What's up with her?" I thought to myself.

Then I realized why she was staring. Groaning inside, I said to myself, "This *can't* be happening."

Incredulous, I leaned over and asked Louie in a hushed but anguished whisper, "Louie, are you eating pretzels out of your coat pocket?"

"I got a sugar thing and it's lunchtime," is all he said.

"But Louie, one of the jurors is staring at you!"

He didn't seem embarrassed as he stared back at the juror and replied, "That's because she's a big girl. She probably wants some of my pretzels for herself."

Noticing he was returning her gaze, the juror looked away quickly, pretending to be interested in something else. Louie tried hard not to laugh at his own joke. As bizarre as his behavior was, I found myself fighting to stifle a laugh over the idea of a weight-challenged juror coveting Louie's pretzels.

Then he got serious. "You did a good job ruining that guy. He hurt you, but you hurt him back pretty good. Now tell the judge we want to break for lunch," Vernell kept whispering. "You don't want me passing out over here, do you? Then they'll *really* have something to stare at."

He actually had *me* looking at his suit pocket, longing for a pretzel. Louie was such a character. It wouldn't have surprised me if blood sugar played a role in his Carbone debacle the day before and perhaps in all of his roller-coaster behavior. One day he'd have the energy of three men and a day later he'd be in a manic-depressive-like slumber. He was excitable, brilliant and loveable one minute, and then he'd morph into a mood-swinging idiot the next. Maybe that's why I liked him. He reminded me of myself.

To Louie's relief, Tyson called for a lunch break. After almost everyone had left, Mike the bailiff came up to me in the hallway and said, "John, some of the jurors have been complaining about Louie."

"What's he done now?" I asked, with no idea of what was to follow.

"John, he was spitting on 'em in voir dire, 'cause he was talking to the jurors up-close and all. And he's still spraying 'em when he's next to the jury rail, asking questions of the witnesses."

"You're kidding me, right?" I asked, contorting my face.

"In fact, John, one of the jurors said to me, 'Can't you guys do something about this? Hey, I don't mind the wind, but the rain is kind of rough!'"

Mike was laughing hysterically. Soon, Cindy and Jim joined him. They had heard us and walked over to see what was so funny. Thankfully, Mike had the sense to wait till the jury was out of earshot before telling the story.

"Bob Behan told the jury he was going to buy 'em all plastic shields."

The visual was too funny not to laugh, but after a minute, I felt guilty and stopped myself.

"Mike, poor Louie probably didn't know he was spitting. Why didn't one of you guys tell him?"

"Hey, it's not my turn to watch him!" Mike said, laughing. "Besides, what would that do? He has all that extra saliva. It's gotta go somewhere. Why don't *you* tell him? After all, you're the one sitting next to him. Unless you like that he cools you off with it!"

He was howling at his own joke.

"Very funny," I said with resignation. There seemed to be no end to the Louie trip.

Chapter 21

Mrs. Immunity

When we returned from lunch, there was more rank hearsay on tap. This time, it would come from Rebecca Carbone, who was married to Michael Carbone at the time of the murders. She and I quickly became fast enemies, though I have to give credit where credit is due. She divorced Michael a year after the murders, so I had to give her an "A" for the good judgment to "get rid of him," as she told the police.

You could see what drew them together initially, though. They were each about as charming as a box of rocks. Then again, in fairness to Rebecca, I wasn't very nice to her, which might have had something to do with her surly attitude.

Michael Carbone told police that he came home after the murders in a cold sweat, crying to his wife about everything Gil had allegedly done. Supposedly, the events of the night were a complete surprise to Carbone. Since he claimed to have cried to Rebecca in a heightened state of fear that he was deathly afraid and that Gil said he'd kill him, his wife and his kids if he ever talked, the prosecution called Rebecca to corroborate his testimony.

This testimony would create a terribly damaging visual, and Molloy and company knew it. They *wanted* the jury to visualize it. Worse yet, they wanted the 10 women on the jury to feel what Rebecca was alleged to have felt: the paralyzing fear of being stalked by an evil killer.

The prosecution introduced her testimony under the "excited utterance hearsay exception," which allows otherwise obvious hearsay statements to be admitted into evidence if they were made while excited or under duress. Tyson allowed this crap into evidence, despite the fact that it was rank hearsay. The prosecutors would elicit from Rebecca that Michael did, in fact, come home and "excitedly" tell her these frightening things. But from my perspective, it was just more trumped-up eleventh-hour hearsay excrement that was being used illegally to buttress Carbone's otherwise uncorroborated story.

The courtroom was packed as Rebecca Carbone took the stand. She said the usual "I do" in response to Beth's rote question, "Do you solemnly swear to tell the truth, the whole truth and…"

"…nothing but what the prosecutor wants," I said facetiously to myself, refusing to listen to this mantra that witnesses too often ignore.

There was more noise than usual on this day. Tyson had to direct his attention to the spectator gallery several times and ask for quiet before it finally became so silent you could hear your own heartbeat. Thankfully, Louie was out of pretzels.

Jim Lewis approached the witness stand and after greeting Rebecca, he said, "Could you please tell us the name of your ex-husband?"

"Michael Carbone," she replied.

"Mr. Immunity, you mean," I said to myself. I always thought of the two of them as Mr. and Mrs. Immunity. As far as I was concerned, her ex-husband had somehow convinced her to lie about Gil, so she had no more credibility than him.

"And were you married to him in April 1983?"

"Yes, I was."

"OK, thank you. Can you tell us what Michael's state of mind was when he came home in the early morning on April 2, 1983?"

"He was scared and a little panicked."

"OK, now, please tell us what Michael said to you," Lewis said.

I objected for the record to Tyson's earlier ruling allowing for this hearsay testimony. I wanted to preserve the issue in case it could be used on appeal. But I didn't want to call too much attention to what might be perceived by the jury as my attempt to keep something from them. Some of the audience members on the defense side of the courtroom knew what was coming. A few made derisive remarks under their breath until Tyson shot them a "don't even think about it" look.

"He said there had been a drug rip-off that night, and that Gil and Tommy asked him to drive the drug dealers out to the Everglades. He said they wanted him to hold one of the victims, and that they wanted him to hand him over so Gil could shoot him. This didn't surprise me. Michael's a follower who always does what he's told."

Gil stared at Rebecca, his expression never wavering. I could hear some of the people sitting on the defense side getting more restless as she continued.

"Gil got mad at Mike when he didn't want to hand over the guy he was holding, so he told Tommy to bring him. Tommy went over to where Mike was standing, grabbed the tied-up guy and pushed him into the water."

Rebecca looked increasingly agitated as she told the story. She took a deep breath and then said, "The next thing Mike knew, he heard a shot, then a scuffle in the water, then another shot. Mike was pacing the room when he told me this. He was totally freaked out. He practically screamed at me, 'Gil shot him in the f***ing head!'"

Rebecca's eyes darted around the courtroom as she dropped the F-bomb. It might have been hard for the jury to tell whether her shifty appearance was because she was lying or because she was truly unnerved by what her ex-husband had told her. She took another deep breath. Calmer now, she went on to say, "He told me that Gil said to get rid of his clothes and muddy sneakers. So he threw the sneakers and his clothes in the dumpster behind the Wendy's drive-through."

"Thank you, Mrs. Carbone. Now, could you please tell us who Michael said was supposed to profit from this drug deal?" Lewis asked, looking for her to slam Bert, too.

"He told me that Bert and Gil would get the largest cut of the money from the sale of the cocaine because Bert set it up and Gil did the job."

The crowd on the defense side of the courtroom was clearly showing their disrespect for Rebecca's testimony. Tyson's face was turning red in response to the chaos that kept trying to break out. He was about to address the noisemakers again when, elevating his voice to be heard over the noise, Jim Lewis said, "Your honor, I have no more questions for this witness."

Then Tyson stood up and said forcefully, "Ladies and gentlemen, you will be quiet or I will clear this courtroom!"

As the room quieted down, Tyson sat down again and said, "Mr. Contini, your witness."

Examining crossly

As I got up to begin my cross-examination, Neli smiled and gave me a look of encouragement. Gil's parents were still holding hands and supporting their son. Christie's ex-wife and daughters gave me the thumbs-up as several of Gil's friends audibly muttered what sounded like more encouragement. Not afraid to show my complete disdain for Rebecca's testimony, perhaps I approached her too aggressively.

"Mrs. Carbone, isn't it a fact that Michael Carbone beat you with his fist right in front of your daughter?" I thought this nasty visual was a good way to start, especially with 10 women on the jury.

"That's right." She said too fast, with real defiance in her voice. Apparently, she was ready for a fight.

My strategy was to expose Rebecca Carbone's earlier, victimized life with Michael the Terrible, in the hope that it would cause the jury to disregard most, if not all, of what she had to say. I wanted the jury to draw the inference, right or wrong, that she was afraid of Michael and would say whatever she could to keep from getting another beating. She might have been a nice person in real life, but on the witness stand she came off like a bigger thug than Michael. She was a regular Ma Barker caricature of a wise guy's wife.

"You like it rough?" I asked, regretting the question as soon as I asked it.

Some of the court personnel covered their mouths and looked down, shocked at this outrageous remark. Even though my intent was born of a desperate effort to save Gil's life, I nonetheless felt bad about saying something so crude. But that didn't stop me from doing whatever I could to destroy her testimony.

Many of the spectators were snickering — all but the victims' families. Tyson looked upset yet again. Squinty-eyed and red-faced, he was *really* over me by now. Seeing that he looked like a volcano ready to blow, the people making the sounds stopped abruptly, covering their mouths to silence their chuckling.

I continued, saying smoothly, "Who is living in the house with you and your children?"

"My boyfriend."

"And what's his name?"

She said his name but I didn't really care about the answer. Shamefully, my agenda was anything but pure. Traveling over this guy's bones to further besmirch her character was all I cared about. It was all about planting some additional seeds of reasonable doubt in the minds of the jurors.

"He's in organized crime with Michael, isn't he?" I asked, acting as if this weren't a rude question.

"No, he's not," she said with a flash of irritation.

Sensing her obvious defensiveness now, I arrogantly asked, "Mrs. Carbone, isn't it a fact that Michael Carbone is a pathological liar?"

"I guess he could be," she said, trying to sound bored so she could mask her anger.

"Did you *not* say that before?"

"Yes, I might have said that," she said defensively.

"Did you *definitely* say that?" I pressed.

"I *might* have said that," she retorted, proving she was stronger on the stand than Michael.

I pulled out a copy of Rebecca Carbone's deposition and started to read. "'He's actually not very bright. Whenever he feels it is appropriate or serves his best interest, he will tell a lie.'"

"I'm sure he probably would but I never said he's a pathological liar, sir. *You* did," she said with a sneer, her voice elevating.

"But in your deposition, when I asked you if he was a pathological liar, you said, 'Yes, at times.'"

My voice got louder as I continued to go after her, "Isn't it also a fact that he'd told you five times that he *hated* Gil Fernandez because he was a police officer and police officers sent him to prison?"

"No, sir!" she said loudly.

"You're not denying that he said that, are you?" I yelled, making sure she understood my words were meant as an accusation.

"No, I'm denying that he said that to me *five times*," she yelled back.

"All right. So you can count. Good," I said with all the condescension I could muster.

There was muffled laughter from some of the spectators and a few of the jurors. I shot a quick glance at Tyson and wondered how much further would he let me go.

"You fear Michael Carbone, don't you, ma'am, the same Michael Carbone who beat you in the mouth in front of your daughter?"

"No, sir, I *don't*," she said, becoming increasingly angry at my aggressive line of questioning.

"You don't fear him at all? You're sandwiched in this organized crime family between Michael Carbone and your new extortionist boyfriend, the new guy we've already talked about," I said forcefully, mocking her.

"Objection, your honor!" Jim Lewis said loudly, so he could be heard above the catcalls that were again coming from the audience.

Rebecca answered anyway, not giving the judge a chance to speak. Ma Barker was really pissed now, not allowing the judge to even rule on Jim's objection. "I don't know where you get your information! I'm not sandwiched between anybody. I got rid of Michael seven years ago!"

Then she said angrily, "I didn't even want to be here today."

A few people in the crowd on the defense side were muttering insults at her. Tyson, who now had a red furrow that started at the top of his forehead and went down to the top of his nose, had reached the limit of his tolerance for these fireworks.

"That will be *enough!*" Tyson yelled. "Counsel, approach the bench, please."

As Jim, Doug, Cindy and I approached the bench, Tyson said in a low tone, trying to calm things down, "That's enough, Mr. Contini. I've given you plenty of latitude in this regard. I want you to stand behind the podium and keep your voice down. You have a right to *cross-examine* but not to examine *crossly*. That's all. Thank you."

"Great line, judge," I thought to myself. Before he got to the dismissive, "Thank you," I thought, "Maybe if I ever decide to be a judge someday, I'll use that 'not to examine crossly' line and *not* give you any attribution." But my words belied my thoughts as I responded respectfully to the judge, apologizing for my complicity in the chaos and outbursts. While I stood in front of Tyson throughout the sidebar, I said all the politically correct stuff. But I had zero intention of letting up on Rebecca. I headed back to the podium to get in her face once again, though in a less objectionable way.

Accessory to the fact

"Isn't it true, Mrs. Carbone, that your ex-husband would do or say *anything* to save himself from the electric chair?" I asked very calmly, pretending to be cordial.

"No, I *don't* think that's true," she said defensively, still maintaining her nasty tone of voice.

Some in the audience laughed at her, knowing that any five-time convicted felon would say whatever it took to beat the electric chair. Ignoring the laughter and raising her voice, she practically yelled, "No, I don't think he would lie to save himself from the electric chair!"

"Now that was a fairly ridiculous thing to say, Rebecca. Any felon like Michael would lie to keep from getting fried in the chair," I ridiculed.

She said some kind of nonsense over me as I spoke. Everyone on the jury and in the audience had to be thinking what I was thinking: If he will commit a series of extortions, hold people at gunpoint with a Tommy gun for hours and do multi-kilo trafficking deals, why would we think he's too moral to tell a lie to stay out of the electric chair? Some of the spectators were now actually groaning in response to this tortured stretch of her testimony.

Tyson came down hard again on the people in the gallery for making a continued ruckus: "You will be quiet in this courtroom or I will hold all of you in *contempt*!"

This latest blast by Tyson calmed the audience down for the moment. Then I felt it was time to let the jury know why I thought of her as "Mrs. Immunity." Like her ex-husband, I wanted the jury to know that she demanded immunity before testifying.

"Before you ever agreed to talk with these folks..." I said, and then paused for effect. "Let me ask it differently, ma'am. You're not going to deny to this jury that the state gave you immunity, are you?"

"No, sir, I'm not," she replied, appearing quite proud of it.

"In fact, you came with an attorney to the prosecutors' office, didn't you?" I asked, acting quite suspicious of her while stealing a staged glance at the jury.

"That's right, I did," she exclaimed unapologetically.

"Before you would agree to talk about anything, you wanted immunity for lying to the police. Isn't that correct, ma'am?" I teased.

"That was because I was told I could be held as an accessory to the fact," she retorted almost apologetically. She turned toward the jurors, looking for their empathy and understanding.

"Right. And you were very upset when Michael talked to the police, weren't you?"

"Yes, I was." We were both pretending to have a civilized conversation now.

Then I approached her a bit too menacingly. "You were upset because he was going to *expose* you and..."

"I was upset because I told him I wanted him to take this to his grave!" she bellowed.

Then Tyson interrupted us. His red forehead furrow had receded a bit but I could see he was still agitated. There was no doubt about it; he was upset with me again. We'd have made the perfect old married couple.

"Mr. Contini, get behind the podium. Both of you — keep your voices down!"

But that didn't stop Rebecca, as she continued, "I was upset because he told me that Gil told him he would kill his wife and children. *That's* why I was upset," she added while sneering mischievously, thinking she had gotten away with something.

She looked proud of herself because she thought she had given the jury some information they didn't have. But Tyson and I had already gone to the mat on this issue. In spite of my objections, Michael was allowed to testify to the prejudicial and improper "evidence of collateral crimes," which is what the alleged death threat from Gil could be considered. Details about these inflammatory and vague alleged threats should never have been admissible, as they constituted hypothetical evidence of future murders. Juries aren't even allowed to hear details about *existing* crimes, other than those in the current indictment. So, it was ridiculous that information about crimes that hadn't even occurred yet — and might never occur — would be allowed.

Challenging her assertion that she was afraid, I asked while smiling insincerely at her, "If you were afraid, then why would you need immunity, ma'am?"

The jury looked at her funny at this point. Giving it her best lawyer-like response, she replied, "I needed immunity because they said I could be held for 'accessory to the fact,' because Michael told me about it and I never went to anybody."

"You mean 'accessory *after* the fact,' right?"

A few jurors stifled a chuckle.

"Whatever! You're the lawyer," she snapped.

Almost done with her, I suggested that she had complicity with Michael in making up the whole thing. "How many times did you talk to Michael in prison on the phone?" I asked, looking at the jury, not her.

"A few," is all she said.

"You got your stories together?" I asked, still ignoring her and looking at a few of the jurors. The jurors were looking back and letting me know with their demeanor that they understood where I was going with this. Nobody really paid attention to her disavowal. The point had been made. The spectators on the defense side of the courtroom were leaning over to one another, whispering and chuckling, as Tyson just stared.

"Your Honor, I have no more questions for this witness."

As I sat down, I reflected on whether Rebecca was lying to cover her ex-husband's butt or if she was telling the truth. She might really have believed Michael's account of Gil's alleged threat to kill her and the kids, assuming for a moment that Michael really came home and said these things. And if that were the case, she truly would have felt she and her kids were in danger if Gil were to be acquitted. If that's what she believed, then I really couldn't blame her for testifying strongly to save her kids and preserve her own life.

From her perspective, if the alleged threats really were made, that would mean Michael had thrown her and her children under the bus when he carved out his personal immunity deal. According to his own assertions, Michael's act of speaking about the murders to the police put his family in danger. Maybe this profound selfishness is why she divorced him shortly after the murders.

Because of my own selfish goal of saving Gil, I wanted the jury to believe all day long that she was lying to cover Michael. But even if she weren't lying, Tyson should have never permitted her hearsay testimony. This sort of inflammatory testimony could quite easily send someone to the electric chair. Though I was vaguely cognizant that it was a betrayal of my emerging faith, I detested her for making it damn near impossible to win this thing.

Pathological lying

Next, up, it was Louie's turn at Rebecca. Tyson looked worn out as he said, "Mr. Vernell, do you have any questions for Mrs. Carbone?"

"Yes, Your Honor, I do." Louie said as he approached the stand. In an incredible combination of smoothness and mocking ridicule, Louie asked, "Mrs. Carbone, do you think your ex-husband's pathological lying has rubbed off on you?"

Showing some of his old prowess, Louie delivered the question sweetly, as if it weren't overwhelmingly insulting. As Rebecca attempted to respond, the crowd went wild. Flashbulbs arced like mad and the decibel level escalated so much that Doug Molloy had to shout when he made a motion to have the courtroom cleared. Tyson turned him down. But once again, more forcefully now, he commanded that there be quiet in the courtroom.

When the crowd calmed down, Louie kept questioning Rebecca, unfortunately asking too many of the same questions I had already asked. At length he finished and a break was called. Tyson wisely knew that it would be beneficial to disburse some of the pent-up emotion in the room.

Before being swarmed by reporters looking for our take on the day's proceedings, I overheard Molloy saying to Tyson, "I've never seen a display like that of John. Respectfully, I think he's playing to the crowd."

"You got that right, Doug," I thought. Molloy was right. He usually was, if I really thought about it.

The next day, the *Sun-Sentinel* printed several articles about the incendiary display in courtroom 970. One of the articles, titled, "Witness Taunted in Court: Spectators Laugh During Murder Trial," described some of the high-energy exchanges between the defense and the woman I lovingly referred to as Mrs. Immunity. Not that I was gloating — well, actually, maybe I was. Either way, I was glad there was a public account of her testimony. I wanted everyone to see what I saw.

Tighter reins

After the fireworks with Rebecca Carbone, Tyson knew he needed to put tighter reins on the media. Not only did he want less exposure for the circus-like proceedings, he didn't want the participants to be distracted by the noise made by the camera-toting mob at the back of the room. There was already enough noise coming from the witness stand.

Tyson decreed that anyone could be in the courtroom when the jury wasn't there. But when the jury was present, only one representative from the television news contingent and a few still photographers would be allowed. He left it to the media outlets to find a way to share their film, so all the stations and newspapers could cover the trial equally.

Media liaison Craig Burger, who wore a lanyard around his neck with an ID card that pronounced him as the media gatekeeper, was in charge of the delicate task of deciding which media reps would be allowed in court each day. It was his job to make sure the scene didn't degenerate into a paparazzi field day.

For the rest of the trial, Craig assigned positions to media representatives, consigning to the hallway those who weren't chosen to be in court that day. This meant that every time someone connected to the case walked out the courtroom door, five or six microphones and half a dozen lenses extended out to us like sticks with marshmallows over a fire. And I ate them right up, just like the boy scout I never was.

Chapter 22

Kid Gloves

I returned to the courtroom the day after Rebecca Carbone's testimony, ready to cross-examine Linda Allard. Rebecca had been punished for being connected to Michael and the murders. She became a victim of the "Carbone prejudicial spillover effect." Linda, on the other hand, had the benefit of the "Nicole sympathy spillover effect," given that she was victim Dickie Robertson's girlfriend and more importantly, the mother of his daughter, Nicole. Unlike Rebecca Carbone, Linda required the use of kid gloves.

Linda was the key to helping me prove our assertion that Paul Combs was lying. Even though she was a prosecution witness, I knew her testimony would help us. She could testify that Dickie said he was doing the drug deal with other people and that he never mentioned a Hollywood bodybuilder named Gil.

But first, we'd have to listen to her sad recounting of the last night she spent with Robertson, the night before he was murdered. Linda took the stand and was sworn in. Jim Lewis approached her politely and proceeded to question her. Throughout their lengthy dialogue, Linda and Jim were effectively cleaning up Robertson's image. Together, they created the vision of a retiring drug dealer who wanted to settle down and take care of his little girl and her mother.

Linda started to cry as she looked over at her 14-year-old daughter, Nicole. "He promised me this was it. This was going to be his final deal and then he was going to get out of the business. He said he wanted to use some of the money from this last job for Nicole's future."

"Did you believe some of the money was going to be earmarked for you and Nicole?" Jim asked.

"I guess so," she said, taking a long, deep breath. Then she said, "The last morning I saw him, I felt uneasy. I don't know if it was women's intuition or what, but something wasn't right. I think he felt something, too. He told me he loved Nicole and me, and that we meant everything in the world to him. I said, 'stop!' because he made it sound like we were never going to see him again."

Jim took a moment to allow Linda, who was now crying, to regain her composure. "Thank you, Ms. Allard. That's all I have for you," he said deferentially. "Mr. Contini now has some questions he'd like to ask you."

Forcible abduction

That was my cue. Gil leaned forward and turned to his left as I squeezed behind him on my way toward Linda. He said quietly as I passed, "Show Lewis what time it is." That was Gil's way of reminding me to drive home the point that Allard's story had been well documented in sworn statements to the police. We really didn't need anything more than her words to the police just after the murders to get some serious mileage on cross.

What she told the police in 1983 was critical for the impeachment of Combs because she could single-handedly expose his pathology. The jury had just heard Combs' incredible denial that he had put a gun to her head. Now, they would hear from the far more credible Linda Allard that Paul Combs put a gun to her head and forced her to take him to the new house she had just bought with Dickie. It would show Combs to be the liar I believed he was.

My intent was to repeatedly cover in detail yet another statement Linda gave to police in 1989. This repetition was necessary so the jury would know that her story was credible, precisely because it had been consistent from the time she spoke to the police until now.

"I won't be long, Ms. Allard," I said as I smiled.

"Is it true you told Detectives Mike Kallman and Joe Damiano on April 25, 1989 that Paul Combs put a gun to your head?"

"I don't remember the exact date…"

"Let me refresh your memory," I said kindly. "The police report reads, 'On Saturday morning, Allard stated she was at her mother's house, at which time she was contacted by Paul Combs. Allard stated that Combs was accompanied by unknown subjects. Combs told Allard they were looking for Robertson all night long and that they had tried to beep him on several occasions with negative results. Allard stated that Paul Combs repeatedly asked her, 'would he f*** us over?' referring to Robertson ripping Combs off. Allard also stated that Paul Combs stated, 'we'll have lost a lot of f***ing money if he doesn't show up.'"

"Pardon the cursing, Ms. Allard," I said as the sound of self-conscious laughter came from some of the spectators. I saw one of the jurors elbow the person next to him. "That language was used in the police report," I said as I waved the report for effect. "Do the words I'm reading sound right to you? Is that what happened?" I asked.

"Yes," she said, nodding.

"Then please permit me to continue for just a moment. The police report also states, 'Allard stated that both she and Robertson feared Paul Combs. Allard advised that Paul Combs began to interrogate her regarding Robertson. Paul Combs then became upset and produced a 9-mm semi-automatic pistol, pointed the firearm at Allard's head and demanded that she take him to the Griffin Road house. Allard stated that she refused, at which time Paul Combs and the aforementioned associates forcibly abducted her and forced her to give them directions to the Griffin Road house. Allard advised that she complied as she feared for her life.'

"Now Ms. Allard, is it a fact that you told police that Paul Combs produced a 9-millimeter semi-automatic pistol and pointed the firearm at your head and demanded that you take him to the new Griffin Road house?"

"Yes."

"How did you know it was a 9-millimeter semi-automatic pistol that he put to your head, as opposed to a .38?"

"Because my father has a gun collection and I know what certain guns are."

"Were you extremely frightened when you had a gun to your head?"

She looked around the courtroom to see if Combs was there and then said, "I knew Paul… of his reputation… and he made me feel afraid."

"All right, regarding his reputation, is he extremely violent?"

"He was serious. He didn't fool around."

"Did he forcibly take you?"

"Yes."

"Isn't it a fact, ma'am, that because of who Paul Combs was, you felt you needed to cooperate?"

"Yes, I felt the need to cooperate."

"And isn't it a fact that he told you, ma'am, and I quote, 'it would be smart for you to cooperate'? Do you remember that?"

"Yes."

"And if Paul Combs told this jury yesterday that he never put a gun to your head, he would be lying, right?"

"Objection, Your Honor," barked Lewis.

"Objection sustained. Next question," ruled Tyson.

Linda started to cry. Hearing the cold reality of the police reports underscored the horror of the events at that terrible time surrounding her boyfriend's murder. She looked at the jury as she said tearfully, "Dickie promised me this was it. He was going to get out."

Linda then looked up at me and glared. It was obvious she didn't appreciate being used by the defense to muddy the waters. She knew our questions were designed to destroy Combs and create the reasonable doubt needed to save Gil. Just as disconcerting, she knew we weren't interested in the cozy Norman Rockwell-like image of the recovering drug dealer yearning to settle down by the hearth with his girls. That was Lewis' visual, not ours.

146 • *Chapter 22*

Decimating the dead-men's talk

"Ms. Allard, do you remember going to a party at Dwight Tolpher's house with a lawyer, Archie Ryan, on the night after the murders and saying that Colombians shot Richard Robertson in the head?"

"I remember telling people at the party, because that's what I thought then."

"Do you recall, ma'am, telling the police that Robertson told you he felt safe when he met about the drug deal at Tommy Adams' house? Did you tell the police that he said there was a family atmosphere, with a woman and a child, a money-counting machine and a million dollars in cash?"

"Yes, but…"

"Isn't it also a fact, ma'am, that despite everything he told you about Tommy Adams' house, the family atmosphere, the woman and child, the money-counting machine and the million dollars in cash, and all this stuff, he never mentioned Gil Fernandez? Isn't that true, ma'am?"

"True."

"Thank you, ma'am. I have nothing else."

Linda Allard was important in the state's overall equation. They wanted to humanize Dickie and let the jury know that he was a decent guy who wanted out of the drug business. They also wanted to show he had a good heart, was a good father and that he wanted to provide for Nicole's future. And all of that may have been true.

As far as the defense was concerned, however, she was important not for what she had to say about her family, but for how effectively she helped decimate the "dead-men's talk" that Paul Combs was peddling. After hearing from Linda about her frightening kidnapping ordeal, the jury had to dismiss Combs' assertion that he never put a gun to her head. After all, she had nothing to gain by making up the whole Combs affair. And he had everything to gain by denying it. We also reasoned the jury would have to seriously consider rejecting his other claim: that Robertson told him about two Hollywood bodybuilders, named Gil and Tommy.

My closing argument was already running through my head: "Ladies and gentlemen, if Combs would lie right to your faces about putting a gun to Linda Allard's head, then what else would he lie about?"

Chapter 23

The Witness Parade

Beginning the day after Linda Allard testified, a number of other witnesses queued up to provide visual, forensic or technical details about the case. The prosecution's witness list originally numbered 180 people. This forced Beth the clerk to read all those names to the jury members before being sworn in. The pretense for reading the 180 names was to see if the jurors knew any of the prospective witnesses. In reality, the prosecution simply wanted to poison the well early on, leading the jury to the impermissible inference that these guys *must* be guilty just because the witness list was so long.

To obtain such a long list, the prosecution added as many names as they could from all the other unsolved homicides for which they suspected Gil. They had to have known that the jury might reason, "Could these 180 people know terrible things that we don't?"

Perhaps the proof that they tried this maneuver lies in the fact that the list had been whittled down to 20 by the time of the trial. This drastic reduction might have constituted reasonable doubt on its own, I opined. One could argue that the absence of all these other folks was a measure of the prosecution's failure to meet their burden of proof, which is an essential requirement for any criminal conviction — especially when men's lives are riding on the outcome.

It was particularly significant that the prosecutors didn't call the lead Broward County and Dade County homicide detectives. They knew that in spite of substantial efforts to investigate the murders, these law enforcement professionals had nothing to say that would help the state's case. Even some of the witnesses who made the final list offered up a mixed bag of testimony that reinforced reasonable doubt, as far as I was concerned. The rest just offered details about the crimes themselves, making for some sickening testimony as they described the gory details.

Just watch

The morning these witnesses were set to testify was rare for me. Miraculously, my newborn son Johnny had slept through the night, meaning for a change I got to sleep, too. I was actually alert and ready to go earlier than usual. So, I called my bodyguard du jour, Bill Kelly, and asked if he would mind driving me to court a little early.

Before the proceedings began, Bill and I ran into bailiff Mike Ruvolo in the hallway.

"You'll never believe what Gil did yesterday afternoon," he said.

Naturally, my curiosity was piqued. "Oh?"

"You know the leather braces on the shackles?" he asked, not waiting for an answer. "Two days ago, I noticed the top one was kind of shredded. I didn't say anything to Gil about it. But I thought about it overnight. I said to myself, 'I've got to check into this tomorrow.'

"So, yesterday, when I put the brace on him, I said, 'Gil, what's going on? When I put that leather strap on you, it was fine. Is that belt defective? I need to know because I only have three of these things.'"

"Gil said, 'Mike, if you want, I'll show you. I'll snap it right here.'"

"I said, 'Come on! You're talkin' to *me* now.'"

"Gil said, 'Just watch.' He flexed the muscles in his thighs to such an extent that I could see the leather stretch — and then it snapped.

"I joked with him, 'Look, I only have two of these left. You snap those and I'm going to sic Bob Behan on you. You know I'm paper-weight next to him,'" Ruvolo said and then laughed at his own joke.

"But I'm not worried about him," Mike continued, more seriously now. "If he were going to run, he would have already done it. Besides, Bob already told him, 'We're not supposed to even try to tackle you if you attempt to escape. We're just supposed to shoot you. There are two undercover guys sitting in the courtroom. Both of them have bullets with your name on them. If you can run faster than a bullet, I'll be happy to let you go.'"

"That'd stop me from trying," I said, laughing.

"Yeah, me, too. Like I said, I don't think we have to worry about that with him. Gil was made a jail trusty. He even trains the deputies to lift weights. He's got it good, relatively speaking. He can walk around inside the jail; get his laundry done, you know, that kind of stuff. I'm sure he'd rather be outside but I don't think he would cause trouble to do it."

"Yeah, I think he's a changed man. Obviously, not everyone agrees," I said.

Bill Kelly chimed in with, "That's an understatement."

Then Mike looked at me and said, "You might be right about him changing but Tyson called over to the jail anyway. He wanted to check with the deputies to see if they thought it was a good idea for someone on trial for three murders to work out so much. I kinda nudged him to do it. Gil seems to be a gentleman but it wouldn't be the first time a prisoner tried to deceive the court. Just in case, Tyson told the deputies to restrict how long Gil can work out."

As Mike spoke, I felt something creepy, like there was someone standing just a little too close to me. Sure enough, as soon as Mike paused, I heard a voice say from right behind me, "Mr. Contini, may I ask you a question?" A second later, a microphone came from behind me and was suddenly in my face, soon joined by several others.

Putting my hand up and smiling to indicate to the reporters that I would speak to them in a moment, I said to Mike, "Guess I've got to go. See ya, Mike."

Sompin flotin' there by the weeds

After giving the media the sound bites they wanted, I maneuvered my way through the crowd and into the courtroom. Several minutes later, the jury was brought in and we were ready to begin the state's witness parade. My job was to rain on it.

First up was Michael White, a strange guy who testified that he and some friends had been ATV-ing in the area of Danger Road when they came across three dead people. He was the one who alerted the police to the murders. Michael, who clearly wasn't from the more cosmopolitan end of Broward County, had his own unique way of describing the area around Danger Road.

"Ain't nuttin' else out there," he said, looking at the jury. "Gets sa dark out, ya can't see yoursef."

"This guy is getting off on scaring the jury," I thought to myself.

"All ya kin hear are them-there crickets, en maybe a wild hog en sum birds," he added.

"Get to what you saw, Billy Bob," I moaned impatiently to myself. I felt like objecting and saying, "What's he doing Your Honor, writing a book?" I wondered if I could get the jury laughing again, and away from the scary picture White was painting, if I added, "this guy thinks he's on the set of *Deliverance*." But I thought better of it. I didn't want him getting pissed and pulling a Ned Beatty squeal-like-a-pig deal on me in the parking lot.

"En then we was four-wheelin' en seen sompin floatin' there by the weeds en the rocks, so we looked up closer. En then we seen 'em – the dead men. We was scared."

"There, you got your Oscar and 15 minutes of fame," I thought. "I'm sure *Hee Haw* will be calling soon. You can go pinch some more chew now."

But Michael was right about Danger Road being dark and isolated. I'd been there myself, so I knew it consisted of dirt and gravel, with nothing but muck, saw grass and rocks straddling it. It looked like one of those places where someone might quip, "nice place to lose your life." No one would ever know how to find this "road," which doubled as an extra-wide walking path, unless they knew about it already. Even though it was located less than an hour's drive from Miami, there was no legitimate entrance to it from U.S. 27, which was the closest paved road. Locals — or someone with a reason — had created an obscure off-road, hairpin opening in the saw grass that branched off the shoulder of the road. This opening curved dramatically south of the Broward-Dade county line.

As if the name of the road weren't prophetic enough, there was a cemetery opposite the opening on the curve. With the full moon only four nights before the murders, there was still plenty of moonlight on April 1, 1983. If they had been paying attention, the murderers probably would have seen the eerie shadows of dozens of headstones in the decrepit graveyard as they drove the victims to their deaths.

Most vehicles, unless they were made for off-roading, would take a beating while traversing the knee-high mounds of rock-hard dirt surfacing this deceptive ingress. About 30 yards into the road, a gate-like, thick wire cable prevented access by car. The killers had to have parked the car, then taken the victims through this barrier and walked at least a quarter-mile down the narrow dirt road before the murders took place beneath the power lines. The men and their vehicle would have been invisible to the motorists on U.S. 27, because Danger Road dipped way below street level.

Forensic facts

After the colorful and disturbing story told by Michael White, the testimony elicited by the state from Metro-Dade crime scene investigator Daniel Wigman was relatively uneventful. The jury had already heard the gory details about the crime from Michael Carbone; so getting matter-of-fact forensic facts from the crime scene investigator was anticlimactic, in addition to being a little technical for jurors who didn't have degrees in forensic science.

"They were bound, gagged and blindfolded," Wigman testified, "along the water's edge, about a quarter- to a half-mile northeast of Jones Fish Camp. The bodies were in full rigor mortis and the lividity was consistent with the body positions. Rigor had been setting in for 9-19 hours. We weren't able to lift any fingerprints from the scene."

My cross examination of him went well. It, too, was uneventful, other than the little bit of fun I had by creating some more evidence of reasonable doubt. I got some mileage out of the whole "lividity and rigor mortis" thing, committing Wigman to a time of death. My goal was to agree with whatever Wigman and medical examiner Mittleman said about the time of death, because it differed from the time in Carbone's story. I made a mental note to add the time of death to the list of conflicts in the evidence, to be used the next time I had the chance to beat the drum of reasonable doubt.

Detective Mayhew, the lead detective who secured the crime scene, then testified to what the jury had already heard from Wigman. He echoed that all three victims had been shot in the head, and that two had additional torso shots. He also talked about rigor mortis and that there were no prints. The only thing new he brought to the party was his testimony that police divers found nothing of evidentiary value in the canal.

Diapers overboard

Essentially, Mayhew was just another warm body for the state. They needed legitimate guys like him to shore up and sanitize their all-star, paid-for felon roster. Otherwise, they might have been left with just purchased testimony. If I had known just how uneventful Mayhew's testimony was going to be, I might have relaxed and succumbed to my sleep deprivation.

My son Johnny was a natural antidote to sleep. He was born a few weeks less than 12 months after the birth of Kathleen. But Johnny was much more punishing with the use of his lungs and his refusal to lie down than Kathleen ever was. Our rented house in Victoria Park was too small for Johnny to have his own room, so he tortured us in ours. When he wasn't screaming at us from the foot of our bed, he was throwing diapers at us over the railing of his crib. Come to think of it, I was getting the same treatment from Tyson. Johnny by night, and Tyson by day; no wonder I was sleep-deprived.

Exhausted or not, I had to wake up the next day for Dr. Mittleman, the medical examiner. He testified that he responded to the murder scene at 3:50 P.M. on April 2, the day after the murders. His testimony echoed that of crime scene investigator Daniel Wigman and Detective Mayhew regarding the full rigor mortis and the time of death. This provided more evidence of conflict with the Carbone story. Aside from that, Mittleman didn't do much to help the defense.

He testified that Walter Leahy had been shot twice in the head and once in the torso, and that one of the bullets through the head was not recovered. Leahy had Valium and Quaaludes in his blood, according to the doc. He then testified that Alfred Tringali was shot twice in the left ear, with both bullets recovered. Tringali also had Valium and Quaaludes in his blood, which was irrelevant for our purposes. Richard Robertson, he stated, was shot three times, once in the head, once in the upper neck and once in the stomach.

"No drugs were found in Mr. Robertson's blood," he added, as though that were important. It would not have been an appropriate defense to claim that the victims somehow deserved their deaths because they were drug dealers, so this information did nothing for us. It probably made Robertson's family feel better, though.

He concluded by saying, "Cause of death for all three victims: multiple gunshot wounds."

No surprise there, except that he said it so cavalierly. He talked about this horrific and sad event as though we were in science class. Suddenly, I became sad. The murders were depressing enough, but speaking about them in these clinical and antiseptic terms just made it worse. I couldn't even imagine how the victims' families were feeling, listening to all this casual horror. It made me wish I were back in our dark bedroom listening to Johnny and fielding his flying diapers. That was easier to deal with, because at least it had to do with being alive.

Ballistics

Ray Freeman, a firearm examiner, testified that he received six of the eight bullets involved in the murders for ballistics testing. He was the forensic firearms and ballistics expert whose scientific findings were the source of Mayhew's assertion that two guns were involved. He informed the jury that both guns were .38 Specials and that the projectiles were fired from two distinct firearms.

Freeman educated the jury about the nature of ballistics testing. He explained that the barrel of each firearm is unique in its "rifling" or markings within it, and that these markings result in distinct fingerprint-like "lands and grooves" when a projectile is fired.

"Mr. Freeman," I began, "isn't it a fact that two distinct firearms were used in these homicides?"

"That is correct."

"Is it also true that even if the same gun were loaded with the two distinct kinds of ammunition found within the victims' bodies, it wouldn't be possible that only one gun was used in these killings?"

Freeman replied, "That's true. One gun could have been reloaded but these homicides involved two distinct gun barrels. We know that from the rifling, or the lands, grooves and marks within the two barrels."

The jury was sitting up a little straighter now. "Thank God you people are paying attention. Drive it home, John, while you've got their attention," I thought to myself.

"Are you sure about that, sir?" I asked solicitously, just to hear him tell the jury again.

"There *had* to be two separate guns, given the distinct markings. Someone could reload the same gun countless times, but there still had to be two guns involved."

"Can this jury have absolute certainty that no two guns or gun barrels leave the same markings on spent projectiles?" I asked, kicking myself afterwards.

"Wait a minute, John," I joked to myself, "you're confusing yourself with this whole 'absolute certainty' thing. I was used to making sure the jury *wasn't* sure of anything, as a prerequisite for creating reasonable doubt. In reality, the only thing I ever wanted the jury to be sure about was that they *weren't* sure about anything — except that they had a reasonable doubt.

"Can they have an absolute certainty, is that the question?" he repeated.

"Yes, can they be entirely sure, sir?"

"Yes, because forensically, or scientifically, it has been proven that each barrel, like fingerprints, has its own unique markings. These are referred to as lands and grooves or rifling. Every projectile fired from a specific barrel is going to be left with the same exact markings."

Freeman started sounding pretty smart, so I decided to keep him on the stand and co-opt him as a defense witness.

"Really?" I said, suggesting by my eyes and head tilt that I wanted him to pontificate some more. There's nothing sweeter than turning one of their witnesses into one of your own. It was fun for me to get more mileage out of him for my cause than he ever produced for the prosecution. After a time, the jury would forget which side called this guy. If pressed, they'd have assumed later that I called Freeman. After all, I was the one camped out with the guy, using him to educate the jury about ballistics and firearms.

"And that's how you knew two distinct guns were used in these killings, when you compared the bullets and the markings on each of the bullets against each other?" I asked rhetorically, throwing him a fastball down the middle that he could hit out of the park.

"Exactly," Freeman replied, with heightened excitement in his voice. He appeared to appreciate that somebody was interested in knowing exactly what he knew and why. This was his turn to do his thing. Now he wasn't just in the lab but in a classroom of sorts. We had turned the courtroom into a lecture hall and Freeman was the professor.

"And when we examined the projectiles found within the three victims' bodies, we determined that three of the projectiles were fired from the same gun. The markings on those three projectiles were identical, just like fingerprints. Whereas, the other three projectiles found within the victims' bodies were fired from a separate and distinct firearm, leaving distinct markings from the initial three. Those latter three were entirely different from the former, but they were identical to one another. In this way, we were able to determine with certainty that two distinct firearms had to have been used in these homicides."

Great job, Professor! The prosecutors looked miserable. I'm sure they would have preferred to skip this particular class.

"Mr. Freeman, would you please tell us more about the lands and grooves and right-hand twists you refer to in your report?"

It was almost enjoyable pretending to be just another one of the jurors, wanting the good professor to educate us all. The prosecutors knew what I was doing — essentially hijacking their witness — but there was nothing they could do about it. They were smart enough to know that if they objected to any of this Firearms 101 stuff, they'd only annoy the jurors who were clearly enjoying it. Only a moronic prosecutor would knowingly annoy the jury. Even with all I had against the prosecutors, one thing I would never call them was moronic. Quite the contrary, they were all very sharp.

Freeman replied, "The lands and grooves are simply impressions or markings on the projectiles I've been describing. These markings are left on every bullet after it has been fired from a gun. As I explained, each firearm barrel has these same fingerprint-like markings, referred to as rifling, along and within its individual barrel. When a bullet is fired, it spins down and around the barrel as it's expelled, resulting in rifling impressions being left on each projectile. These impressions are the lands and grooves referenced in my report."

"And these right-hand twists?" I prodded.

"The right-hand twist you referenced refers to the fact that the projectiles were spinning to the right as they were expelled from both firearms. That's not always the case. Some firearms expel projectiles with a left-hand twist."

"So, there's certainty now, for all the reasons you've told us, that two distinct firearms were involved in these homicides. Is it also true, Mr. Freeman, that all six recovered projectiles, labeled A through F, were .38-caliber bullets? What else, if anything, can you tell us about the ammunition?"

Class was too much fun now to end early. I didn't want to release the students, especially since the prosecutors appeared to be aging right in front of me, shifting repeatedly in their seats and looking at the clock. My retaliatory thoughts were damn near audible now, as I asked in my head, "Why aren't you smiling now, Jimmy?"

"That's true, Mr. Contini, and just to back up a bit, projectile A was recovered, according to Dr. Mittleman, the medical examiner, from the body of Mr. Leahy. Projectiles B and C, we're told, were recovered from Mr. Tringali and were the same brand as projectile A. These three projectiles, though recovered from two bodies, were nonetheless fired from the same gun, which was a .38 Special with eight lands and grooves and a right-hand twist. The bullets used were 158-grain lead, round-nose projectiles made by Winchester Cartridge Company.

"Projectiles D, E and F were recovered from the body of Richard Robertson, according to the medical examiner. These three projectiles were fired from a different .38 Special with five lands and grooves and a right-hand twist."

I made a mental note that one of the other two people present at the scene might very well have killed Robertson, even if the victims' families insisted on believing that Fernandez killed all of them. All three of the projectiles found in Robertson came from a distinct gun. Could it have belonged to Tommy Felts, whom Carbone said was in the water with the victims and Gil? Or could it have belonged to Carbone?

Then, anticipating more fun, I asked, "Isn't it a fact, Mr. Freeman, that the prosecutors requested, as recently as this week — after the testimony of Mr. Carbone — for you to test still more firearms in connection with these murders?"

"I'm not sure when Mr. Carbone testified. But yes, it's true that we were asked to test two other firearms this week, to see whether they might have been used in these homicides."

Thank you, Mr. Freeman, for helping me to show that the state was still investigating this case eight years after the murders! They would never concede this, of course. Instead, they'd argue that these other guns were tested this late in the game only to give me less to shout about in closing argument.

"In fact, weren't you given a .38-caliber firearm this week that was once seized from Michael Carbone in connection with his 1985 arrest?"

"I'm not sure about the arrest you're referring to, but yes, we were asked to test a firearm. It was a .38, and I see here in my report that it has Michael Carbone's name adjacent to the serial numbers."

"Your ballistics report, Mr. Freeman, reflects the fact that you weren't able to specifically exclude this firearm as being used in these homicides. Isn't that right, sir?"

"Well, yes and no. I was able to exclude this firearm in reference to projectiles A, B and C, but not for projectiles D, E and F."

The last three were the Robertson projectiles.

"So Mr. Carbone may have killed these victims with three bullets, and not six, with another shooter or another gun involved…"

"Objection, Judge. That's argument, and it assumes facts not in evidence," protested Lewis.

"Sustained," bellowed Tyson.

"Gee, that was a surprise ruling, Judge," I thought cynically.

The jury was wide-eyed with attentive curiosity as they watched this exchange. "Good jury," I thought, imagining myself patting them on their heads. In truth, Lewis and the gang were right. Had they *not* tested all these other guns, they could almost hear me in their sleep complaining in closing argument, "Why didn't they test Carbone's .38 from his 1985 arrest? What if that was one of the firearms used in this case?"

I couldn't wait to get home to Elizabeth and my babies after a good day with Professor Freemen. "Who knows," I thought, "maybe my night will go as well as my day and I'll get to enjoy Johnny when he's happy, before he starts his lung exercises." Sure enough, when I got home Johnny was laughing and crawling around the rug with Kathleen, the two of them competing to see whose knees were redder. They were a joy to watch. But then night came and the drama king started up again. Life with Johnny was a trip. He was full of life and laughter, and he brought me great joy. But after he screamed again all night, he had me hating life the next morning. I had to strap four cups of coffee to my face before I could even think about facing our 9 A.M. start time in court. On the drive into court, I couldn't help but think that Johnny was just getting me in shape for more time with Tyson.

More witnesses

In spite of feeling like I had been dragged to work underneath a bus, I somehow managed to haul my tired body into the courtroom the next day. First up was Elizabeth Brown, who testified that she was the supervisor of personnel for the Metro-Dade Police Department, as it was called during the time when Gil was a police officer. She said that Gil had two weapons while he was on the force: a two-inch Smith and Wesson revolver that he wore on his ankle and a four-inch Smith and Wesson revolver that he wore on his shoulder. Both weapons fired .38-caliber ammunition. The fact that Gil's guns fired bullets with the same caliber as the murder bullets seemed damning, but there was never any evidence that his particular guns were connected to the crimes. Nonetheless, the prosecution obviously wanted the jury to draw that inference.

Next was Sergeant Whitfield, a diver for the Broward Sheriff's Department. He testified that he dove off the Sheridan Street Bridge in 1990 to look for guns but none were found. Michael Gast, a diver for the Metro-Dade Police, testified that he also dove the north bank under the Sheridan Street Bridge. He likewise reported that this search produced no results. Both said that because of moving sands and rapid water currents, it would have been difficult to find a firearm even one day after it was thrown in. Their position was clear: Since the dives took place seven years after the weapon or weapons were allegedly thrown over the bridge, it would have been a miracle had they found anything.

My favorite witness of the day was Chris Inks. Inks was Paul Combs' cousin who pled guilty to a drug case with Paul in Philadelphia and lived with Combs at the time of the murders. Inks testified that he and his cousin had moved thousands of Quaaludes, thousands of pounds of marijuana and many kilos of cocaine in their careers. He reported that he and Paul had testified against others in separate cases in Ohio and Pennsylvania and received probation instead of prison sentences for their efforts. Like Combs, Inks said he overheard Dickie Robertson say to Paul that he was going to do a drug deal with a couple of bodybuilders from Hollywood, named Gil and Tommy. This was just more dead-men's talk that couldn't be confronted on cross-examination but Tyson let it in anyway. Again, no surprise.

"So you were convicted with your cousin Paul Combs, is that right?" I asked Inks.

"Yeah, that's right."

"Kinda like that saying, 'the family that gets *convicted* together, *stays* together?'"

He just ignored me while the jury laughed. The prosecutors started to object, but I just moved on with another wisecrack.

"Do you guys always do everything together, in the exact same way, Mr. Inks?"

"No," is all he said.

"Oh, really. Let me ask you again in another way. You both moved all that dope and you both got convicted. Then you both testified in Ohio and Pennsylvania, blaming other people. As a result, you both got probation for moving more dope than is trafficked in most small Latin American countries..."

"Objection, Judge" barked Lewis.

"I'll rephrase it, Judge," I offered.

"Then you both got immunity here, and now you're both testifying for Lewis. So, are you *sure* both of you aren't programmed to do and say the same things?" I had fun asking that one.

"That's ridiculous," he replied, looking to Tyson for help.

There was the usual objection, resulting in the usual ruling. Then we moved on to Scott Calvis, a cocaine-distributor associate of Paul Combs. Calvis testified that he had been friendly with Dickie Robertson. He was yet another person who testified that Dickie had told him about a drug deal with some bodybuilders from Hollywood, one of whom was named Gil.

This was even *more* dead-men's testimony, with fingers pointing from eternity. It was already impossible to confront, but now it was piling on, allowing Inks and Calvis to corroborate the impeached Combs. Allard had helped to destroy the credibility of Combs, but now with Chris Inks and Scott Calvis essentially reverberating what Combs said he had heard from Dickie, the cumulative effect was becoming insurmountable. Like a pile-up on the freeway, there was just so much carnage; it was looking like it would be harder and harder to get around.

After Calvis was done testifying about his warm-and-fuzzy, *Kumbaya* friendship with Robertson, it was my turn to cross-examine him.

"So, Mr. Calvis, you were the accountant for Mr. Robertson and our good Samaritan, Paul Combs?" He was almost as much fun as Inks.

"I did some accounting for them, yes," he replied, quite guardedly.

"Those would be some fun books to look at, now wouldn't they, sir?"

"I resent your implication," he said, figuring the best defense is a good offense.

"No, you're right. I'm sorry. Shame on me for mistakenly assuming that two drug dealers sharing the same accountant would make for some wild and funky accounting. Can you see where I might make that mistake, sir?"

"No, I can't," he snarled.

"Dickie Robertson was your friend, wasn't he?" I continued.

"That's right, he was." Calvis replied defensively.

"And of course, if law enforcement gave you their opinion that a particular person killed your friend, you'd do and say whatever you could to try to get that person convicted. Wouldn't you, sir?"

After about a half-hour of suggesting to the jury, right or wrong, that this guy had been in the business of jockeying drug money numbers, I was done with him.

Say a prayer for me

After Calvis was through, Melissa Felts, the wife of the murdered Tommy Felts, testified. She said that Tommy, Gil and Bert were close friends and that they all had the same tattoo design. She informed the jury that Gil was the best man at her wedding to Tommy; that Bert, Gil and Tommy often stayed out all night together; and that Bert was the dominant figure in the group. The prosecution wanted the jury to think the defendants were inseparable, so if they thought one was guilty, there would be a prejudicial spillover effect onto the others.

On cross-examination, however, Melissa admitted that Gil and his wife, Neli, lived in a $68,000 two-bedroom house that didn't have central air conditioning. She said they didn't even have enough money to get their car out of the shop. The jurors had to be told these important points again in closings, I reminded myself with asterisks and notes on my myriad legal pads.

When I cross-examined her, I asked, "Ma'am, big-time drug dealers making the kind of money made in this case don't have problems getting their cars out of the shop, and they don't live in $68,000 two-bedroom houses with no central AC, do they?"

Once again, the usual objections were followed by the usual rulings. It was time to move on.

Eugene Martinez, who was a friend of victim Wally Leahy, testified next. He stated that he drove Leahy to the Rustic Inn on Ravenswood Road at 4 or 5 P.M. on April 1, 1983. This testimony was important because it contradicted Mike Carbone's story that the victims were already bound and gagged by 1 P.M. My notes reflected my intention to remind the jury later in closings that it would be awfully hard to bind and gag victims four hours *before* they had even showed up for a drug deal.

Then came Mike Nadoka, Al Tringali's roommate, who backed up Linda Allard's testimony. Mike, too, had heard all the details about the safe family environment with a woman and a child, the million dollars in cash and the money-counting machine. That only helped us, I felt, in exposing the reasonable doubt surrounding the alternative Carbone story, which included no woman, no child, no million dollars in cash and no money-counting machine. Michael's account contained none of the so-called "safe family environment." On cross-examination, I helped Mike Nadoka reiterate *this* end of the dead-men's talk. Two can play the hearsay game, I reasoned.

If Al Tringali told his roommate Mike Nadoka about a money-counting machine, a million dollars in cash, a woman and a child — the exact details that Linda Allard said Dickie had told her — then Louie and I could take advantage of Judge Tyson's illegal decision to allow this testimony. Nadoka and Allard's testimony gave us license to hijack this same kind of hearsay dead-men's talk and beat it to death in our closing arguments. After all, the prosecution was cherry-picking and using the other end of what the dead men said by trumpeting that now-tired line about "two Hollywood bodybuilders, named Gil and Tommy." Why shouldn't we also use what the victims supposedly said for *our* side, even if legally speaking, it was the same kind of hearsay.

It was amazing to me that so much of the "testimony" in this case came from murdered men who seven years earlier had become unavailable to testify. Each side cherry-picked and used the hearsay they liked, while ignoring or explaining away anything they disliked.

Some of the most moving testimony was saved for the end of the day. It came from Doug Eddy, Al Tringali's best friend. He testified that he used to drive with Al to pick up cocaine from Tommy "No Fingers" Felts. He also told jurors that Al shared with him that he was excited because he was going to make a million dollars in a drug deal. Eddy had been a friend of Tringali for years and they were very close. In an emotional moment, Eddy broke down and said that Al must have known something bad was going to happen.

"Al told me the night before the murders, 'If I don't come back, say a prayer for me.'"

Chapter 24

Channel Switching

Louie and I felt like we were winning throughout the trial. And our perceptions were only strengthened by comments we received from court personnel. Bailiffs Mike and Bob often told us at the close of the day's proceedings that in their opinion things had gone very well for us. Even more telling, we got reassuring nonverbal cues from the jurors when they nodded or shook their heads at just the right times. From what I could see, they didn't appear impressed with the prosecution's case.

The defense had this going for it, in spite of Tyson raging at us while simultaneously enjoying his love fest with the jury. From all appearances, he treated the jurors like his extended family. It seemed like he had befriended the whole gang of them. He invited them to use his chambers in his absence at lunchtime, so they could order in whatever they wanted. He even let them use his personal bathroom and play with his daughters' little plastic toys that were displayed across his credenza.

By this point in the trial, the jurors had almost camped out in his office every day for lunch and bathroom breaks. That might seem relatively harmless under most circumstances, but since he often raged at the defense — albeit mostly at Louie — it appeared as though he favored one side over the other.

It was downright dangerous, in my opinion. I was afraid the jurors would become victims of the infamous Stockholm syndrome, whereby hostages fall in love with their kidnappers. The jury essentially had been held hostage for months. During that time, Tyson had all the power in the world over them. And they all knew it, even if only subconsciously. The jurors had to be thinking, "The judge is upset with the defense. He knows something we don't. He must know these guys are guilty. Or maybe there's a lot of evidence we're not being allowed to see because the defense lawyers have fought to keep it out. Judge Tyson is such a sweet man and he's *so* nice to us. I wish those defense lawyers wouldn't upset him so much. They're hiding a lot from us and Judge Tyson knows it all. He just can't tell us and maybe that's why he's so frustrated."

This is the exact reason why a judge's temperament is so important in the judicial process.

You're up!

So many people wanted to see what was going on that a huge crowd formed outside the courtroom door once the room was full. Even my mentor and pastor O.S. Hawkins showed up, surprising me. He was lucky he even got a place to sit. As one person would leave the packed, noisy courtroom, someone from the hallway would slip in and take the seat. If a guy got up to use the bathroom, he would immediately lose his spot.

It's hard to describe what it felt like when the judge called on me to present the defense closing argument. He looked at me as if to say, "you're up!" Ready or not, that was my cue. Gil gave me an encouraging squeeze of my hand, as the court reporter looked at me expectantly, fingers poised above the keys of her machine. The jurors also gazed at me with anticipation — along with my opponents.

There was no more time to reflect on what I was going to say. It was always this way when I made a closing argument, but this time it felt almost like slow motion. Every millisecond seemed frozen just long enough to notice small details: the nervous looks of a juror trying not to signal encouragement, the hateful stare of a victim's family member, Neli holding hands with Gil's parents or the second-hand on my watch.

The trial spectators, including the ones who hated me, managed a hushed silence out of respect for the process. That only made the moment more surreal. It was time for me to get up off my seat and start running my mouth. Gil's life was on the line and now it all came down to me.

Let's Make a Deal

"Good morning, ladies and gentlemen of the jury," I began, building up confidence with each word. "You're going to be listening to lawyers all day. And try to bear with us. This process is extremely important for the State of Florida, of course. But it's particularly critical for these two gentlemen over here," I said as I pointed at Gil and Bert. "Their lives are riding on everything we'll be saying — or God forbid — on what we *forget* to say."

My goal was to make them actually feel the burden I carried as the lawyer, so they'd quietly root for me. It also was important for them to see me moving the podium out of the way while I talked with them. I did this to show that nothing would be between us, and that I was comfortable just standing before them while working the room. There could be no hiding behind the podium if I was determined to control the proceedings. Not if I wanted the jury to feel my confidence and comfort.

"And remember, you promised *not* to hold it against the defendant if the lawyer is trying very, very hard to expose something that he feels is the truth. You all swore an oath before the judge and before God that you wouldn't hold it against the client when his lawyer is feeling passionate about the case. You swore not to hold it against the defendant if the lawyer gets in the face of a particular felon. You swore to understand that you would expect nothing less from an attorney defending a man whose life is at stake. And that's why every one of you was chosen, at least from the defense standpoint.

"The judge will instruct you that after weighing all the evidence, if there's not an abiding conviction of guilt, or if the conviction you have wavers and vacillates, then the charge is not proven beyond a reasonable doubt. In that case, you *must* find the defendants not guilty, because the doubt is reasonable."

I could sense that I had to get away from the legalese for a moment and make them aware of the game — or more accurately, the game *show* — being played by the prosecution.

"Ladies and gentlemen, over the last few weeks, you heard two completely different theories or stories from the prosecution. It was almost as if the prosecutors had a remote and they were switching channels on TV. On one channel, you heard one story. Then they'd switch to another channel and you'd hear a different story.

"Then while they were changing channels, the remote got stuck on *Let's Make a Deal*. The lead prosecutor over here, Jim Lewis, is kind of like Monty Hall."

It was a good time to pause for effect. The cameras were clicking away as I was pointing at Lewis. He just sat there frowning at me, looking smug and pretending not to be worried.

"Monty Hall over here," I repeated as I pointed to Jim, "is actually presenting *two* competing theories on behalf of the state, each behind separate doors. He has 'door number one' and 'door number two.'

"Behind door number one, we have Michael and Rebecca Carbone, Paul Combs and Chris Inks, all of whom said they heard in one way or another that Gil was involved in the drug rip-off and murder. Ladies and gentlemen, let's look at the credibility of these people. Michael Carbone sat right here in this witness seat and suggested that the victims, who can no longer defend themselves, were lying."

The jury followed me attentively with their eyes as I walked over to the witness chair and actually sat down, mimicking Carbone for effect.

"He sat right up here and said, 'I saw no money counting machine; I saw no million dollars in cash. I saw no woman, no child. There was just Tommy, the Gil and Bert characters and me.' This story completely conflicts with the victims' stories, which are inherently more believable."

Then I got up to walk in front of the jury box again, specifically looking at each of the female jurors. I wanted them to pay special attention to what I was going to say next.

"On top of this, Mr. Carbone admits he beat his wife with his fist in front of his daughter. What kind of a person would do this? The same kind of man who would sleep with a murder victim's sister and further victimize her. It's not enough that she lost her brother. No, he had to use her, too. He lied to her about being in prison in 1983 when the murders happened. In reality, he didn't go to prison until 1985. He then sleeps with her to get what he wants. Nice guy.

"Mike Carbone is a five-time convicted felon, a pathological liar and arguably sociopathic. On the most horrific night of his life, how could he forget who was driving the death car? Even with all this, you might still be asking yourselves, 'Why would this guy lie?' This is the value system of this gentleman — or this *man*, I should say. This is his belief system. You can't try to figure out why an arguably sociopathic person who has no conscience would lie.

"The forensics expert said two firearms had to be used in this triple murder. Science has proven this. Thank God for science. Forensics has proven that Michael Carbone is lying about the gun. He either lied to the Grand Jury or to you. So, to which jury did he lie? We've got two different stories about the guns, told to two different juries. Since we know he's lying about the gun, what else could he not be telling us? What else is he attributing to others? If he's lying about the gun, and it's a scientific fact that he is, could he be lying about anything else?

"There's more evidence against Michael Carbone than there is against Gil Fernandez. I urge you to dismiss his purchased testimony. It's tainted. Think about it: You're being asked to possibly fry people on *his* word?"

That line seemed to really affect a few of them. The look in their eyes said, "no way!" This gave me a boost of greater confidence as I moved on to Carbone's ex-wife. "There's also Mrs. Carbone, Mr. Immunity's former not-so-better half, behind door number one. She's no Rebecca of Sunnybrook Farm — more like Rebecca of Wise Guy Palooka Farm, if you ask me. Her testimony is on a par with his; it's just as worthless.

"And what about Paul Combs and Chris Inks? These professional testifying felons are accustomed to selling their stories to save their hides. They did it in Ohio and they did it in Pennsylvania, and now they're guests of the State of Florida, peddling their new story, the one they read in the newspaper.

"How do we know that Mr. Combs is lying to you? Because Linda Allard came up here and told you that Combs put a gun to her head. She, in fact, gave a statement to the police and swore to God before you in this courtroom that Combs put a gun to her head. She has nothing to gain by telling you that. And what did he tell you? 'Absolutely not; I never put a gun to her head.' He has everything to gain by denying it. This guy was lying. He admitted that he didn't come forward until he read a *Miami Herald* article about this trial. He saw the defendants' names mentioned in the article and suddenly he came up with, 'yeah, Dickie mentioned two bodybuilders from Hollywood, named Gil and Tommy. Yeah, that's what Dickie said. Yeah, that's the ticket.'

"If he had only been a little straight with you. If he had been more forthright, he would have said, 'Yeah, I was upset. I owed my connection a half-million dollars, so yeah, I put a gun to Linda Allard's head.' If he had been just a little straight with you people, maybe you could rely on what this felon has to say.

"But he had the audacity to take an oath before God to tell the truth, the whole truth and nothing but the truth, and then lie. How can you help but reject the rest of his testimony? How do you know what else he's lying about? How do you know?

"Linda Allard helped prove he's a liar. He told us the source of his information: a *Miami Herald* article from eight years after the crimes. He's stupid enough to admit that under oath. And then he demands immunity!

"As if the Carbones and Paul Combs weren't enough, behind door number one we also have Chris Inks, Combs' cousin. Inks didn't even flinch when I said, 'the family that gets convicted together, stays together.' Combs, Inks and Scott Calvis all testified to the same thing — and all for the same reason: immunity!

"So, we have all these outstanding citizens behind door number one. Now, behind door number two, we have the story that came from the victims' families and friends. Mike Nadoka, who was Al Tringali's roommate, testified that Mr. Tringali told him there was a meeting held in a family atmosphere where a woman and a child were present. He also mentioned that Al told him he saw a million dollars and a money-counting machine. Linda Allard stated that her boyfriend Dickie Robertson told her the same thing. Gil Fernandez was never mentioned in either of these conversations with the victims. Door number two.

"The testimony of these witnesses is inherently more believable because the victims were still alive at that point. They told their loved ones these things in a conversational way. There was absolutely no reason for them to lie!

"Behind door number two, we also have Eugene Martinez, who said, 'I drove Walter Leahy to the Rustic Inn on Ravenswood Road at four or five in the afternoon.' Michael Carbone sat up there and told you, 'No, I had these three guys bound and gagged at one in the afternoon.' When I asked him, 'How could you have them tied up at one in the afternoon when Walter Leahy's friend said he drove him to the Rustic Inn at four or five?' Mr. Carbone's only response was, 'I don't know.' The same man, by the way, who said 'I don't know' at least 150 times in his sworn testimony on significant, not trivial, points. Sometimes I can't believe I have to argue these things; that this absurdity has gone this far!

"The infinitely more believable story, ladies and gentlemen, is behind door number two. But the strange thing is, the state doesn't really care which one you pick. Actually, they would have been better off giving you just one theory but they gave you two.

"They're asking you to forget about the tremendous conflicts between these two competing theories. They're asking you to ignore all the conflicts in the evidence and pick door number one *or* door number two, just like Monty Hall would do. Door number one is the Carbone story. Door number two is the victims' version, the more credible one. Go ahead; pick one. It makes no difference to the prosecution which one you pick."

I paused for a moment.

"What they're not telling you, ladies and gentlemen, is that there's a 'door number *three*.' It's called '*reasonable doubt*,' '*not guilty*!'"

I paused again to give them time to absorb what I had just said. Both pauses had the desired effect. I could have sworn I had a few of their heads nodding in agreement. It was a high like no other.

"They're asking you to reconcile competing, conflicting stories. Yet, if you do that, you're going to be torn for the rest of your lives. You're being forced to guess when people's lives are at stake. It's up to you to decide whether the defendants ride the lightning. But remember, you have door number three, which is the path of the clear conscience: '*not guilty*.'

"Did you realize that they hadn't given you the door number three option? Well, they might not tell you about it, but the judge will. He is going to give you some instructions on the law. This will be one of them: 'Reasonable doubt as to the guilt of the defendants may arise from *the evidence*, *conflicts* in the evidence or *lack* of evidence.'

"But wait! In case you didn't happen to like *Let's Make a Deal*, the prosecutors over here are happy to change the channel for you once again. They'd love it if you would play the game *The Price is Right* with them. Bob Barker over there," I said, pointing again to Jim Lewis, "said to Paul Combs, 'Oh, you want immunity, even though you're on federal probation? Fine. No problem. *Come on down*!'"

Jim was slumping in his chair now, glaring at me. Doug and Cindy wouldn't even look at me, feigning complete disinterest in what I was saying.

They weren't fooling anyone. They couldn't have been more interested, hoping I'd screw up.

"Can you see the prosecutor and Combs on the phone? Bob Barker over here calls Combs and says, 'Hello, Paul? It's me, Jim. You just read the *Miami Herald* article? Great! You say you didn't put a gun to Linda Allard's head? Good, you go ahead and deny that. You lied to this jury a day before Linda swore to the jury it happened? No problem! That's OK! You're a federal felon who has been convicted of trafficking thousands of pounds of marijuana, thousands of Quaaludes and multiple kilos of cocaine? Great! You want immunity even though you're on federal probation? No problem. *Come on down!*"

Jim just kept eyeballing me. I almost said, "Come on Jimmy, lighten up. I didn't make faces when you were pulling those stunts with your buddy Combs and all that dead men's hearsay crap."

"Tempted by these immunity gifts from Monty Hall, Bob Barker and all their prosecutor friends, Combs jumped all over it. And he'd be an idiot *not* to. But now we're forced to listen to him and all the other immunized felons.

"Ladies and gentlemen, all sarcasm aside, the defendant is not required to prove a thing. The law is clear: It's not necessary for the defendant to disprove anything. This is the law. Nor is the defendant required to prove his innocence. It's up to the state to prove guilt. Judge Tyson is going to read you the jury instruction regarding 'the defendant not testifying.' His honor will instruct you as follows: 'the defendant exercised a fundamental right not to be a witness in this case. You must not view this as an admission of guilt or be influenced in any way by it. No juror should be concerned about whether the defendant did or did not take the witness stand.'"

"Yeah, right," I said to myself. We all knew that juries wanted to hear from defendants, especially from a former cop who ought to know how to testify. I knew he'd be held to a higher standard because of this. Worse, he'd be cross-examined about the photographs that showed him partying with Tommy Felts, Michael Carbone and Bert Christie. He'd also be questioned about his Metro-Dade Police Department employment records, specifically regarding March 31 and April 1, 1983, when he may or may not have called in sick.

There was no way we could allow for that cross-examination. The "guilt by association" phenomenon would have been devastating, giving new meaning to the old saying, "association brings about participation." The only solution? Beat to death with the jurors that they'd be expected to deliver what they had promised in jury selection: They had to understand and agree that a defendant was not required to testify and that they didn't need to hear from him.

"We talked ad nauseum during jury selection about how when you give a speech, you're not your best self. This is a nerve-wracking atmosphere. You each said you weren't expecting to hear from the defendant if his lawyer advised him not to get up here. That's because I don't want to let the prosecutors attack him and get in his face. And you all agreed that it was understandable that Mr. Fernandez wouldn't want to subject himself to that. His life is on the line. He's not going to be his best self. You all agreed in jury selection that you were not going to require that. Just like the law says, the defendant is not required to prove a thing — or to even get up here.

"The judge also will give you this instruction on circumstantial evidence: 'The circumstances themselves must be proven beyond a reasonable doubt, and must be consistent with guilt and inconsistent with innocence.' You'll hear Judge Tyson tell you in so many words, if there are two reasonable scenarios, one indicating guilt and one indicating innocence, you must accept the one indicating innocence. You must not convict unless you are first able to exclude every reasonable hypotheses of innocence. That cannot be done here.

"You've heard tremendous conflicts in the evidence. The judge will tell you that a reasonable doubt may arise from *conflicts* in the evidence. The judge also will tell you a reasonable doubt may arise from a *lack* of evidence. Ladies and gentlemen, the lack of evidence in this case is rivaled only by the conflicts in the evidence!

"Talk about lack of evidence! Melissa Felts admits that Gil and Neli live in a two-bedroom house. Gil Fernandez is some million-dollar player, right? They can't even get their car out of the shop, according to Melissa Felts. I'm beginning to wonder who called her up here. It seems like she's working for our side. I'm glad they called people I already had under subpoena. Gil and Neli couldn't get the car out of the shop. Melissa, who was the prosecution's witness, told you that. This is a million-dollar-cash guy, right? I mean this is ridiculous! No central air in a $68,000 house. The state has all the records to back this up. But you haven't seen them, because they don't want you to see them. It's called lack of evidence.

"They also didn't call Detective Diaz, the lead Metro-Dade detective, and Detective Kallman, the lead Broward detective. They didn't because they know they failed miserably in their burden of proof. You're going to get instructions on manslaughter, negligence and other lesser-included offenses. Read them and try to keep a straight face, folks.

"You would have shaken your head with disgust had they called Kallman. You don't get to hear from Kallman because they know that the defense lawyers would have had a field day with his testimony. Michael Carbone lied to Kallman and then changed his story when it suited him.

Kallman would have no choice but to say, 'Yeah, Michael lied to me when I first confronted him about the triple murders but I think later on he would have told me the truth.' They don't call him to testify for you, and yet it's *their* burden.

"When you weigh testimony in your mind, you have to follow the judge's instructions, which require you to ask yourself the following questions:

"Was it proven that any of the witnesses had been convicted of a crime? Try five felonies for Michael. Chris Inks, Paul Combs — more felonies.

"Do the witnesses have some interest in how the case should be decided? Michael Carbone needed to stay out of the hot seat. He wanted to stay out of prison, where he surely would have been sent for the rest of his natural life. Did that witness have some interest in how the case should be decided? You bet he did! His ex-wife demanded and received immunity, too, before agreeing to speak to you. Mr. and Mrs. Immunity; they must've met in charm school.

"Do the witnesses seem to have accurate memories? I've lost count but I believe there were around 155 'I don't knows' in Mike Carbone's various sworn statements.

"Did the witnesses have opportunities to see and know the things about which they testified? Remember all that hearsay? This is a hearsay case.

"Did the witnesses' testimony agree with the other testimony and evidence in the case? Remember door number one versus door number two — Carbone's story versus the victims' stories? These were two completely different stories.

"Has the witness been offered or received any money or preferred treatment? Can you say 'immunity'? This is ridiculous. 'Money or preferred treatment'? This question is part of the jury instructions for cases in Florida. I didn't write the question, but if I did, I couldn't make it fit this case any better.

"The legislature and the Florida Supreme Court knew that testimony that would put a man away had to be from disinterested human beings with nothing to gain. You don't send somebody to the electric chair or to life in prison on testimony from felons who expect preferred treatment; who demand and receive immunity. Remember, these are the rules that govern your deliberation. As the prosecutors get up here again, remember that the defendant is *not* required to prove a thing.

"Ladies and gentlemen, this case is unique in that it has all three elements that cause reasonable doubt: *lack* of evidence, *conflicts* in the evidence and the *evidence itself.* You only need *one* of these elements for reasonable doubt. This would almost be comical if it weren't so damned tragic."

I went on for over an hour, passionately accentuating certain key words and legal phrases. I brought up anything and everything that would remind the jury of the reasonable doubt I hoped was in their minds. My job was to either expose reasonable doubt or create it. It didn't matter at that point, either would do.

"You have to be comfortable with the verdict here. You have to know in your heart, mind, soul and spirit; and have an abiding conviction of guilt — one that doesn't waver or vacillate — before you can find a defendant guilty. The instructions are very clear: 'If you don't have an abiding conviction of guilt, you must find the defendant not guilty.'"

Once I finished begging them for the not guilty verdict, I simply said, "thank you" and headed back to the defense table, exchanging smiles with Gil. Louie and Bert were grinning big, too. But I wasn't getting any love from the state or their friends in the peanut gallery. They all hated me at that point — everyone but my wife and my pastor, who stuck around to support me; and of course, the guys at the defense table and their families. It was a weird feeling, being sandwiched like that between love and hate.

Just as I was sitting down, Mike Ruvolo handed me something. On a small piece of paper, my mentor O.S. Hawkins had written, "I pick door number three!" I spotted O.S. in the crowd and smiled at him as he was leaving. The note brightened my day, all right. But truth be told, the real reason I was happy was because my closing was over. Finally, after weeks of arguing, I didn't have to be "on" anymore.

Chapter 25

Plots Hatched in Hell

The prosecution brought out their best guns in response to my closing. Doug Molloy and Jim Lewis both delivered final closing arguments for the state, even though it was illegal for them to split their remarks like this. Under Florida law, the state was supposed to have only one closing argument, not the two bites of the apple that Tyson gave them.

According to law, calling defense witnesses or introducing physical or documentary evidence would have precluded our team from having a rebuttal closing. So, Louie and I, with the consent of our clients, decided from the gate not to introduce new witnesses. We assumed this strategy would give us the opportunity to address the jury one more time, giving us the last word. But Tyson essentially gave the prosecution two closings by allowing them to split their remarks. This defeated our strategic purpose for holding back. We erroneously believed that we'd be given two closings and the state would get only one. Louie and I objected to this clearly illegal maneuver in advance but Tyson allowed it anyway.

The jury was with me when I sat down; this I knew. Then Doug delivered a strong closing argument, following mine. I watched the juror's faces as they slowly warmed to whatever he had to say. His smooth allocution definitely hurt us. Ironically, when Doug delivered his closing, he talked a lot more about me than he did Gil Fernandez. But I suppose that was his assigned role in the prosecution's agreed-upon division of labor: to attack Contini's arguments, one by one.

And that set it up nicely for Jim's end of the deal. Lewis calmly got up and delivered his own methodical closing, which, unfortunately for us, also was an excellent recitation of the evidence — from his perspective. I sat in frustration, forced to watch part two of the state's double feature.

Jim started by saying to the jury, "Sometime tomorrow you will get this case and begin the awesome responsibility of determining truth — the truth about what happened on that canal bank in 1983. Surely there can be no doubt, based on the crime scene evidence alone, that these three killings were premeditated. Each of the victims were blindfolded and gagged, and then their wrists were bound behind their backs with rope. It's obvious this didn't occur in the darkness of night. It occurred at some other location — before the victims were brought to that desolate Danger Road, where they were executed, one-by-one.

"Walter Leahy was shot twice in the head at point-blank range. He also had a third shot in the back. Dickie Robertson was shot twice in the head at point-blank range and had a third shot in the stomach. And like the others, Alfred Tringali had two shots point-blank in the head. There were eight premeditated acts designed solely to kill three human beings."

Many members of the victims' families were quietly crying. Even though they had already heard the crime details many times during the trial, Jim's deliberate, theatrical description elicited gut-wrenching reactions.

"The three victims in this case were friends. They knew each other from school. Admittedly, they came together for a drug deal. And if you believe Mr. Robertson's girlfriend and the mother of his child, this was going to be Dickie Robertson's last deal before he got out of the business."

The weeping was more audible now. I imagined the woman who was crying the loudest had to have been Linda Allard. She had every right to cry, as this was her day, too. The clicking sounds of the photographers' cameras let us know they were seizing upon her grief to sell tomorrow's newspapers. And these guys asked me how I could do what *I* did?

"Speaking of the drug business, that takes us to the testimony of Paul Combs, the supplier of the cocaine. Mr. Robertson told Mr. Combs that the buyers were two bodybuilders from Hollywood, named Tommy and Gil. I don't ask you to like Paul Combs, but what possible reason does he have to come into this courtroom and lie about that? What benefit is it to him today?"

Looking at the jury, I was hoping one of them would use all three parts of his brain and think what *I* was thinking: "Hey, Sherlock, how about to help *you* out, and by doing so, to salt the mine for the next time he's jammed up. Or, how about this one: You've already got him dead-to-rights for trafficking the kilos connected with these murders, thereby subjecting him to guilt under the felony murder rule. Why else would he need complete immunity?"

"If Mr. Combs were to lie under oath, he would violate his federal probation and go to prison. That's for sure. So, why does he come in here? Of what benefit is it to him to come in here and testify about 'Gil and Tommy, bodybuilders from Hollywood'? He didn't want to be involved in this case. Being involved with cocaine, the supplier of the cocaine, as he was, I'm sure you can't blame him for not wanting to be involved as a witness in this case.

"Just like I don't think you can blame Rebecca Carbone for not wanting to be a witness in a case like this. Nobody wants to be here. Scott Calvis is an accountant now in Coral Springs. He has no connection to Paul Combs anymore. What reason does he have to lie?"

The jurors either had good poker faces or they were dumb as stumps. Either way, they were hard to read while they listened to Jim. They had little emotion, lazy body language and blank stares. Occasional coughs were the only visible signs of life. And it wasn't Jim's fault; he was doing an excellent job. It might have been that he was the third lawyer out of the box. They might just have been sick of listening to lawyers. At least I hoped they were tired of listening. I didn't want them to pay too close attention, because Jim was doing a good job.

"Even the defense must admit that Michael Carbone was present for these killings. Carbone had never seen the crime scene evidence. It would have been improper for us to show it to him. If we had shown him these things, they would have said he's being given the evidence to give to you. But he was never given access to this evidence. What he knows, he knows from being there, from seeing these things.

"He knew about the black Z28 belonging to Mr. Robertson. He knew about the rope. He knew about the blindfolds. He knew about the gags. He even knew that the gag had fallen out of Mr. Tringali's mouth on the trip to the canal bank. He knew about Mr. Robertson's beeper was going off when Ms. Allard or Mr. Combs were trying to page him that evening. He knew about that. How else could he know about that if he weren't present?"

I yelled in my head, "Of course he was present! He was probably in the water with the victims! No one doubts he was there, Matlock. Do you really think he stayed on that canal bank?"

Fortunately, Jim couldn't hear the ridicule in my head. He continued, saying, "The defense said Mr. Carbone has been given a script. They made that accusation when he was being questioned. Occasionally he would forget something and ask to back up because he wanted to tell the whole truth. But they said that I or someone else had given him a script.

"Why would there be inconsistencies in Michael Carbone's statement? He gave over 650 pages of sworn testimony over a period of years. Altogether, he'd given seven formal statements. There have been questions proposed every different way in this case. I believe there were over 350 pages of cross-examination alone. Mr. Carbone was asked to remember the minutest detail of something that happened eight years ago. And you can bet it was not a calm happening. It was hectic. If every one of Michael Carbone's statements had been the same throughout this case, I submit to you that they would have been fabricated. *That* would have been a lie.

"Then there was the two-gun inconsistency. The evidence shows there were two guns involved but Carbone originally said there was only one. According to the defense, this is proof positive that Michael Carbone is a liar and a killer. In fact, that inconsistency rings of absolute truth. If Michael Carbone were the killer by his own hand that night, he would know the number of guns used. If he had two guns himself or if there were two killers and each one had a gun, he would absolutely know that there were two guns.

Don't you think when he was getting his story together for fabrication that he would have told you about two guns?"

"Touché, Jim," I thought, in spite of myself. I hoped the jurors were still asleep at the wheel. But then again, had Carbone said there were two guns, the chances of an indictment would have been much slimmer. Nobody would've known *who* caused the deaths. And with Felts being murdered and Carbone getting immunity, the uncertainty as to the shooter may have been too problematic for the Grand Jury. I felt *that* was the real reason Carbone never mentioned the other gun.

"Carbone tells you that all this happened in the darkness. And ladies and gentlemen, you talk about a desolate place. There were no lights out there. It was dark. There was no view of Danger Road from the nearby Jones Fish Camp. It was desolate and tucked away behind trees, away from any major road.

"We know eight shots were fired because there are eight wounds. Mr. Carbone, he's not sure but he believes six. Is that an inconsistency? I submit to you that while this was happening, Mr. Carbone had other things on his mind besides counting the number of gunshots. Is that an inconsistency or is it believable that he wouldn't remember the exact number of gunshots? Michael Carbone told you he held these men for some six hours at gunpoint. If he were fabricating the story, would he tell you about that?"

Again, I was screaming in my head. "Because he wanted us to believe *he* was the one in the dark! He wants everyone to believe that he's the big flunky in this deal, like Sergeant Schultz from *Hogan's Heroes*. 'I know *nutting*!'"

"Michael Carbone is a criminal and he thought like a criminal. He did what he was told. In his criminal mind, he couldn't let those men go. He thought, 'they're going to go back to whoever gave them the cocaine and they're going to come back with their friends and guns.' Don't you think Tommy and Gil would have been upset with Michael Carbone if he let these men go? He would have had trouble from both sides. He was caught in the middle.

"And ladies and gentlemen, as he testified, he had just seen what Gilbert Fernandez was capable of when he stuck a revolver down the throat of Dickie Robertson. Carbone told you he was hoping that what they told these men was true; that they were going to go see the boss. In his mind, though, he certainly suspected the worst: that these men, in fact, were going to be killed. But in his criminal's mind, he had passed the point of no return."

I couldn't help but go off on a tangent, once again talking to the guy in my head: "Jim's hanging out in Carbone's criminal mind? No wonder Lewis isn't likeable." But I hadn't been either since the trial started, so I realized I shouldn't slam him too hard.

"And how can you possibly explain the testimony of Rebecca Carbone? That night after the murders, from the minute he comes in the door, she knows he's upset. And he tells her what happened, what he had just been involved in. Does Rebecca Carbone have a reason to lie? She apparently has no love for Michael. She divorced him. She's upset; she wanted him to take this to the grave. She did not want to be involved in this. She's upset with him because he told the police. By doing this, he made her a witness in this case.

"The cross-examination in this case has been a defense of distraction to prevent you from focusing on the evidence that comes from the exhibits and the witness stand. Ladies and gentlemen, you can't base your verdict on what lawyers say during the trial. You can only base it what comes from that witness stand."

"Boy, if that were true," I thought, "Gil's gonna walk. If you want a conviction, Jim, you'd better hope the jury bases its verdict on what you're saying and not on what your merry band of felons have said from the witness stand."

"The defense in this case has attempted to create reasonable doubt where none exists. What does Melissa Felts tell us? That Gil and Tommy were very close. Gil was the best man at Tommy's wedding. That Bert, Gil and Tommy, they went out all night, stayed out all night. That Bert was the boss, the dominant figure in the group; that they all share the same tattoo. Tommy Felts, Gil Fernandez and Hubert Christie all had the same tattoo!

I had a twisted thought as I sat there, almost delirious from listening to stuff I hated hearing: "Wouldn't it be amazing if there were a tattoo that read, "Whatever you do, don't trust Mike"? Jerking myself out of my stupor, I thought, "Back to reality, John. Snap out of it."

"Melissa Felts told you about Mr. Christie's dominance over Felts and Fernandez. Clearly, he was the boss. Tommy Felts referred to Bert in terms of having to give him the largest share of the money. After the murders, Mr. Christie meets them at a gas station. All he wants to know is, 'Is the job done?' And as soon as Mr. Fernandez and Mr. Felts get back in the car with Mr. Carbone, threats are given. Mr. Fernandez told him, 'If you tell anybody, I will kill you. I will kill your wife and your children. You can go to China, but I will find you. I will kill you and I will kill them.'

I couldn't keep my mind from wandering. "Could you picture Carbone in China? He'd blend right in — a bodybuilder toting a Thompson around Tiananmen Square! Come on, John, you're doing it again. Stay focused. He's almost done."

"If you don't like Michael Carbone's immunity deal, let me just say that *nobody* likes deals given to criminals. But if you believe the testimony of Michael Carbone and the testimony of the other witnesses in the case, that these men committed the crimes for which they are charged, don't give them the benefit of your anger about those immunities. Giving criminals immunity or a deal to testify is not a rare thing. It's not a good thing, but sometimes it's a necessary thing.

"I'm not the first one to say this, but it's never been more true: You can't expect angels as witnesses to plots hatched in hell."

"Yeah," I thought, "that may be true. But Carbone and Combs were about as far from angels as anyone could ever be."

Waiting

Molloy and Lewis had each done an outstanding job. Though they scored a lot of points with the jury, I hoped we had exposed quite a bit of reasonable doubt, enough to win an acquittal.

To his credit, Louie gave a very effective closing argument on behalf of Bert Christie. There didn't appear to be a whole lot of evidence against Bert, so Louie seemed to shine again, like in the old days.

"Gil and Bert might actually walk," I thought privately. I was much cockier with the media, though. The day before I had told them, "My guy's gonna walk."

Tyson gave the jury lengthy instructions before they went off to the jury room to begin deliberations. We could hear them arguing behind the closed doors. That's always a good sign.

"There has to be more than enough reasonable doubt for them to be arguing like that," I reasoned to Gil.

"They're probably arguing over the lunch menu," joked Gil. How he could find humor at a time like this was amazing to me.

Tyson had decreed that the jury would be sequestered during the deliberations, so they knew they were going to be spending nights away from their families until they reached a verdict. I thought this might help give them incentive to come in with a quick decision. That didn't turn out to be the case. The jury members deliberated in the jury room by day and were driven to a local hotel for sequestration each night. As they battled it out in that tiny room during the day, friends and family of the defendants sat nervously on a bench in the hallway north of the courtroom. Relatives of the dead men kept their own tense vigil in the hallway south of the courtroom. There was no way these two groups wanted to mix.

During the day, I wanted to stay very close to wait for the verdict. Beth had the phone numbers of all the attorneys in case the jury had a question. She also was obliged to call us right away if there was a verdict. I sat in front of the Courthouse Deli, located directly across the street from court. Neli and Gil's parents greeted me there with hugs in the morning, and they'd stop by again around lunchtime and before dark. Somehow, they were still hanging in there.

For three days, I sat at the same table on the sidewalk in front of the deli. I drank cup after cup of hot coffee, in spite of the mid-August heat and humidity. As I sat there, people I knew drove by, raising their palms in the air, using impromptu sign language to ask, "What's going on with the verdict?" I would just shrug my shoulders and shake my head.

If I had a dime for every time someone asked me about the verdict while I sat at that table on the street, I'd have had enough money to take them all to lunch on Las Olas.

Chapter 26

The Verdicts

Finally, my cell phone rang. It was Beth, hailing me back to the courtroom. As I ran across the street, Doug, Cindy and Jim entered the building just ahead of me. When I went into the courtroom and sat down next to Gil, the first thing I said was, "The jury must have had tremendous doubt to be out for three days."

"I've been praying you're right," Gil replied, looking nervous for a change. He and his family exchanged hopeful, yet anxious looks. My hope was that they'd soon be embracing each other and crying joyful tears of unmitigated relief.

Tyson soon called the courtroom to order and the jury was brought in. Several of them were crying. That was a great sign. But then again, they weren't looking at any of us at the defense table. *That* was a bad sign.

I waited patiently as the jury foreman handed the verdict form to Mike, who then passed it to the judge. After Tyson read the verdict silently, he handed the form to Beth. She stood up at her desk, located to the left of Tyson's seat at the bench. She held that determinative piece of paper in front of her, hands shaking visibly. Even this experienced professional couldn't help but be influenced by the gravity of the outcome. Her voice trembled as she read the verdicts:

"We the jury, in the case of the *State of Florida v. Gilbert Fernandez*, find the Defendant is Guilty of First Degree Murder, without a firearm."

"We the jury, in the case of the *State of Florida v. Hubert Christie*, find the Defendant is Guilty of First Degree Murder, without a firearm."

My heart sank. I was breathless. Then my mind exploded. "*Without* a firearm? How was that possible? The victims were *shot* to death!" I screamed inside as I looked incredulously at the jury. These verdicts made no sense, legally or factually.

The indictment charged Gil and Bert with shooting these men *with* a firearm. Yet, somehow the jury managed to find them guilty on three counts of shooting people *without* a firearm.

"You've got to be kidding me," I muttered.

"Nobody's kidding anybody," Gil answered, thinking I was talking to him.

We didn't even look at each other. Instead, we looked at the visibly affected jurors. Neither of us looked at his family, either, as that would have been too painful. This verdict was only possible because an additional option had been added illegally to the verdict form. Along with *"not guilty"* and *"guilty, with a firearm,"* jurors were given the option of choosing *"guilty, without a firearm."* I can only assume that the option to convict without a firearm must have looked like some sort of lesser offense to the jurors. That's the only explanation I could think of because the verdict made no sense. It was a factual and legal impossibility for murder victims to be shot and killed by bullets *without* a firearm. The only way for this verdict to be reached was if the jury disregarded the instructions Tyson gave regarding reasonable doubt as to *each* element of the indictment, the firearm element being only one of them.

If the jurors had a reasonable doubt that Gil shot the victims, they were instructed to vote "not guilty." The doubt should never have been about whether the victims were shot; that was a matter of record. The doubt had to occur about whether they thought Gil was the shooter or whether he committed the crimes at all.

It wasn't that much of a stretch to say the jury members were looking for any way to convict Gil and Bert, in spite of their obvious reasonable doubt. As I had feared all along, it appeared as though the jury had indeed fallen victim to Stockholm syndrome. Tyson had essentially held them hostage, which is typical in lengthy trials. But a judge is required by law to be neutral and detached and to act accordingly. That obviously never happened in this case.

This judge had an obvious preference toward the state, allowing in all that illegal "dead-men's talk." According to Paul Combs, his cousin and his accountant, those poor dead guys pointed up from the grave to finger Gil and Tommy. But they never mentioned Bert. So why was Bert being convicted, too? To me, that was just more proof of the unfairness and absurdity of it all.

Another factor influencing the jurors, in my self-serving opinion, was that the victims' families were seated right next to the rail that separated the jury from the spectator gallery. This meant the jury members had a chance to see and feel the families' pain, up-close and personal. Because the jurors weren't sequestered during the trial, they probably also were exposed to the relentless onslaught of incredibly damaging and highly inflammatory daily press coverage about Gil. It seemed like all my motions found their way onto the front page of the newspapers. Ironically, my well-intentioned efforts to protect my client might have actually caused the additional press coverage that further affected the jury's perspective.

Given all the factors that came into play, the verdict wasn't actually that much of a surprise. But that didn't stop me from feeling absolutely terrible.

No sooner had I exited the courtroom doors when a half dozen bright lights and TV camera booms were in my face.

One of the smarter reporters asked, "Do you feel robbed?"

My response to the guy in my head was a resounding, "Abso-f***ing-lutely." But what came out of my mouth was just, "What do you think? *Absolutely.*"

All trial lawyers know that it almost never gets lonelier or more dismal than when you're making that walk down the courthouse hallway after a big loss in trial. Angry, I told the mob of journalists in the hallway, "There was no forensic or physical evidence whatsoever in this case. No saliva, no hair, no blood, no fingerprints, nothing whatsoever suggesting that Gil Fernandez was involved in these homicides, except for the purchased testimony of a five-time convicted felon who got complete immunity for these murders. The state bought and paid for this felon's testimony, along with the testimony of a few more immunized felons. How many repeat felons wouldn't sell out their mothers to get complete immunity for multiple murders and escape the electric chair?"

Barfly

Floored by the verdict, I proceeded to numb my feelings and drown my sadness in more than a few glasses of red wine. Dave Blood and I sat at a darkened corner table in The French Quarter restaurant, located a block from Las Olas Boulevard. While we were there, Elizabeth called to hear the verdict. I couldn't even lift myself from my despair long enough to talk to her. So, I handed the phone to Dave and asked him to help me. He told her I was despondent but otherwise in good hands with him.

"May I have some more wine?" I asked the waitress.

"Pardon me?" she responded.

"We'll have two more glasses of wine," Dave said, speaking for me.

"She couldn't even hear you, because your voice is so soft right now. You really *are* depressed about this, aren't you?"

I just looked at him. I wasn't exactly sipping my wine. I alternated between staring at it one minute, and then taking big swigs the next. A few minutes later, the waitress brought two more. All I could manage was a weak smile in her direction, in lieu of thanking her.

Dave interrupted my fog when he asked, "You know I've been getting into the Bible recently, right?"

I must have nodded, so he continued.

"Last night I read in the book of Proverbs, 'the Lord detests the acquittal of the guilty.' I'm not saying I believe Fernandez is guilty. It's just that if he *is*, that verse is something you might want to think about."

At that point, I was a fair-weather Christian, at best. I put on a good show on Sundays but when the rubber hit the road, I hit the road, too. I knew I should be paying attention to Dave but I really didn't have it in me. I didn't know if I was sadder for Gil or for his family. Maybe I was just sad because my pride was wounded from losing. Whatever the reason, I *was* sad.

Dave quickly realized I was beyond reach. So, he just said to the waitress as she walked by, "We'll have two more, and then the check, please."

Chapter 27

Life

Still reeling from the guilty verdict, I had to somehow find the strength to continue the fight for Gil's life. I knew if he were sentenced to death, I would never get over it. A death sentence would mean Gil would sit for many years in a tiny cell on death row. Unless he received clemency — and the chance of that was slim to none — he would eventually be escorted to Florida's ancient wooden electric chair, nicknamed "Old Sparky." This archaic device, which had ironically been manufactured by prison inmates, sometimes malfunctioned, causing the head of the condemned person to catch on fire before death. Needless to say, this definitely would be a violation of the inmate's Eighth Amendment right to be protected from "cruel and unusual punishment." The thought of Gil sitting in that chair — and my role in keeping him out of it — made it very hard for me to eat or sleep.

I called 17 witnesses to testify in this phase of the trial, including four BSO jail deputies; four pastors from the local community; Gil's long-time friend, Vince Forzano; Gil's wife, Neli; and his mother, Emma. Everyone who testified said the same thing: Gil had changed markedly because he had become a born-again Christian.

A watery grave

Reverend Dominick Avello said that Gil was baptized on Aug. 13, 1989 at the Cornerstone Church in Hollywood, Florida. Not realizing it, his well-intentioned testimony opened the door for the prosecution to emphasize the plight of the victims.

"When I baptized Gil, I dipped him in water to cleanse his soul and leave his sins in a watery grave."

"Did you know Mr. Fernandez in 1983 when these three victims gave *their* lives in a watery grave, left there among the old tires and trash in that canal?" asked Jim Lewis during his cross examination of the pastor.

"No, I did not," Avello said sadly as he realized the morbid double meaning of his words.

This shot by the prosecution was tempered as Pastors Dwight Allen and Harry Keith of the Miramar Church of God, and Pastor Phillip Kenneth Loring of the Armor of God Tabernacle, also took the stand. They, too, testified to Gil's transformation and his selfless work with people who needed help.

Then I brought Neli Fernandez to the stand. Showing her characteristic strength, she confidently said, "Gil is the best father in the world and the best thing that ever happened in my lifetime. Since the day we got saved, we read the Bible every day. I don't need to beg for his life, he's got Jesus. He'll be with the Lord if he stays and he'll be with the Lord if he leaves. We're not afraid of death."

Gil gazed adoringly at her from the defense table and mouthed an "I love you" as she left the witness stand.

Next I called the four jail deputies to the stand. Most of the jailers liked Gil, although they didn't necessarily want people to know it. Gil was actually appointed a trusty in the jail. This meant he had more privileges than other inmates. He received better food and was allowed to walk around more freely within the facility. The deputies respected his abilities as a bodybuilder and trainer, so various guards would pull Gil from his cell up to six times a day to train with them in the gym. He could squat up to 500 pounds, so the deputies, along with everyone else in the jail, were in awe of his raw physical power.

I knew subpoenas would be necessary for the jail deputies for CYA purposes, so they wouldn't get into hot water with Sheriff Nick Navarro, their boss. Navarro had been on a dogged crusade to nail Fernandez and wouldn't have taken too kindly to BSO deputies willingly testifying on Gil's behalf. Sheriff Nick was definitely larger-than-life and no one who worked for him wanted to get on his bad side.

To their credit, the four deputies honored the subpoenas and testified. Each told compelling stories of seeing Gil holding hands and praying with inmates who had AIDS. At the time, there was a lot of phobia surrounding how AIDS might be transmitted. Hardly anyone within the county jail, other than doctors and nurses wearing gloves, would touch AIDS victims, let alone hold their hands. Gil's willingness to do this was not only evidence of his compassion but also of his fearless belief in God's protection.

One of the deputies also testified that Gil saved a cellmate's life. Only 24 years old and a diminutive five-feet-four, the man was known by the intimidating nickname of "Commander." But his nickname didn't have much to do with his having a commanding presence; it was based on the name given to him at birth: Charles Commander.

"Fernandez saved his life by cutting him down when he tried to hang himself," Deputy John Ferguson testified.

Another deputy told the jury, "Gil Fernandez does a lot of wonderful things in the jail. He preaches, leads the other inmates in Bible study and runs the services. He's well-liked and well-respected by inmates and staff."

The jury got the picture. The deputies respected and admired him, not for what he had done in his past life, but for how he was managing his new life since he came to the jail.

After all the other witnesses had testified on Gil's behalf, I placed Gil's mother on the stand. Emma Fernandez sat stoically in the witness seat holding several crumpled, soaked tissues in her balled-up fist. Soon, tears ran down her cheeks and her pleas for mercy were punctuated by deep sobs.

"He was a good son and a good father to his own two sons. I can't understand what happened," she said, bending over and resting her elbows on her knees. She looked as if she could no longer support her own weight. "If you let him live, I will visit him always, until I die. Please don't send my son to the electric chair!" she begged, now weeping uncontrollably.

As his mother sobbed on the witness stand, Gil's wall of emotional suppression crumbled. For the first time since the trial began, Gil slumped his shoulders, bowed his head and cried like a little boy. The jury stared at him. They had never seen this side of Gil throughout jury selection or at any time throughout the lengthy trial.

Some of the jury members, along with many of the people on the defense side of the courtroom, were crying, too. Only the cruelest and most cold-hearted person could have kept from feeling something as they watched Emma beg for her son's life. As she cried, I noticed the jury members kept looking at Gil, only occasionally stealing a glance back at her. She was too hard to look at; her pain was far too intense. It was probably easier for them to watch Gil cry.

My goal in putting Emma on the stand was fairly obvious: Tug on the jurors' heartstrings and cause them to believe that the mercy I wanted, was really what *they* wanted, too. It was my mission to prevail upon them to enter that jury room and conclude, "Well, I suppose we could spare his life for her. She's so sweet and she's hurting so terribly. Let her visit him in prison until she dies."

When Emma Fernandez finally left the witness stand, she walked slowly. Anyone could see the emotional exhaustion had taken its toll. She looked at Gil the whole way from the witness stand to the spectator gallery, tears streaming. But Gil didn't even know she was looking at him. His head was resting just above his shackled arms, which barely reached the table because of the chains. His massive shoulders shook slightly as he cried, still feeling the residual effect of his mother's testimony.

"Mr. Lewis, you may deliver your argument now," Tyson said.

Each of us was entitled to present arguments for or against the death penalty. Lewis was up first, and thankfully, my argument would follow his. This time, I wouldn't be sandwiched in by another state argument.

Four good reasons

Jim Lewis stepped from behind the prosecution table, dressed to impress.

"Thank you, Your Honor. Ladies and gentlemen of the jury, at the close of these arguments you'll retire and complete your jury service in this case. You'll make a recommendation regarding the appropriate penalty for each defendant, for each count in the indictment for which they have been convicted. Judge Tyson will pass sentence, but he will give your recommendation great weight and consideration.

"If the aggravating circumstances justify the imposition of the death penalty and outweigh all mitigating circumstances that exist, it is your duty to follow the law and to recommend a sentence of death.

"The aggravating circumstances you may consider in this case are, number one, that the defendants have been convicted of another capital offense. This applies because we have what we call simultaneous killings. This aggravating circumstance allows you to consider that not just one human being lost his life but that three separate individuals died.

"The second aggravating circumstance is that the crime for which the defendants are to be sentenced was committed for financial gain. The evidence is uncontroverted that the motive for these crimes was to steal an ice chest full of cocaine. Three men died for cocaine and for money. They died for greed, even to the extent that their jewelry was taken. The defendants in this case could have just robbed the victims and taken their cocaine. They could have let them go but they didn't.

"The third aggravating circumstance is that the crime for which the defendants are to be sentenced was especially wicked, evil, atrocious or cruel. Wally Leahy, Alfred Tringali and Richard Robertson were pounced on immediately when they entered that house. Defendant Gil Fernandez stuck a gun to the mouth of one of the victims. Their hands were tied. They begged for mercy to the extent that they were gagged with paper towels, which were wadded up and stuffed into their mouths. Then their mouths were taped on the outside to ensure their pleas could no longer be heard. Michael Carbone held them at gunpoint for some six hours as defendants Fernandez and Felts discarded the victims' vehicles.

"They were driven out to the Everglades until they reached Danger Road. The three men were taken out of the car in the darkness and marched down that road for some way. Mr. Tringali's gag somehow came out of his mouth and he asked, 'Why, why are you doing this?'

"Surely, the victims knew as they walked down that road that their lives were in peril. The defendant, Gil Fernandez, ordered his victims to kneel in the water. As that first victim's feet touched the water of that canal, he must have been in terror, absolute terror. As he got wet, could there be any doubt in his mind that he was about to die? Then finally, there was a gunshot.

"And then there was a second victim. Having heard the previous shots, he must have known his fate as he was taken to the edge of the water and told to kneel. Defendant Gil Fernandez then took a weapon, placed it directly to the head of that individual and at point-blank range, shot him dead.

"But the carnage wasn't over. A third victim was taken down to that canal bank, knowing that he, too, would soon be in darkness; absolute, eternal darkness. The third victim struggled. But Gil Fernandez, with almost professional cruelty, once again put a gun to the head of this man and shot him at point blank range, causing what the medical examiner called 'internal decapitation.'

Walter Leahy, Richard Robertson and Alfred Tringali were then shot a few more times by Gil Fernandez to be sure they would stay in their watery graves. Then they were just left there, among the garbage in the canal.

"The fourth aggravating factor for which you may consider in this case is that the crimes for which the defendants are to be sentenced were committed in a cold, calculated and premeditated manner without any presence of legal or moral justification. Can there be any doubt that these murders were well planned? Can there be any doubt this was meant to be a drug rip-off from the inception?

"The second night, April 1, 1983 — April Fools day — when the victims showed up, there were ropes and blindfolds, and everything was ready. Were these murders calculated? They were calculated in a way that only a policemen could conceive them. There was no physical evidence. He was sure to wear gloves so there would be no fingerprints on the victims' vehicle."

In spite of the graphic images Jim evoked, the crying we had heard throughout the trial was nowhere in evidence. There was now just silence coming from the spectator gallery. I stole a glance at the victims' families. Many of them held hands or had their arms around one another. They all looked stunned. It had been too much for too long.

"You can wash away your sins, but you can't wash away these murders. We have talked about the Bible during this trial and there is something in the Bible that just stuck out when I heard some of this testimony. 'The wages of sin is death.'

"Lewis is cherry-picking the Bible," I said to myself. "Here he goes, hijacking half a scripture verse for his own selfish agenda." But then I thought, "Wait a minute John, haven't you done that, too?" Listening to Jim was actually easier on my conscience than listening to me, so I tried to quit giving audience to the truth-teller in my head.

"The punishment must fit the crime. That's why the death penalty exists: an eye for an eye, a tooth for a tooth, a life for a life. It's a hard thing to do, to come in here and expect you to make an impassionate decision based on the law and the evidence, but that's your duty. God forgives, but it's your duty to follow the law.

"Three human beings had a right to grow old. They had a right to enjoy the fullness of their lives. That has been taken away and can never be replaced. These two defendants took away those lives, in a cruel and calculated way. And why did they do it? Was this some heat of the moment, passion-type killing? Was this some retribution-type killing? No. It was for an ice chest of cocaine. It was for money. It was for greed. And the wages of sin is death.

"Your decision should not be for anyone or against anyone. It's human nature to show mercy, but there was no mercy shown that night on that canal bank along Danger Road. First-degree murder is the ultimate crime. Is life in prison enough? We know a recommendation of death will not bring back Alfred Tringali, Richard Robertson and Wally Leahy. But it *will* bring justice and that will have to be enough.

"Thank you."

You could sense the jurors had taken Jim Lewis's words to heart. How could anybody not? You could almost imagine the struggle going on inside some of their heads as they weighed his words against whatever compassion they had developed for Gil and Bert.

Don't put out the fire

It was now time for me to present the jury with my argument against the death penalty. Lewis would be a hard act to follow. Frankly, I was angry with the jury for convicting Gil, given all the conflicts in the evidence. So, I didn't have any qualms about going the extra mile to make them feel the emotional pain that Gil's son, Gillie, might someday feel if his father were executed.

I opened by making a passionate plea for the jury to allow Gil to continue to be a family man. I wanted the jurors to visualize Gil's first-born son, then eight, as the frightened little boy asking his mother about the death of his father. Making my voice sound like a frightened little child's, I mimicked little Gillie and said, "Mommy, why did daddy die in the electric chair?"

As I imitated little Gillie's hypothetical question for the jury, I let a teardrop run down my cheek, ever so slowly. I then once again asked them to spare Gil's life, if only for the sake of little Gillie. As I spoke these words, tears started to run down both cheeks. I didn't wipe them off, even though I wanted to. One of my cheeks was itching and felt uncomfortable, but I knew

I wasn't as uncomfortable as the jurors, some of whom had dropped their heads to their chests and were weeping.

Playing to the jury's sympathy is clearly impermissible and therefore arguably unethical. Feigning ignorance, I suppose, could help a lawyer like me stay out of jail on a contempt-of-court charge. But at that point, I didn't even care if my statements resulted in a weekend or two in jail.

They didn't play by the rules, I reasoned, so why should I? I felt Tyson and the prosecutors had essentially robbed us throughout the trial, by allowing clearly inadmissible evidence, rank hearsay and "dead-men's testimony" from Combs and the others. In my anger, however, I was oblivious to the pain of the victims' family members who had to sit and listen to me beg for Gil's life. I can only imagine how hard that must have been for them.

As some of the jurors wiped away their tears, I went on to say, "I have lived with this case for 13 months, every day; and rather obsessively at that. Even *I* don't know all the answers because there have been way too many stories. We had to try to figure it out and I still don't have all the answers. So, I don't know how *you* can have all the answers. You must have had a heck of a lot of doubt to keep you out for three days, though. That's a long time. Enough doubt that you knew the lies of Mr. Carbone were out of control. Somehow, though, you resolved that doubt by deciding that he was guilty *without* a firearm. You cannot, however, carry that doubt to the chair.

"There are some things in life for which you *have* to be 100 percent certain. You can't allow even one percent doubt when the electric chair is involved. That is not the place for a question mark, however small or remote.

"I don't personally believe in capital punishment. Those are my feelings and I know they don't count. But in society, I think we have to respect the sanctity of human life. You have already determined that people have killed in this case. What happened was atrocious and horrific, but it's no less horrific than society choosing to kill people in return.

"By placing Mr. Fernandez in the electric chair, the state would just be taking another life. As a society, we're supposed to be better than that. If we execute a man because he killed another with premeditation, how does that differ from his original crime? How is our act any less sociopathic than his? As a society, aren't we supposed to value the sanctity of human life more than the killer does? If we don't, how are we any different than him? Each of us is supposed to have feelings and a conscience. Perhaps I have too much feeling and that may be my problem. And I *did* make some mistakes in this case. The biggest one that I made was getting close to my client and his family. That was a mistake. I still love his family and they have met members of my family.

"Contrary to what you might think, lawyers aren't like pastors who get to hear everything when someone confesses to them. Again, I don't know the answers here. So, I don't know how you could know. You simply cannot let that doubt take Gil Fernandez and Bert Christie to the chair. Some things in life require 100 percent certainty. You can't be 99.9 percent sure when the people in question are facing the reality of having a steel cap put on their heads that causes their eyes to pop out…"

"Objection," Molloy snapped.

Tyson called us over to the bench, where Molloy stated in a hushed voice, "I object to Mr. Contini giving a description of what happens during electrocution. This information has been specifically held by the Florida Supreme Court to be prohibited in closing arguments. I didn't want to interrupt because I wanted to give Mr. Contini as much latitude as possible but the Florida Supreme Court already ruled on this subject. You cannot argue residual doubt to the jury."

Then, repeating it for emphasis, he said, "You *cannot* argue residual doubt."

Tyson then ruled, "Objection sustained." It didn't matter. The jury had already heard the gory details of electrocution.

Continuing, I argued, "Many advocates say the death penalty is needed as a deterrent to murder. But ladies and gentlemen, when was the last time you heard of a would-be murderer who stopped short of killing someone for fear of the death penalty?

"The killers in this case were well aware of the death penalty in Florida. They had probably even heard that at one point Florida had executed more people than any other state in the nation, with the possible exception of Texas. Obviously, the death penalty has not been working as any sort of deterrent to murder in our state." They seemed to be going with me on this, so I kept it up.

"And what of the people who say that putting a murderer to death saves the taxpayers money? Did you know it cost over $11 million in Florida tax dollars to pay for Ted Bundy's seven death-row appeals? And did you know it takes less than $40 a day to keep a person confined in prison? It can literally save millions of dollars to keep an inmate incarcerated instead of putting him to death.

"If saving money and deterring future murders are not justifiable reasons for putting him to death, then the only reason left is vengeance. If you feel vengeance is warranted, then put my client in prison so he can think about what he did for the rest of his life! And while he's doing that, you would be giving him the opportunity to help others, which, as the witnesses today have testified, he has already proven he wants to do and can do.

"Please recall why some of you were weeping when you came back. Recall that. Recall the question marks in your mind. Recall the arguments you had with each other. Recall all that and ask yourself if Michael Carbone's various stories didn't cause you to have doubt. Something caused you to be out three days while you deliberated. There was a reason you came back feeling emotional and chose 'guilty, without a firearm' on the verdict form. That speaks for itself. Men can't be electrocuted based on that kind of doubt.

"Perhaps you're weighing that doubt against the question of why my client was driven to God. You think, 'Some people are driven by guilt.' But in reality, people are driven for various reasons. They might want to help others or to turn their lives into something positive.

"You ask 'what drives them?' If it's guilt, it's actually immaterial now. You heard from all those pastors. I'd never even met them before. There is no way their testimony could have been presented to elicit emotional impact. I had never even met these men before, yet, they all said Mr. Fernandez is a changed man.

"Even as a former prosecutor — and I was a prosecutor for a number of years — I had never seen deputies come into court on behalf of a defendant. *Never*. It's probably unprecedented that deputies would testify about how an inmate saved another inmate from hanging himself.

"There would be no way someone could create evidence like this. I couldn't hire deputies, put them on the witness stand and get them to say the right things. They are deputies I've never met before in my life. These are sworn police officers telling you what they have witnessed on a daily basis.

"Ladies and gentlemen, even guards come to Gil Fernandez for problems in the jail. He ministers to them as well as to the inmates. He brings about a real peace and a calm to the prison. I heard it; you heard it. And you know that's where he's going to spend the rest of his natural life if you recommend life imprisonment.

"Think of the thousands of people he might put on the right track — not hundreds, but thousands. God knows; we have a prison problem in Florida. Prison is the perfect place for someone who is so good at doing prison ministry. That's where he belongs.

"Wouldn't it be more helpful to society for Mr. Fernandez to spend the next 25 years in prison? That way, his kids can still get to know their father. They'll never have to ask their mother, 'Why did Daddy die in the electric chair?' Why not let them know their father and feel proud of him as a minister in prison?

"And he wouldn't leave early, believe me. Prison for life means just that: he would be there for life. They don't parole these guys. Florida is tougher than most states about this. Florida leads the nation in per capita prison population. We're fourth in the nation in prison population, following Texas, California and New York. But in actual population, we're 10th, making us first in prison population, per capita. Prisoners can't even make applications for parole for 25 years. They can't even ask lawyers to apply for them.

"Remember, he turned around a lot of people in the last 13 months. And there were even more that he helped in the year before he was arrested, including youth-gang members. That desire to help is a fire that's still burning in his soul. At least it would burn in the right place in prison. Let's not put that fire out. *Please*, let it burn in the right place — in prison for the rest of his natural life."

I had nothing left to argue and was emotionally wasted, so I just said, "Thank you."

Gil thanked me upon my return to the defense table, giving me an affectionate squeeze on the forearm. His family was gracious, too, each mouthing an appreciative "thank you" from the second row. My wife, who was sitting behind the Fernandez family, encouraged me, too, rooting for me to hang in there.

Louie Vernell then presented additional defense witnesses on Christie's behalf. He then asked another attorney to enter a limited appearance for Christie as co-counsel of record. Based on decades of friendship with Bert, Louie wanted to testify for the jury about Bert's character. This would have been impossible if Louie had continued on as Christie's attorney throughout the sentencing phase. A lawyer can't be both the attorney and a witness for the client, and Louie chose to be a witness.

Once Christie's defense argument was presented, there was nothing for us to do but wait.

On behalf of the victims

Up until this point in the sentencing proceedings, nobody had spoken on behalf of the victims. The reason was simply because under Florida law, victim impact testimony was not yet allowed for presentment to the jury. Only the defendants could present testimony from character witnesses.

But the U.S. Supreme Court had ruled just the month before in a Tennessee case that testimony from victims' relatives *should* be allowed at penalty phase hearings. So, prosecutors were allowed to present — albeit outside the presence of the jury — testimony from friends and relatives of the victims.

After the jury was ushered out of the courtroom, Linda Allard, who had already testified during the trial, sobbed on the witness stand. "There are no words to describe how it feels to tell a six-year-old girl that her father has been killed and that she will never see him or talk to him again."

I looked over and saw Robertson's daughter, who was now 14 years old. Linda Allard's story about telling this young girl that her daddy was gone and that she would never see him again was unforgettably sad and very compelling.

Patricia Leahy Compton, sister of Walter Leahy, also cried as she testified, "My family lives with the knowledge that my brother knew he was going to die. He begged for his life. The psychological, emotional and physical pain my entire family feels is as intense today as it was eight years ago." Her testimony was equally powerful. Nobody in his right mind would question the truth of the pain she described.

Then Luana Tringali said, "My family is devastated by my brother's murder. I've never seen my father break down like he did at the funeral. It nearly killed him."

Listening to Luana would have made any lawyer wish that he were in a position to help her dad and the rest of the Tringali family. In truth, listening to all the victims' family members testify made me wish that I had gotten to know all of them. In a perfect world, that would have been possible. But this wasn't a perfect world.

Although the jury was barred from hearing the testimony, everyone in the overflowing courtroom listened intently — especially Judge Tyson. It was for his benefit that this testimony was presented. Since he was the one who ultimately had control over the sentence, it was up to him to weigh what he heard from the family members against the sentencing recommendation made by the jury. That was a scary thought, indeed.

Chapter 28

Sentences

Just before the jury returned with their sentencing recommendation, 20 deputies flooded into the courtroom. Wherever you looked, there were uniformed men with guns — even more than there had been throughout the trial. This show of force caused an increased sense of anticipation in the courtroom, even though the trial participants should have been used to it by this point. I guess the average person could never get used to the sight of lots of burly men with guns.

The presence of the deputies signaled that the verdict announcement was imminent. As if directed to do so by some silent force, everyone in the courtroom quieted down and moved to the edge of their seats, almost in unison. Bailiff Bob called the court to order and asked everyone to rise as the judge entered. As we sat down again, all eyes were locked on Tyson. When he was seated, he said to Mike, "Bring in the jury. Defendants, please rise."

The jury filed in slowly as Gil, Bert, Louie and I stood up. I tried not to squirm during the seemingly endless time it took for the jury to take their seats. Some of the jurors looked tired and some had red-rimmed eyes from crying. You could see they had not taken the penalty deliberations lightly. In contrast, Gil was relaxed. Apparently, he was stronger than the rest of us. He seemed ready for whatever.

"I hope they're feeling guilty for doing the wrong thing before," I told myself, thinking angrily about the convictions. My thinking was so self serving and one-dimensional that it bordered on retaliatory.

The jury foreman passed the advisory sentence recommendation to the judge. After he reviewed it for a long moment, he passed it to Beth, who read the sentence recommendations aloud.

Nervously, she said, "Count I, the jury advises and recommends to the court that it impose a sentence of life imprisonment upon Gilbert Fernandez, without possibility of parole for 25 years."

"Wow!" I said to myself, as Gil smothered me in a bear hug.

"I love you," he said as he embraced me.

"I love you, too," I said. He then turned to Neli, smiled and said, "I love you."

The room seemed to split in two as some of the people on the defense side of the courtroom jumped to their feet, yelling with glee. In contrast, the looks on the victims' families' faces ranged from impassive to sad to enraged, as they absorbed the sentence recommendation for the first count. The noise continued as Beth read the sentence recommendations for the other counts:

"Count II, the jury advises and recommends to the court that it impose a sentence of life imprisonment upon Gilbert Fernandez without the possibility of parole for 25 years.

Count III, the jury advises and recommends to the Court that it impose a sentence of life imprisonment upon Gilbert Fernandez without the possibility of parole for 25 years."

Then the exact same text was read for Bert Christie, replacing Gil's name with his. Beth looked straight down at her feet as she returned to her seat. She knew she couldn't show any emotion, no matter how she felt about the sentences.

Gil and Bert were given the only possible penalty other than the electric chair: Life in prison with a minimum 25 years before either could be considered for parole. In this case, it would actually be 24 years, because they had already served one year in jail.

Tyson was scheduled to give his final ruling on the sentence in over a month. He had two choices: consecutive or concurrent sentences. If he allowed the sentences to run concurrently, Gil and Bert would be out in 24 years. With Bert's health, however, even the minimum penalty of 24 years would be equivalent to a death sentence. He was already 58, so no matter what the outcome, it was likely he would die in jail. Not so, however, with Gil. In 24 years, he would be only 62 years old.

The other option was for Tyson to slap them with three consecutive 25-year sentences — one for each of the murders. With credit for time served, the resulting 74-year penalty would mean essentially that neither would be a free man again.

Mike came over and stood at the defense table, fingerprinting Gil and Bert. This was standard procedure after verdicts were announced.

"Congratulations, guys. I'm happy for you that they said 'life,' instead of, well... you know," Mike quietly said while doing their prints. Bob Behan soon joined him, echoing equally warm congratulations.

"Thanks, Mike," the four of us replied, almost in unison. "Thanks, Bob."

The jury members then left the courtroom with a phalanx of deputies surrounding them. None of them even glanced at anyone as they walked quickly from the courtroom, some still in tears. Neli, who also was crying, smiled and tried to thank them for their recommendation as they filed out, but they couldn't see her. Most of them looked down at their feet or at the back of the jurors in front of them. Gil's parents didn't even try to get their attention. They couldn't forget that these were the same people who returned the guilty verdict — the one that would forever separate them from their son.

Elizabeth hugged Gil's parents, just before she left to get back to our babies. Before she fled the mad scene of reporters and navigated her way past the television cameras and extension cords, she blew me a kiss and mouthed the words, "I'm so happy!"

As the excitement and paparazzi activity died down, my bodyguard du jour, Dave Blood, overheard Luana Tringali tell a *Sun-Sentinel* reporter, "I didn't get my hopes up. I would have been happier with the electric chair. There is no doubt in my mind that what he did was premeditated. My brother didn't deserve what he got. But my dad's happy. He thinks Gil will suffer more in jail."

When the victims' families filed out, it was my turn to run my own mouth before the cameras, giving them the usual self-serving platitudes.

Congratulations!

Courthouse banter travels fast, so it was only a few hours after the jury's recommendation was announced that Judge Bob Fogan called me and said enthusiastically, "Congratulations!"

"Thanks, Judge," I replied.

Surely, Bob, a real friend and one of the few judges who once made his life as a criminal defense lawyer, would understand my feelings. So, I poured my guts out.

"I'm relieved, but I still feel rotten. You know the deal, Bob. We won in the penalty phase but we still lost the trial. I can't get over the fact that the jury was out for three days, arguing the whole time. How was that *not* reasonable doubt?"

I figured Bob would empathize with me and agree that I was robbed, but instead he said, "John, if any case in the history of this courthouse ever cried out for the death penalty, it was this one. If it's even half true what the papers have been saying, these murders definitely met the legal standard for being heinous, atrocious and cruel. You know that. And when you have multiple victims and execution-style murders… come on, my friend. They said each man was made to kneel in the water and the last guy had the horror of listening to the others being shot. All of this after being tied up and gagged for hours. How much more heinous could it get?

"The very fact that your guy will be able to live out the rest of his life after doing what he did is a tremendous victory, my boy. You saved this guy's life. Congratulations! Cheer up."

All I could say after that was "Thanks, Judge."

But he must've sensed that my vision was still altered by the lens of pride. He was quite perceptive. He probably remembered what it was like when he was criminal defense lawyer for those 30-some-odd years. So, Fogan wasn't done with me yet. "You and I sit in church together sometimes, so let me ask you: Have you ever stopped to think that God doesn't want him to walk on these murders? You're a good lawyer but you might have gotten a little too close to this particular client."

Bob Fogan, judge or no judge, was like the rest of us in the system. Perhaps he had become jaded from seeing too many guilty defendants over the course of too many years. He assumed Gil was guilty. But this wasn't the right time to discuss it.

"Remember, my boy, only God knows why He allows these things to happen. You did the best you could and that is your responsibility. But that's *all* you're responsible for. You're not responsible for the outcome, OK?"

"OK," I replied. Thank God for Fogan, I said to myself.

It wasn't more than a minute later that O.S. Hawkins called.

"Judge Fogan must have called you," I said.

"He did, my boy, and I hear you could use a little encouragement."

It dawned on me that both of these men called me, "my boy." Smiling inside, I replied, "I feel a little better after talking with Bob but I'm still upset about all the unfairness that went down in this case. I think we were robbed. The way the judge treated us and the fact that he let in all kinds of inadmissible evidence; it was a whole kangaroo court thing…"

He cut me off, as he must have known I was just going to continue doing my hyper-verbal manic number on him.

"It's God's will that all those prisoners need to hear the gospel, and there may be no better guy than Fernandez to reach them." Spoken just like a preacher.

"But in the note you passed to me in court, you wrote that you picked 'door number three,'" I persisted. "You, too, had a reasonable doubt after listening to all that testimony."

"I was just providing some encouragement for you, John. I didn't hear all the evidence in the trial. But if Gil Fernandez committed these crimes, he has to be held accountable for what he's done, just as you and I are accountable for what we do. The newspapers printed the violent and illegal things he admitted to at all those church youth groups. Those admissions came out of his own mouth."

I tried to get a few words in, but O.S. was on a roll.

"God is a God of mercy and grace, John. And by all appearances, Gil is sincere in his faith and appears to have truly repented. But let's not forget, God is a God of justice, too. God's will might be that Gil doesn't get to walk away without answering for his crimes. Better yet, God's will might be for him to be a minister to thousands of prisoners. Remember, God loves them, too."

He was getting ready to hang up now; I could always tell when O.S. was through talking. And I knew there was no resurrecting the conversation, either. This preacher could out-lawyer any lawyer I knew.

"Thanks, O.S., I love you," I said.

"I love you, too. Hang in there, my boy!" he said and then he hung up.

More whine

In spite of the wise words from Bob and O.S., I couldn't shake feeling bad about the unfairness of the trial. It got my goat that Mike Carbone, Paul Combs and their merry band of scumbags were ever even allowed to testify. It also pissed me off that the jurors were sitting right next to the victims' families — when they weren't eating lunch in the judge's chambers, that is.

True to form, I headed for my favorite bar to anesthetize my feelings. I asked Dave Blood to help me with my numbing and narcissistic-pride campaign, to which he readily agreed. When we got to the bar, I didn't even have to order my usual merlot. The cocktail waitress saw me at the door. Seeing the look on my face and knowing my drug of choice by heart, she had a glass waiting at the table by the time I got there.

After staring into my wine glass for a while and feeling sorry for myself, I couldn't help blurt out, "Thank God he got life, for sure, but I still feel robbed. I don't want to be a sore loser, but man, it's just not fair."

"You need to 'let go and let God' on this one. You did your best," Dave said to me. "Gil is probably right where he richly deserves and *needs* to be, in prison. Remember, there are a lot of people he can help there."

Feeling a little better after this reminder, I begrudgingly said, "Yeah, maybe you're right."

Then I really started to feel ashamed of myself. "What are you complaining about?" I told myself. "What happened to you was *nothing* compared to what happened to the victims and their families."

I paused a moment to take in the enormity of how many people were effected by the trial. Then I remembered that first meeting with Gil's parents. At that point, there was still hope that Gil wouldn't be convicted. I had to shake off this image. It did no good to indulge in it now.

The final ruling

Before Tyson made his final penalty ruling over a month later, I was given the opportunity to present arguments in favor of concurrent sentences. I tried to convince him that all the murders took place during the same criminal episode, which would allow him to treat the murders as if they were one crime. I cited all the applicable case law. Also, I made what I thought was a compelling case for the fact that the three days of deliberation meant jury members must have had a lot of doubt.

"Your Honor, I don't believe those jurors see my client as the shooter. Otherwise, they wouldn't have had such a hard time with the deliberations," I pleaded with him.

In spite of my passion and arguments, Tyson gave Gil three consecutive 25-year sentences. Several days later, Tyson made it official that Bert would receive the same penalty.

None of us were surprised. After all, it *was* Tyson making the decision. But even I had to admit that one 25-year concurrent sentence for three murders — which would result in the defendants serving only a little over eight years for each death — was inadequate. Human lives are worth a whole lot more than that, by anyone's standards.

Chapter 29

Union

Gil and his appellate attorneys have argued seven state and federal appeals since his conviction in 1991. None of them were successful. Twelve years after he was convicted, I drove six-and-a-half hours to visit him. The long drive allowed me to process why I felt so compelled to tell him what was on my heart.

Since his conviction, Gil had been in a total of five prisons. He had served time in Cross City Correctional Institution, Baker Correctional Institution and two other facilities. He had recently been transferred once again, this time to the maximum-security Union Correctional Institution, affectionately known as "The Rock" to those who live there.

There is often no rhyme or reason to why a prisoner is moved. In some cases, if he gets friendly with the guards, the senior corrections staff at the warden's level will transfer him. This helps cut down on the security risks that might occur when a prisoner gets too chummy with prison personnel. Gil's exemplary behavior didn't make him a security risk, but his beliefs often ran him afoul of the religious leadership at the prison. Gil had already been kicked out of the "faith-based" dorm by the time I saw him at The Rock. He was deemed inappropriate to be housed in this separate unit in which prisoners participate in mandatory daily devotional periods, specialized counseling, and religious services and study.

Even though it was obvious that Gil was responsible for introducing hundreds of inmates and even four guards to Christianity, the prison chaplain didn't go for Gil's belief in speaking in tongues or the laying on of hands for healing. Gil wouldn't compromise his belief in these aspects of scripture or practice them in conformity with the chaplain's standards; so, right or wrong, he was moved back to the regular population.

Nowheresville

To get to The Rock, I had to bear right, somewhere near Nowheresville, Florida. I then had to go past another maximum-security prison in the town of Starke, before reaching the rural prison town known as Raiford.

Showing up early when you're a guest in someone's home is considered rude; but when you do it at the prison home of an inmate client, the guards pretty much tell you to leave and come back when you were scheduled to be there. When it comes to maximum-security prisons, rules are in; flexibility is out. This forced me to have to kill some time.

There is no better way for me to get my head right than to go running, so that's what I decided to do while I waited. The fresh air and total freedom from work, vibrating cell phones and a million other little interruptions are my antidotes for stress. It's just God and me when I run. I suspected this would be especially medicinal before this particular visit.

The locals who ran the nearby gas station convenience store allowed me to do the whole Superman-quick-change thing in their dirty bathroom, so I shagged my running clothes and shoes from the gym bag I always carried in my trunk. When I emerged from the bathroom — a little worse for wear from the smell of disinfectant and who-knows-what — I hung my clothes in the back seat of my car and started running. There's nothing like an hour or so in the noonday heat to get that runner's high.

The road ahead of me stretched between the buildings that comprised the prison compound. Death-row inmates were housed on the right of the road and the rest of The Rock was on the left. As I ran, I thought about all the letters Gil had sent me over the years. Each one was more inspiring than the last. I also thought about the irony that even though he was in prison, he seemed to have more freedom than most people. He would always say that his relationship with Jesus Christ is what allowed him to reject the cares of this world. And it was clear to anyone who knew him that something had given him the ability to look through the bars, not at them.

Gil had been ministering to people inside and outside of the prison walls ever since he was incarcerated. He definitely had a unique ability to reach people, and he demonstrated that skill nearly every day. Although I was in awe of his compassion and willingness to serve others, a nagging feeling came to me as I ran. I couldn't help but feel we needed to talk about the victims and their families.

Unbelievably, in all these years of exchanging letters, we had never brought up the subject of the families' loss and grief. I'd been telling people for years that Gil had a radical conversion experience, and that he'd been transformed and lived to serve others. Yet, we never discussed these families. I began to wonder whether he was as sensitized to their pain, loss and grief as he was to everyone else's.

And today I was going to ask him about it. But first, *I* needed to confess to *him*. It never sat right with me that I wasn't straight with him about the extent of my faith during the trial. Gil and his family wanted a Christian lawyer to represent him. I told them I was a Christian — and everyone thought I was, based on my appearance in church each week. But I knew the truth. And the time had arrived to come clean.

I knew this visit could either be very nice or it would be something I would regret. I might just wish I had never lost my mind and decided to do the whole confession thing. I was actually a little apprehensive about Gil's reaction. So, as I ran I said a quick prayer: "Father, please help me be real with Gil and tell him the truth about my earlier deception. Help him to understand and forgive me for being dishonest about the extent of my faith in the old days."

My mind then turned to Gil's appeals. Even Gil acknowledged that he had only one appeal left. By legal standards, the likelihood of its success was doubtful. In most cases, only two years are allowed before an otherwise meritorious appellate issue is time-barred because of the statute of limitations. Even though many more years than that had passed, Gil was still hoping that his last appeal would work. I had done whatever I could to help Gil and his assigned public defender with his first appeal, and now I was doing whatever I could to help Mike Gelety, Gil's private appellate lawyer, with his last.

I only mentioned once that the likelihood of success for this final appeal was remote, because I knew Gil's beliefs didn't allow for negative thoughts. Based on the Bible, he embraced that "*all* things are possible with God." This was giving him continued hope that God would somehow find a way to release him.

Off the hook

After a good run in the heat, it was just about time for my scheduled visit. I had to figure out how to take a whore's bath over the filthy sink in the men's room at the gas station — without actually getting dirtier. Somehow, I managed. I changed back into my regular clothes and was good to go.

Once I went through security and was inside Union, I hit the vending machines in the visiting room in preparation for a long stay. I loaded up on junk food and then bought some healthy stuff, like coffee, chips and candy bars. The visiting room was predictably dreary, even though it overlooked the oddly park-like setting of the prison courtyard. The steel table and metal chairs in the room were a stark contrast to the expanse of green grass outside.

Soon after I arrayed all my junk food on one of the tables, a guard brought Gil into the room. Gil stood right inside the doorway, smiling, wearing prison-issue blues and shiny black boots. His short hair was slicked back. He still looked great and was incredibly fit, although a little less cut and pumped up. There also were a few gray hairs along his temples, as you would expect from someone in his early fifties.

He hugged me as naturally as he'd hug a family member and then we sat down. And before I knew it, he leaned forward and firmly held my hands in preparation to pray.

"Just like the old days," I thought. Only this time, I wasn't embarrassed. It was interesting to experience that his prayers were still as inspired as they used to be. In all this time, I had never heard anybody pray with the same kind of fervor.

When we were done praying, we both leaned back in our chairs. He smiled at me and shook his head slowly, as if to say, "So, what are you doing here?"

I made small talk because I knew I wasn't ready to confess to misleading him about being a more devout Christian during the trial. Following my lead, he teased me about how white my hair had turned and that I looked like his dad. He still looked great; I knew I couldn't get too far with teasing him about how he had aged. So, I continued the chitchat, talking about my kids.

"My two babies are now 14 and 15! Our third, Mary, is adorable, smart as a whip and already nine-years-old. Remember, I wrote to you that she came along five years after the trial? It took that long for me to recover, my friend. And let me tell you, she's got me wrapped around her finger, just like the others did when they were her age."

He was laughing then, which was great to see. We then talked briefly about his family.

"I just got a card and some photographs from Gillie and David," he said proudly. I knew he hadn't heard from his sons in two years, and five years ago was the last time he had seen them. It had been 10 years since he even had a letter from Neli, who had divorced him years after his incarceration so she could go on with her life.

"Neli wrote on the outside of the envelope. Listen to this," Gil said, pulling the envelope and his reading glasses from his shirt pocket. After he put on the reading glasses, he said, "Here's what she wrote: 'Gil, you would be proud of the young men your sons have become. They're exactly what I believe God wants young men to be in this world. Thank you for helping to create these two beautiful young men of God.'"

Gil wiped away a tear after he laid the envelope on the table. I knew he had never stopped loving Neli, so the note from her touched him deeply. I could see he was feeling vulnerable, so I quickly moved on to other kinds of catch-up talk, allowing him to recover his composure. After we talked about a variety of safer topics, finally, I was ready.

"Gil, I've got a confession to make."

He knew when to get serious and I could see I had his attention.

"I wasn't really a true Christian when we first met in 1990."

This was harder for me than I had thought. Looking him in the eye was an effort but I had to do it.

"I went along with your perception that I was a believer like you because I really wanted the case. I wanted it for all the wrong reasons: money, publicity, the challenge. I wanted to represent you. The truth is, I used to feel self-conscious and embarrassed when you held my hands and prayed with me in the jail. I used to worry about what my friends and colleagues would say if they saw me."

Gil just leaned back further and seemed to be studying me more, noticing my discomfort.

"Back then, I was still a major drinking and partying fool. Then over the years, I started noticing all the scriptures I'd conveniently glossed over in those earlier days."

Gil was smiling bigger now, still nodding, essentially telling me that he could relate.

"Will you forgive me?"

He laughed and said, "Yes, of course I forgive you! Father God knows that the road to sanctification is just like the road to success; it's always under construction. Don't you see, John? It's Jesus; only Jesus and His Holy Spirit could get you to come up here and say this. Praise the Lord!"

He could have just as easily laid a major guilt trip on me. He could have used some of his charismatic faith vernacular and accused me of "allowing the enemy into his camp," as I had heard him say about others with whom he stopped associating since his conversion. He could have suggested that I wasn't fully on board with God, thereby bringing the "wrong spirit" to the defense table. But he didn't do any of that. Instead, he just simply forgave me. After so many years, I was relieved to be let off the hook.

Seth

Before I could get up the courage to address the other important issue I thought about while running that morning, an inmate named Jerry approached Gil. He politely interrupted and asked Gil for his help.

Jerry and his girlfriend Sally were apparently at their wit's end. They were seeking Gil's help with encouraging Seth, Sally's suicidal son who had come with his mother to visit Jerry. Gil didn't hesitate to act, after first asking Seth if it would be OK to talk in front of me. He then asked Seth if he could lead him in a prayer. Surprisingly, Seth consented.

"Look me in the eye, Seth. Repeat after me," Gil said. "Father God, close the doors that need to be closed. Satan, I rebuke you. You're exposed, trespassing, unwanted. I command you in Jesus' name to get up and get out…"

This was vintage Gil. Nothing had changed since I first met him. I experienced a flashback of sorts as I saw Gil's large hands clasped around Seth's, which were much smaller by comparison. Even though I had prayed earlier with Gil, I had a different perspective now that I was seeing it from the outside. This was exactly the way Gil held my hands the first time he prayed with me. For a moment, I felt as though I was back with Gil in the Broward County jail in 1990.

It was obvious from Gil's prayer that Jerry had already told him that Seth, though only 16 years old, had been in drug rehab and had thoughts of suicide.

"Do you think you're the only one who has thought about suicide?" Gil asked, keeping his voice low and soothing. "When I was a cop, I used to put my gun to my head and cock the trigger, squeezing it a bit, thinking those kind of thoughts. But I didn't really want to die. I only wanted a little pity party."

Gil's eyes flashed. Anyone could see he was in his element.

"You remember the little kids poem, 'Humpty Dumpty, sat on a wall, Humpty Dumpty had a great fall. All the King's horses and all the King's men, couldn't put Humpty Dumpty back together again'? Remember that one? They were talking about the King's *horses* and the King's *men* — not about the King! My life was wrecked, like Humpty Dumpty's, and only the King could ever put it back together again. And I didn't just wreck my life. I wrecked my wife's life and my parents' lives, and my kids' lives, too, by doing cocaine and being an idiot. And now look at where I am."

We were all speechless and listening intently as Gil continued telling Seth, "My boy, Gillie, wouldn't play sports because he kept waiting for me to get out of prison. He'd say 'I don't want to play until you get out and watch me, daddy.' He just kept waiting. It's almost 14 years later, and because of me, he never played sports."

"The last time I saw my boys was five years ago. My youngest boy, David, was nine then. He cried his heart out and refused to leave when visiting time was over. Even the guards were crying because David kept saying, 'I'm not leaving my daddy!' He put his arms out to stop anyone from making him go through the door. The guards kept telling him, 'It's OK, your daddy's going to be OK.'

"But David didn't even hear them. He just kept saying, 'I'm staying here with my daddy!'"

Gil started crying. We all cried, too. Listening to his pain and visualizing his little boy was heartbreaking.

"My parents lost everything they had while trying to help me. They won't say it but I know it's true. They were successful businesspeople; they owned two salons. They sold everything. They lost their salons and their house, and had to move in with one of my sisters. They lost it all while trying to help me but they won't say it. I was the only dummy in the family. The rest of them are winners — my parents and my sisters."

"Seth, look at your sweet mom; she loves you like my mom and dad love me. You wouldn't let me hurt her, would you? Not if you could stop me, right?"

"Yeah," Seth said immediately.

"You wouldn't let me kill her, but you'd kill her, wouldn't you? Do you know that when she's up all night worrying about you, night after night, you're killing her? I know you don't want to or mean to, but you are.

"Your mom is all you've got. Your friends won't be there for you when all hell breaks loose. You know how it is when you're in trouble: The going got tough and they got going! I'm not saying your friends are bad; they're just blind.

"Your homeboys probably won't be there for you if you get in trouble. They won't tell you the truth about places like this either. They don't tell you that everyone can see you in the shower. They don't talk about the Dear John letter you're gonna get or about the letter from your family, saying they can't send any more money. They also don't talk about the money troubles you're gonna have, like when you get a letter informing you your appeal's been denied — again — and you know it's gonna take a bundle to do another one. Where are your friends then? Are they there when you have to try to hide from the guys waiting to get their mail so they don't see you crying?"

"They also won't tell you that you're given 90 minutes of free time between the head count at 4:30 and dinner at 6. During this time, you have to get cleaned up, and pick up your laundry and mail. Then 90 guys line up to use one phone. You do the math. There are 90 guys and only 90 minutes. There's no way you can tell anyone to hurry up, so you might not get to use the phone that day. If you don't get to use it, you just get in line the next day and try again.

"Sometimes a guy will try to take your food, or maybe he tells you that you're sitting in his seat or he changes the TV station you're watching. You gonna let it go? You gonna give up your food, move your seat, whatever? You gonna show yourself to be weak, pull up your panties and leave? Your friends don't tell you all that. Do they? You'd be lucky if you could even get one of your friends to actually come and visit you in jail.

"You see, Seth, your mother is the only bridge you have. But that bridge only extends so far. I see that with a lot of the guys in here. Some of them don't get visitors anymore because that bridge ran out. If you're lucky, your mother will put up another plank to lengthen that bridge. But if you keep hurting her, eventually she'll run out of planks.

Seth cried as he glanced over at his mother, who was holding onto Jerry, her eyes filled with tears.

"I started out as a good guy. I was a police officer. I had a sweet wife and a great family before it all snuck up on me — the cocaine, the steroids, the women, the bodybuilding championships. Then I became a bodyguard for the Colombians. I realize now it was never about me against anybody else; it was always about good against evil. It was the power of light against the power of darkness."

Seth, now crying, nodded.

"I don't know the trials you've had. It's true that you can't tell another man how to live until you walk in his shoes. But believe me, I've been there."

"Seth, I'm gonna stop now. Know that your mother and Jerry love you. And I can tell you that even though you just met me, I love you as a brother."

Humbled now and looking softer than when we first saw him, Seth walked over and held his mother and Jerry in a silent embrace. I sat somewhat stunned as I watched Gil wrap his huge arms around all of them.

Several minutes later, Jerry passed by me before a guard escorted him, Sally and Seth out of the visiting area. Gil had walked over to say a quick hello to a friend who was visiting another inmate. I seized the opportunity of Gil's absence to ask Jerry, "Is he always consistent like this or does he sometimes…"

Jerry interrupted, "Always like this, helping me and everyone else. *Always*. I've been in prison for 19 years now and I've never met a greater prayer warrior than this man. I've never met anyone like him."

Strong hands

As Gil returned to the dented steel table, I wiped away my tears and took a deep breath. Not only was I nervous about what I came to say to Gil, I was blown away by what I had just seen. But I knew what I had to do. Gil could tell something was up. He knew me pretty well, even though it had been a while since he'd seen me. Typically, he was quite conversant. But now he just sat there quietly, waiting for me to speak.

At length, I finally said, "Gil, I'm in conflict over some issues we've never really discussed concerning things people say you've done in the past."

Gil was studying me more than usual. He started to say something, but I wasn't done. I think he knew I needed to empty my bucket.

"I don't want to continue pretending there's not an elephant in the corner of the room. You know what I mean? We both know it's there and neither of us have ever talked about it. At this point, our relationship can either be superficial or real. We need to get past this."

"It's one thing to have to listen to you clear your conscience about your faith in the old days, and that was cool. But now I have to listen to you talk about elephants, too?" he joked. Then he suddenly became serious and said, "Look, John, you already made your confession today. Are you saying it's my turn now? If you are, I'll tell you what I told you way back when I was accused of Tommy Felt's murder…"

I interrupted, saying, "Before we even talk about Tommy and other things from your past, I need to say something. You know that as your attorney I couldn't and wouldn't be stupid enough to say anything without your blessing. Even if a prosecutor were to subpoena me and suggest that our attorney-client privilege has somehow been waived by the book I'm writing or by the fact that I've talked openly about some of the things we've discussed, my testimony would be the same then as it is now: you've never admitted to any murders, period.

"I'm only saying; if there's truth to any of the other allegations and you want to license me to work out concurrent sentences, I can. I can work with Cindy Imperato — she's a judge now and she's still friendly with..."

"John, let me help you out here," Gil interrupted. "I already get my protection where it counts, from God."

"I know, it's just that..."

"Let me say a few things. You said your thing, now let me say mine."

"OK," I said, "I'll listen."

"The prosecutors had everyone convinced that Bert and I killed Tommy Felts to get rid of him. Then they convinced Carbone that he was next. Remember that? But they also told the jury that Tommy and I were best friends and like brothers. They used my association with him and his association with Carbone against us. At the same time, the cops and the state convinced the media and everybody else that we killed Tommy. You gonna kill your best friend? If I were gonna kill one of them, why would I kill Tommy when I could've killed Carbone? And here's the kicker, John. The same prosecutors have since pled out another guy for Tommy's murder. You told me that yourself. The guy's name is Bobby Young, right? Young admitted he did it. He's serving time for Tommy's murder. Before, they were convinced that *I* killed Tommy. And they convinced everyone else of that, too. Think about it. What else could they be wrong about? They were wrong about a *lot* of things."

"Gil, don't get me wrong. Keep in mind that I'm not asking you to admit to anything or do anything, other than to think about whether you have any information that might help the families achieve closure.

"Now that Bert's dead, is there anything you could say that you couldn't say before? Law enforcement already knows that Harry Van Collier killed Charlinda Draudt and Mitch Hall because he left a fingerprint on duct tape at the scene. But do you know of anything else that might help the victims' families? If you do, wouldn't it be the right thing for you to say something? People are saying that you're not the real deal because you don't talk about the old days. Look, we both know the Gil Fernandez *I* met in 1990 was *not* the Gil Fernandez of the early 80's; the man they say committed other crimes. Frankly, guilty or not, he's a man I never would've wanted to know."

Gil moved his head back and forth slowly, as if to say "no." I wasn't quite sure whether he was saying no to my request to think about these things or if he was just shaking his head because he agreed the old Gil was someone he wouldn't have wanted to know either.

He started to say something but then stopped. My body language told him that I was amped-up and needed to talk some more.

"You talk about 1 Corinthians 5:17 and use that as evidence that you're a new creation in Christ, that old things have passed away. But doesn't the new Gil have to accept responsibility for what the old Gil did, or at least talk about anything else the old Gil might know that might help the families? Do you agree?"

"Are you going to take a breath and let me talk?" he asked, this time sounding understandably impatient with my verbal purgation.

"I'm almost done, I promise. The new Gil, who might as well have a completely different name, occupies the same body as the old Gil. Look, you believe all day long that you're a new spiritual man and that you've been forgiven by God for all that the old Gil did. And I agree with you. But there are still earthly consequences. Forgiveness and consequences are not mutually exclusive. And I know you know that.

"Gil, here's the bottom line: I don't want people to believe that you're just another hypocrite and that you aren't as genuine as I've told everyone you are."

"John…"

"One second. Cindy, Luana and I don't know how many others have been saying that you're not repentant because you haven't confessed to the Tringali, Leahy and Robertson families. You've been convicted, so as far as they're concerned, you should just confess and give up any remaining appeals. They say that you should take responsibility, and if you don't, you can't be a real Christian…"

Gil couldn't wait any longer. When I paused to take a breath, he jumped in and said, "John, first of all, I don't care about the opinions of men. I only care what God says. Nobody knows what I say to the Father. And how do these people know what it takes to be a real Christian anyway?"

"Cindy and most others believe, I'm sure, that when you sin there's judgment…"

"Don't waste a good sermon on me, preacher-man," Gil joked as he interrupted me. "Tell these people the real message of Christianity is not about sin and judgment; it's about salvation and second chances. That's why they call the gospel the good news. Otherwise, they'd call it the bad news. The Bible is clear that we have to confess to God, not man. And besides, confession is not the same as repentance or redemption. I believe people are redeemed because of what Christ did, not because of what *they* do."

"But some people use that scripture in James, "confess your sins, one to another..."

Gil interrupted me to say, "But that's only the first part. They need to look at the whole verse, not just half of it. You should know that, John."

"Yeah, I know," is all I said. I couldn't possibly keep up with Gil's years of concentrated Bible study."

"OK, well, let me enlighten you," he said, teasing me. "Here's how it reads: James 5:16 states, 'Confess your faults, one to another, praying for one another that you may be *healed*,'" Gil said, recalling the verse from memory. "That refers to talking to others about your faults because it's healing for you to get it all out. You know, like they do in 12-step programs."

He then added passionately, "But I *don't* keep stuff inside, John. I go to my Father with everything."

As he spoke, I noticed the guard who stood at the sentry post on the other side of the visiting room window. He was examining his nails, looking incredibly bored.

"I know, Gil, but all that having been said, here's the bottom line question: Does a Christian owe any sort of confession and apology to people he hurt, in addition to confessing to God? I'm not talking about anything specific and I'm including myself in this, too. So, please don't be defensive.

"Even the 12-step programs have a step that requires a person to make amends to those he's hurt. Do you think Christians owe the same type of amends? I believe *I* do, unless of course it only hurts the person more if I say something. I read that in the Alcoholics Anonymous *Big Book*, back in the days when I was beginning to wonder whether I was getting addicted to all that wine I drank."

"Anyway, I learned I had to make amends to some people. At first, I tried to get out of it. I actually scoured the *Big Book* to find any reason I could why I *didn't* need to confess things to people. And I found a section that mentioned we shouldn't say anything if it's going to hurt or affect the person in any way. So, if that's your reason for not wanting to give the families information, then I understand..."

"But John..."

"One second, Gil, I'm almost done. Let me just finish. If the answer is that you don't want to add more pain to their lives or your sons' lives, that's honorable and..."

"I hate to cut you off there, counselor. But these prosecutors who say I haven't confessed, do they confess all they've done? Because the last time I checked, Christ said, 'Now go forth and sin no more.' Have they gone forth and sinned no more? And as for them saying I'm not repentant for what I've done in my life, how can they judge me and know my heart today?"

"Yeah, but Gil, this is about you, not them," I said. "You can't take their moral inventories."

Through the window, I could see a crowd of people who had just been escorted out of the visiting room. As they walked behind the sentry and down the hallway, I could hear the echoing sound of tearful good-byes.

Frustrated now, Gil responded, "Repentance is just a change of mind about sinning, a decision to stop. I've done that. Can my accusers say the same thing? These people want to help God judge me — and they aren't even Christians! How do they know what I'm supposed to do to be right with God and to be a good Christian? Did the Lord tell Apostle Paul 'go turn yourself in'? Paul had done some horrible things before Christ changed his name from Saul to Paul. But God told him, 'just go.'"

I looked at my watch and saw that visiting time should have been up by now. Knowing the guard would be here any minute, I had to speak quickly. So, I sat forward and asked Gil one last question: "You wear that WWJD bracelet. I know that's there to remind you to ask yourself 'What Would Jesus Do?' So, I'm asking you, what do you think Jesus would want you to do with respect to talking about your past?"

Gil stared at me for a moment and smiled, with a look on his face that said, "Are you done? Can I answer now — *without* being interrupted?"

As he was about to speak, we heard the quick footsteps of a guard coming down the hall. I looked at my watch again and saw that visiting hours had been over for five minutes. I had been here for hours without realizing it. Somehow, the guard hadn't realized it either. He had screwed up and let us stay together longer than allowed.

Suddenly there were two loud raps on the metal door by the prison guard. As Gil and I jerked our heads in the direction of the noise, it got eerily quiet; and then there were another two raps to interrupt the silence. Then the door swung open wildly, banging against the dull-colored concrete block wall.

"OK gentlemen, visiting time's over," the guard said as he burst into the room. He was out of breath but spoke in a friendly way. I could tell he liked Gil.

Understanding more than anyone the importance of following the rules in prison, Gil stood up rapidly, screeching the metal legs of his chair across the concrete floor. He stood almost at attention, the way you would expect a private in the military to do in the presence of a superior officer. The guard approached Gil with purpose and quietly said 'Gotta go Gil.' He let us know we had no more time for anything but an abrupt goodbye. Knowing we had run out of time, Gil gave me a quick bear hug and firmly buried my hand in his.

He started to follow the guard out the door and into the hall but stopped short. He turned and said quickly, "Be blessed, John. I love you. And so does Jesus."

As he passed through the door, he paused one last time to turn and smile at me. I could tell from his look that he knew, like I did, that I would be back. This conversation wasn't over.

Epilogue

In retrospect, just about everyone connected with the *State of Florida v. Gilbert Fernandez, Jr.* case was robbed in some way.

Obviously, the victims were robbed of their cocaine. But that was the least of their problems; they were robbed of their very lives. It's almost impossible to imagine the terror they must have experienced that dark, scary night. Two of the victims had to listen while their friend was being shot and sent splashing into a watery grave. Then, the last victim was forced to experience the terror of listening to his other friend murdered, too, anticipating that he would soon be next.

But the victims weren't the only ones who were robbed. There were parents, sisters, brothers, aunts, uncles and even children who were robbed, too. They were cheated out of spending the future with their loved ones. There might not be enough counseling in the world to help these family members process this grief or learn how to *not* think about those last hours of the victims' lives. How does one fashion coping mechanisms from the emotional carnage caused by such unfathomable loss?

As horrific as the loss was for the victims and their families, others were robbed, too. When Gil Fernandez was convicted, his wife Neli was robbed of a husband. Although Gil is still in love with her to this day, he could do nothing about the fact that she was forced to raise their two boys alone. She became a single mom overnight — without the help of alimony or child support. Gil couldn't help her love their boys up close any more, and he wasn't there to reassure her that things would be OK. And as hard as it was on Neli, their boys were robbed of even more. Their father couldn't tuck them into bed at night, teach them how to play sports or even demonstrate the basics of how to get along in this world.

Gil's parents were robbed, too. They lost their business and had to watch their grandchildren grow up without their father. The happy memories they once had of their son were no doubt marred by the pain and wreckage of the last 15 years. Their little boy is now locked away for life.

When I used to think about the incredible unfairness and illegalities in the trial, I would only think selfishly about the fact that I had been robbed, too. But as I've gotten older, I've come to realize that the loss of the acquittal and my perception of malfeasance during the trial doesn't even belong in the same category as the losses suffered by the victims and their loved ones, or the losses experienced by Gil's family.

I also found that all things were not as I originally thought. Through researching this book, I was able to revisit the case from a different perspective. With the objectivity that comes with the passage of time, I realized there was a lot I didn't know in 1991.

The following updates encapsulate the results of my research and efforts to reach out to people connected to the trial. I feel this journey of discovery, which reacquainted me with the past and allowed me to make new friends out of old enemies, was well worth the effort. I hope you will agree.

John P. Contini

UPDATES

Neli and Gil

Obviously, Gil's imprisonment had a profound effect on his relationship with Neli.

Gil told me on one of our visits, "My parents came to see me with my boys in 1998, when Gillie was 14 and David was 7. I knew something was up when my mom asked my dad to take the boys for a soda so she could have a minute with me.

"Once the boys were gone, she told me, 'Neli is getting remarried.'"

"I said, 'Mom, couldn't you think of a better place to tell me?'

"She said, 'Where else am I going to tell you?'"

He laughed as he remembered his mom's remark, but I could tell this was a painful subject for him. He went on to say, "I've had a few other relationships even while I've been in here, with good women I've met through other people. They visit me and we write. But I tell them that I still love Neli and that it would be unfair to them for me to commit. No woman has my heart like my wife. Actually, I should say "ex-wife," but I just can't. My love for her is still so strong."

Gil stopped for a moment, took off his glasses and wiped his watery eyes. After he composed himself, he said, "My love for her has never wavered or weakened. I don't know why God permits this love for her to continue. I still break down over her and my sons." Then after a deep sigh, he said, "And my boys, that's a whole other story. Flesh of my flesh and bone of my bone; they are my life and breath, my very reason for existing."

Gil took another deep breath and then just sat there for a moment. Tearing up again, he said, "That year we got saved together, Neli, Gillie and I; that was the best year of my life."

Bert Christie Joe Damiano
Defendant   *Detective, Broward Sheriff's Office*

Cynthia "Cindy" Imperato
Assistant Statewide Prosecutor, Office of Statewide Prosecution

Bert Christie and his new lawyer, Bruce Zimet, a former federal prosecutor, sought to vacate Bert's earlier conviction based on allegations of "ineffective assistance of counsel," referring, of course, to trial counsel Louie Vernell. Broward Circuit Judge Susan Lebow overturned Bert Christie's convictions and life sentences in 1999. I testified at length at the evidentiary hearing that led to this decision.

Bruce asked me to testify about whatever I could recall about Louie Vernell's antics and performance, or lack thereof, during the trial. As I testified, Bert looked at me with appreciative eyes. I could tell he was very sick; he looked like he was on his last leg. And as could be predicted, his daughters were there to support their daddy, almost ten years after they had turned so many heads during the trial.

Strangely enough, Cindy Imperato was the prosecutor who questioned me on the witness stand. Cindy was still married to the father of her two children, Gabe Imperato, an attorney in the firm of Broad and Cassel. Although she became a Broward Circuit Court judge just after Bert's hearing, at the time I testified, she was the only prosecutor from the original crew who still worked in the Office of Statewide Prosecution.

Cindy was in an unusual position because Bert was seeking a new trial based on Louie's ineffective assistance. She did her level best to suggest by her questions that Vernell did an effective job because she didn't want the underlying conviction reversed. It was her job to defeat Bert's efforts to secure a new trial by minimizing any examples of Louie's screw-ups.

Poor Cindy was in the unenviable position of trying to make a silk purse out of a sow's ear. She tried her best not to laugh when I reminded her from the witness stand, "Come on, Cindy, you and the other prosecutors used to tease me about how Louie ate pretzels out of his coat pocket in front of the jurors! You used to talk about how he was in and out of lucidity, at times charming and sharp, but at other times totally out of it. You used to joke that his elevator didn't stop at every floor. You guys used to take shots at him all the time."

The hearing won Bert the right to a new trial. Zimet also fought to have Christie released on house arrest until that trial could take place. But Bert never went home. His health had deteriorated so much that he died in prison shortly after the hearing. Naturally, Cindy and the victims' families were upset when Bert's conviction was overturned, so on one level, I imagine his death was a relief of sorts for all of them. I'm sure they also felt that his dying in prison was a bit of poetic justice.

Ironically, Jim Lewis told me that he had recommended to Cindy that Bert *should* be released from prison to die at home, believing that Bert would cooperate. Cindy and the victims' family members, of course, didn't share his position on this issue. Jim said he saw Bert's daughters coming out of the jail, shortly after their father died. They were carrying their father's belongings in a white plastic garbage bag. According to Jim, when they saw him, they let him know with their piercing eyes how much they still resented him.

Everything

Cindy told me over lunch in October 2005, "You know, Bert was about to tell us everything right before he died," Cindy said.

"Everything?" I asked.

Detective Joe Damiano, who also had joined us, was sitting across the table from her, nodding his head in silent agreement as she continued. "Bruce Zimet said Bert would tell us everything about the murders because he knew he was dying. He said he'd give it all up if we would just let him out of jail so he could die at home with his daughters."

"Whatever happened with that?" I asked.

"He died before we could put the deal together," Cindy replied. "His only stipulation, other than being allowed to die at home, was that he didn't want anyone to know what he told us until after he died."

"Obviously, the victims' families didn't want Christie out. They wanted him to die in prison. And they got their wish," Damiano added.

Cindy lamented, "It really was a huge missed opportunity."

I was surprised at her remark, given that she was an advocate for keeping Bert in prison. So, I asked, "But is it true what Jim Lewis told me? He said you were the one who wouldn't agree to letting Bert out of jail so he could die at home."

"That's true, because I was honoring the feelings of the victims' family members," she replied. "But when Christie died, the information died with him. We believe he would have given us more than enough to put Gil in the electric chair on the other murders."

"Is that what Bruce Zimet told you?" I asked them.

"I can't tell you that," she said, using her best poker face. "I can tell you there was a concern that he would have held back on talking after he was released. The victims' families were concerned about that, too."

Personally, I doubt that Bert would have said anything remotely negative about Gil, given their strong loyalty and friendship. Bert had already refused a deal to testify against Gil and avoid the chair. And since I helped in the effort to get his conviction vacated, it's doubtful that he would have done something to deliberately hurt me.

Could Bert have been teasing the state into believing he might say things they wanted to hear, just to get home and die with his daughters? Could it be that he intended to give them information that would amount to nothing more than chump change? Could he have been intending to talk about a crime for which the statute of limitations had already expired? That might have been the case — and that's what Cindy and the families feared.

Cindy went on to say, "To change the subject a bit, let me ask you a question. If Gil is a born-again Christian like you say, isn't he supposed to confess to whatever he has done?" Cindy asked.

"That's a legitimate question. There are some biblical verses on this point," I replied. "The fact remains, a lot of Christians scan the Bible to choose the scriptures they want to embrace and those they want to avoid. I know, because I've been guilty of it in the past, too. Lewis did it, too, during the trial. But to answer your question, yes, there must be a confession. But that confession must be to God, not necessarily to police and prosecutors."

Then Damiano said, "I know Gil hasn't admitted to any murders. But if he ever *did* confess, we would need to ask the victims' families whether they would agree to concurrent life sentences. Obviously, we could only ask them this if he accepted responsibility and was willing to be held accountable."

"Joe and I have been thinking about this for over a year now," Cindy said. "We could do the same thing for Gil that we did on the Tommy Felts murder. We pled out Bobby Young, the defendant, so the sentence for the Felts murder was concurrent with Young's other murder sentences. If Gil would just admit to the other murders he committed, we might be able to make the new sentences concurrent and combine them into his existing sentence."

"But we don't want to go to the other families and talk about all this if Gil has no intention of admitting guilt," Joe added. "I have my doubts that he would do that if he still thinks he has a shot at getting out."

"Doesn't he know it's impossible for him to get out? I mean, John, he's had all his state and federal appeals and all the time limits are up, right?" Cindy asked.

"Well, he may file one more appeal, despite the time limitations. But more than that, he chooses to hang on the Bible verses that say, 'all things are possible to him who loves God,' and 'what's impossible with man, is possible with God.' The bottom line is that he believes God is going to release him."

Louis "Louie" Vernell, Jr.
Defense Attorney for Bert Christie

Bert Christie's attorney Louie Vernell was disbarred from The Florida Bar in 1998. This action arose from a complaint filed in 1995 by one of Louie's clients, Howard Rosenberg. This complaint was the last in a long line of grievances filed against him.

In 1989, Howard Rosenberg, a friend of Louie's since the 1960's, retained him as counsel in connection with an eminent domain proceeding involving the Department of Transportation's efforts to condemn and subsequently acquire property owned by Rosenberg.

Louie helped Rosenberg challenge the determination of the property's value, alleging it had a greater value and, if condemned, should entitle the owner to more money. Before the trial, the state had paid Rosenberg approximately $45,000 for the property. After the trial, which Louie won, the jury determined the property was worth $70,000. The Clerk of the Circuit Court issued checks totaling approximately $60,000, payable to Vernell on Rosenberg's behalf. This amount represented payment for the balance due on the property, statutory interest, attorney's fees and costs.

Howard Rosenberg testified that Vernell never notified him of receipt of the checks. Rosenberg and his wife testified that they asked Vernell about the status of the funds and the eminent domain case many times. Vernell was alleged to have told them that the appeal was pending and that the money was "tied up," even after the appeal was concluded. Vernell, they claimed, never paid any of the proceeds from the checks to Rosenberg. Frustrated with Louie's unwillingness to give him his money, Rosenberg finally felt he had no recourse but to file the Bar complaint.

Oh, well, so much for a 20-year friendship. But who knows what Louie's defense might have been. How many times might a lawyer do favors for a friend over the course of 20-plus years? Maybe the client offered to pay him back for all that help over the years with proceeds from recovery in the trial. Maybe Rosenberg asked Louie to work on the case for no charge for a while and not get paid hourly, teasing Louie with a much higher contingency fee if victorious. Do people who are friends for 20 years usually put that kind of thing in writing? More than likely, they don't. Could Louie have legitimately felt the money was his? Possibly. Or, could the whole thing have been dirty all along? Maybe, but we'll never know.

After an investigation, lawyers for The Florida Bar claimed that Vernell had a long history of ethical violations. They noted that he was privately reprimanded in 1964 and publicly reprimanded again in 1974. He was suspended for six months in 1979 because of his convictions for failure to file income tax returns for five years and for conduct prejudicial to the administration of justice. He was suspended for three months in 1987 for conduct similar to that in the Rosenberg case and was admonished in 1992. So they say, anyway. But again, we don't really know the truth.

A Florida Bar referee found that Vernell's history of misconduct "clearly demonstrates his unfitness to practice law." To add insult to injury, Vernell was made to remunerate $5,030.18 to The Florida Bar for their expenditures in connection with his disbarment proceeding.

The referee concluded that Vernell hadn't learned anything from prior suspensions and reprimands, so disbarment was appropriate. But that was his opinion. Louie tried countless cases in his career. How many had that referee ever tried? Probably few, if any, which might be why he's a "referee."

Jim Lewis
Assistant Statewide Prosecutor, Office of Statewide Prosecution

Though I disliked Lewis during the trial, I've since grown to understand him. Not only had I changed, but he appeared to have changed, too. He had been humbled quite a bit.

His humility began when it was his turn as a defense attorney on the high-profile Lionel Tate case. Lewis publicly contended that the 12-year-old Tate had killed 6-year-old Tiffany Eunick while imitating the moves of professional wrestlers he saw on television. The World Wrestling Federation then brought a multimillion-dollar defamation suit against Jim in 2000 because of his use of "the wrestling defense." They claimed he publicly blamed them for causing his client to beat a little girl to death.

Unfortunately, Jim's defense also caused other problems: it put his young client in the state pen for life. Tate was the youngest person in America to ever receive a life sentence. Thankfully for Tate, Richard Rosenbaum signed on as his appellate counsel. After working tirelessly for the boy over a three-year period, the life sentence was reversed. Jim was defeated and humbled, but in the process, he became less self-righteous and arrogant, and therefore more empathic and likeable.

Carrot cake

If someone had told me during the trial that I'd someday sit in a booth at The Cheesecake Factory in Fort Lauderdale sharing carrot cake with Jim Lewis, I'd have said they were crazy. But that's what happened in October 2005.

"Thanks for doing this, Jimmy," I said.

"You're welcome. Come on, John, have some of this carrot cake; it's huge."

We were winding up our lengthy lunch meeting by this time, and I was appreciative of Jim's willingness to share the inside scoop and behind-the-scenes political machinations of the prosecution on the Fernandez case.

"I heard BSO shopped this case to both the Dade State Attorney's Office and the Broward State Attorney's Office before bringing it to the Office of Statewide Prosecution. Even Sheriff Nick Navarro confirmed this, calling it "the turf thing." Hearing you confirm this today just proves what I've said all along — they forum-shopped this thing and forced a square peg into a round hole. It'll always be my opinion that your office lacked the jurisdiction to present this case to a Statewide Grand Jury."

Jim disagreed, even though he confirmed that the other two offices didn't want the case. He not only felt his old office had the requisite jurisdiction, he went on to say, "John, I believe Fernandez killed these poor guys for money. I believe he's got his religion now. I also believe everything you're saying about him being a changed man. God may have forgiven him but I don't think society should. There's no residual doubt in my mind that he was guilty of murdering these three guys. He executed them in cold blood for money. For that, he richly deserved the death penalty. I believed it then and I still believe it now."

"I only want the truth, Jimmy," I replied. "If those are your feelings, then those are your feelings. I'm not into revisionist history here. I'm only looking to get to the unadulterated truth about everything that happened during the trial."

"What else do you want to know?" Jim asked.

"I'll get to that in minute," I responded. "First I want to say that I thought of you as the villain in this case. Even though we're friends now, I didn't like you at all back then."

"That's OK," he said, "I've been the villain before. I'm used to it."

"You need to let me explain why for a minute — uninterrupted — because you'll be tempted to stop me and defend yourself," I said, before wolfing down some more of his carrot cake.

"Go ahead. I'll listen to you," Jim replied.

"I resented you because I believed then, and so did Gil, that you suborned perjury with that whole Paul Combs, dead-men's testimony crap. I thought that was a total bag of feces about how the three victims supposedly told him that 'they were going to meet two bodybuilders, named Gil and Tommy.' If Gil were really planning a drug rip-off, do you think he would have let these guys know in advance who he was and that he was a bodybuilder? Come on Jimmy, you know that's a bunch of crap. Yet, you elicited this testimony from Combs.

"Gil and I always thought that you and Combs got together to concoct this whole thing. The prosecution was fighting a losing battle before you were brought on board a couple of weeks before the trial. Then, lo and behold, up pops this newly discovered eleventh-hour 'evidence.'

"But then you told me in the courthouse hallway yesterday that you weren't the first to have discovered this so-called dead-men's testimony. You said Paul had come into the office..."

"That's right," Jim finally interrupted. "Paul came in a week or so before I was on the case and told Doug and Cindy his story. I pretty much inherited it. And I'll tell you, John, I asked Paul several times over the years whether he made it up. He swore to me that he didn't. I've represented his brother since then and we've got an ongoing relationship now. I think Paul would tell me if he made it up."

"Don't you see that you're proving my point?" I prodded. "The fact that you even asked that question of Combs throughout the years proves to me that you had doubts about his story. You must have known on a certain level that the testimony wasn't true. That's why I always thought you suborned perjury back then. But now you're telling me you inherited this crap from Doug and Cindy. To whom did he supposedly say this first? Do you know?"

"I'm not sure," Jim replied.

"In any case, Jimmy, I'd be lying if I didn't tell you that I'm hoping you can get him to come clean with you. Look, since Combs keeps in touch with you, I'm hoping you can get him to cough up the truth now. Especially since the statute of limitations has run out on perjury and everything else except murder. He can tell us the real deal now without fear of prosecution. He can tell us until the cows come home that he made up that crap and nobody could touch him. And we know it had to be crap, because there's no way the three dead guys would have known Gil's name, assuming for a moment that Gil was even involved."

"Why do you keep saying that the victims wouldn't have known his name?" Jim asked.

"All you have to do is look at Linda Allard's sworn statement to the police. I've got all this documentation if you want to see it again. You'd see that Paul Combs had been beeping victim Dickie Robertson all night to no avail. Combs apparently thought he had been ripped off by Dickie."

"I don't remember all that. I hadn't thought about this trial in years until you brought it up. It sounds like you're reliving this whole thing," Jimmy said. Then he added jokingly, "Hey, I said you could have some cake. I didn't say you could finish it.

"Combs testimony notwithstanding, what really did you in, John, was Louie Vernell. You would make all your points and then Louie would get up and undo everything you did. He made many of my points, too. I remember joking that he was on my side."

"That was brutal," I replied, "because I couldn't object to what he was doing, like I could have done if he had been one of you guys."

"Even then, you *did* object a couple of times! I could see you were trying to distract him from crippling your case," Jim added.

"I hate to even think about when that was happening," I said. "But getting away from Louie, you're right, Jimmy, I am reliving this whole thing. It's part of the process of writing the book. Also, I still visit Gil. He's a friend and I love the guy like a brother. For years, I looked under every rock to see if there was any way to appeal remaining issues.

"I can understand why you don't remember the subplots and all the police reports, like the one involving Linda Allard. You'd really have no reason to after all this time. I've got law enforcement reports I can show you and Paul, if you want. He knows what he did over at Linda Allard's place, just ask him."

"Maybe I will," he said.

"Well, let me just remind you. According to Linda Allard's sworn statement to the police, Paul Combs came over to her place with some goons and put a gun to her head. He demanded to know where Robertson's other house was. They wanted to know where the safe was, once they drove her to the house. She told the police that Ed Fogerty, now a big construction guy and a friend of Combs, opened up the safe. Then she learned there was a kilo in the safe, along with a couple hundred thousand dollars.

"Why is this important? Because it shows by Paul's actions and frenzied, maniacal behavior that he had never been told about 'two bodybuilders from Hollywood, named Gil and Tommy.' Had his buddy Robertson given him those names when he fronted him the kilos, Paul wouldn't have been freaking out, thinking Dickie ripped him off. He'd have known to look for two Hollywood bodybuilders, named Gil and Tommy. He'd have gone looking for them, don't you think?"

"That makes sense. I see what you're saying," Lewis responded. "Now I remember. He *did* testify that the victims told him they were meeting two bodybuilders, named Gil and Tommy."

"Yes, exactly," I replied, nodding. "His own conduct after the rip-off suggests otherwise. Not to mention, there was no way the victims would have known the names of the guys who did this, assuming for a moment it happened the way the prosecution said it did."

"Like I said, I've asked Combs many times if his story was true. He has always maintained that it was."

I thought to myself, "Thou doth protest too much."

"Again, the fact that you asked that question of Combs throughout the years suggests to me that you suspected the testimony wasn't true. I believe you kept asking him because it didn't pass the sniff test, even with you. He maintained his story, because that's all it was — a story. He must have said to himself, 'that's my story and I'm sticking with it!'"

"No more carrot cake for you!" he said, feigning annoyance with my continuing pressure on this subject.

We both laughed. It really did seem as though we'd become friends. If we weren't friends, we certainly were friendly. It almost felt like we were the former presidents of two countries that were once at war with one another, and now we were living in peace and breaking bread together.

Doug Molloy
Assistant Statewide Prosecutor, Office of Statewide Prosecution

Doug Molloy became the Chief Assistant United States Attorney in Fort Myers, Florida right after the trial. He now has the reputation of being one of the Justice Department's leading experts on human trafficking issues. He travels the world preaching an anti-slavery message and teaching police how to detect 21st-century slave trade. In contrast to this very serious side of himself, he also is a part-time lead singer in a Fort Myers-based band, appropriately named "Alter Ego," that plays rhythm and blues, soul and contemporary dance music.

In spite of my somewhat rough treatment of his wife, Cora, Doug and I ended up sharing a mutual respect by the time the trial was over. We both were a bit emotional when we spoke privately about faith and forgiveness, as we waited for the jury's recommendation as to life or death. I really respect the man. I believed then — and still believe — that had Doug not been on the prosecution team, Gil would have walked.

In 2005, Cindy Imperato spoke to Doug and told him I was writing a book. According to Cindy, his comment was, "John can write?"

I guess Doug could always be a comedian, if the music thing doesn't fly.

Cora Cisneros Molloy
Assistant Statewide Prosecutor, Office of Statewide Prosecution

Cora Cisneros Molloy is currently a partner in the law firm of Henderson, Franklin, Starnes and Holt in Fort Myers, where she represents insurance carriers and employers in the defense of workers' compensation claims. She also is a member of the Association of Certified Fraud Examiners, and assists with the investigation and referral of insurance fraud claims to law enforcement. Cora is still married to Doug and they have two sons.

In retrospect, I regret my unprofessional and overly aggressive approach toward Cora. A more seasoned trial lawyer wouldn't have treated her that way. My anger was simply masqueraded fear, I'm sure. It's too bad I didn't enjoy the experiential wisdom back then that I covet today — the kind that's acquired the hard way — from the trials and tribulations of life.

Dave Blood
Friend and Impromptu Bodyguard

Dave was a true friend during the trial and after. Once a barfly like me, he has since turned his life around. He went to seminary at Emory in Atlanta and is now the pastor at New Hope Christian Fellowship on the gulf coast of Florida, in Port Charlotte.

When I spoke to him recently, his memories about the trial were still vivid. He said to me, laughing, "I was pretty judgmental back then. I remember thinking that every witness on the stand was slimier than the last. Although I wouldn't put it this way now, I remember feeling at the time that I couldn't wait to go home and take a shower after listening to those slime balls and dirt bags all day."

Mike Ruvolo
Court Deputy

Beth Kessler
Court Clerk

Denise Hughes
Judicial Assistant

Robert W. Tyson, Jr.
Judge

Mike, Beth and Denise were kind enough to join me for lunch in December 2005 so we could discuss the trial. We met at my home away from home, The Cheesecake Factory in Fort Lauderdale, which is down the street from the courthouse where Beth and Denise still work. Mike is now retired from the court system.

"Did Gil joke around with you guys?" I asked Mike, who arrived before Beth and Denise.

"Yeah, he would kid with us," Mike said. "One time, I told him that all I have to do is push a button and I would have 24 guys there to take him down. He joked, '24? I can handle five or six but 24 might be too many for me.'

"In my opinion, he wasn't really that *bad* a bad guy. He was a good cop who went bad; so there was some good in him. My experience was that he was always a gentleman. We had an understanding. He said, 'You guys have a job to do. I gotta do what I gotta do and you guys gotta do what you gotta do.'"

"Did he ever try to share his faith with you?" I asked.

"He started talking about being a born-again Christian. I told him I didn't want to mix religion with the judiciary. He wanted me to switch my religion. I told him I was happy being a Catholic and that I didn't want to talk about it with him. He said, 'OK, if that's what you want. I won't talk about it.'"

"Four deputies testified in the life and death phase that they would see him holding hands and praying with inmates who had AIDS. Do you recall that?" I inquired.

"Oh yeah, he did that. The jail had a holding cell on the third floor. He would get together there with other inmates and pray. Among other things, they prayed that the trial would go his way the following day."

"Did you think he was sincere about his faith at that time?" I asked.

"Yeah, I thought he was sincere," he answered.

"Did you think, as some people have said, that Gil and Bert looked like killers when they sat in courtroom?"

"No, they really didn't. They were well behaved throughout the entire trial and the penalty phase. Even after they were found guilty, they still behaved well."

Judge Tyson

"They acted a lot better than Tyson," I said, laughing and only half-kidding.

"Oh yeah!" Mike said, laughing. "He used to tear the heads off attorneys. He'd say, 'Counselor, did you do your homework? Are you *ready*? Are you *sure* you're ready?'"

"I remember his face would get red, especially when Vernell would upset him. He would get rough with him. He used to get upset with me, too. What do you think it was, that I just knew how to push his buttons?" I asked.

"No," Mike said. "I think Vernell would push his buttons and you would get the wrath. Believe me, Tyson actually worked at being neutral. After some of his proceedings, he would ask me, 'Mike, do you think I was too harsh on that guy?' If I agreed that he might have been, he would say, 'Put that guy on the docket for next week. Let's get this straightened out.'

"He also listened to the probation people. He would sit for an hour in the morning reading the probation reports before he made his decisions. He did everything he could to be fair."

"He didn't seem that way to me," I said. "It seemed like he became a father figure to the jurors. He let them eat in his chambers and use his bathroom."

Finally, I had a chance to say something about this pet peeve that had bothered me ever since the trial.

Mike defended Tyson by saying, "He didn't eat with them. He would let them use his chambers when he would go out for lunch. He never stayed in there with them. He only did it out of courtesy and because he wanted to prevent a mistrial. He felt by letting them use his chambers, where there were no TVs or radios, he could control the situation. If they wanted a walk, we had a deputy we'd send out with them."

"I laughed and said, "Yeah, I used to call those 'the strolls.' I didn't want the jurors walking around where they could see newspapers because the feds had just indicted Gil on a new extortion charge during the time the jury was deliberating. It was front-page stuff."

"Don't worry," Mike said. "We always made sure there was a deputy with them. We never let more than two or three go at a time and no one was allowed to talk to them."

I replied, "That really made me angry at the time. I really felt Tyson was biased toward the state. How do you think he felt about me? I was pretty aggressive during the trial. I wonder if he thought I wasn't showing enough respect toward him."

Mike said, "You were just doing your job. Actually, he mentioned to me that he thought you were a good attorney. Let me tell you, I think you're an excellent lawyer and so did the jury. I've seen a lot of lawyers in my forty-some-odd years in the courts. You did your job like you had to do it, regardless of whether Gil was good, bad or indifferent. I'm sincere about that, really."

It was nice to hear that Mike and the jury thought I was a good attorney. But I was *very* surprised to hear that Tyson thought so, too. For all these years, I thought he didn't like me.

"Do you talk to Tyson?" I asked.

Mike nodded and said, "Yeah, I talk to him every month or so. He's about 73 and he's up in Jacksonville. He's not doing well. He has the progressive type of multiple sclerosis, which is bad. With that type, a person goes through three or four stages and then he expires. The last time I spoke to him, his wife got on the phone after a while and said, 'Mike, he's got to rest now.' Even talking on the phone wears him out. It's a terrible disease.

"He also had MS during the trial but few people knew it."

This was a revelation to me. Honestly, I thought he had been drinking during the trial because of his rage. Also, some days he would seem foggy and there were times I saw him stagger.

As if reading my mind, Mike said, "I don't know how many people told me over the years that they thought he was drinking."

"Absolutely, I thought his volatility, grogginess and staggering were because of alcoholism," I said.

"I'm not sure about the volatility but the grogginess and staggering were from the MS. It affected his balance. In someone who has MS, the coating that protects the nerves comes off and the person starts to react differently. My daughter has it, that's how I know."

I was sad after hearing about Tyson's physical condition. Mike, who is a naturally "up" kind of guy, also became overtaken by sadness for a moment. He said, "It makes me emotional to speak about Tyson because I was very close to him. I felt he was a perfect gentleman and I admired the way he worked at being fair. It's hard to know that he's suffering now."

The mood had turned serious. I said, "I wish someone had told us back then about the MS. I would have had more empathy for him." Then I asked, "Is he incapacitated now?"

"The MS has really affected his walking. For a while, he was in a wheelchair but he found that his legs were atrophying. So, he started trying to walk around the house with a walker to keep his legs strong. That didn't work out too well, either. He only uses the wheelchair now when he goes out," Mike said.

Trying to push away the image of Tyson not being able to walk, I changed the subject and said, "I remember he loved dogs."

"Oh yeah!" Mike said. "He loves dogs. Once, on a drug case, he had the drug-sniffing dogs brought into the courtroom because he wanted to see them. And when the dog he owned during the trial died, he went to the animal shelter and got a new one that's throat had been cut by someone because he barked too much. Tyson has a big heart."

"Wow. This is a totally different view of the man than I had in 1991," I said, shaking my head.

Just then, Beth and Denise arrived, having walked over from the courthouse on their lunch break. As Tyson's in-court clerk during the trial, Beth sat right next to him and took care of anything he needed during the court sessions. Denise worked behind the scenes in Tyson's office, answering phones, handling all the legal motions and correspondence, and generally ensuring that the administrative end of the judge's job went smoothly.

Louie Vernell

After warm greetings were exchanged all around and we ordered lunch, I asked everyone, "What do you think would have happened if we had gone to trial without Vernell and Christie?"

Mike answered quickly, "You would have had a better shot, let's put it that way. For every two steps forward you took, Vernell took you back four. You would make progress with the jury, and then Louie would get up. First, he would spit all over them; second, nobody understood his gibberish! Louie always tried to be charming but his elevator didn't go all the way to the top."

"Louie was really comical," Beth said, laughing.

"We liked him but we were embarrassed for him. And I could see the embarrassment on your face because you had to sit next to him. Honestly, I don't know how you tried that case with him there. We couldn't do anything but shake our heads at him," Denise said.

"Yeah, Louie definitely made that trial much more difficult for me. But I still liked the guy. Regardless of all that, why do you think the jury went for life imprisonment instead of death?" I asked.

Mike answered, "I think the fact that you brought out that he's a born-again Christian was part of it. You showed that he had turned around. In other words, he wasn't a thug like they portrayed him. I think the jury believed it. If not, he would have gotten the chair."

Then I asked Mike, "Do you remember the jury asking the difference between the elements for second- and third-degree murder?"

"Yeah, I do," he replied.

"I was excited when I heard that. I thought at the time, 'They're certainly not looking at first any more.' But that didn't turn out to be true. I was so disappointed when they found him guilty."

Mike said, "Well, they weighed the elements, which is what they were supposed to do. They were a very good jury. If they didn't understand one of the elements, they sent out a note to the judge."

Denise said, "I didn't know what to think about the verdict. As much as I might have thought Gil and Bert were guilty, I liked them."

Beth interjected, "Gil was such a gentleman in court, always. He was very nice, soft-spoken, low-key. There was never any kind of a problem. As bad as you thought they might be, we cried at the end for them. I was upset and very emotional because they were so nice in court. I had to hide my feelings. I thought people would think, 'they're murderers and you feel *sorry* for them?'

"Even after all the evidence was presented, there were still so many questions. I really didn't know what to think. We wanted them to get a 'not guilty' verdict because we liked them. We got to know their families. Gil's wife would come in; Christie's daughters would come in. I remember going to court every day and everyone knew us by our first names. I even got a Christmas card from Bert Christie after he was sentenced. When you're with people every day, you don't think about the other side. All you see is how they are to you every day.

"When I heard bad things in the testimony about Gil, it would bring me back to the reality that he was in the courtroom because he was accused of murder. I still remember people describing the crime. I don't even want to talk about it while we're eating," Beth said, looking sad. "Whenever the murder details were mentioned, I thought, 'Wow. Was Gil capable of that?' But I still had compassion for him as a person because I didn't know who he was in 1983.

"I was worried because I thought they might get the chair. And I didn't think they had even proven Christie's case." Then Beth added, "It was really hard to be in that position. I felt funny being nice to Christie's daughters and Gil's wife. I was cordial and said hello every day. When I was nice to them or Gil, the victims' family members would look at me like, 'How dare you?' I understood how they felt but it was *hard*."

Then I interjected, "I can understand that it must have been hard for you. It wasn't quite as difficult for me because I had no choice but to block out the victims' families. I couldn't have done my job if I hadn't. I feel bad about that. Even though there was nothing I could do at the time, I really do feel for them now and I can only imagine their pain.

Talking about the victims' families reminded me that my own family grew during the trial. "My son was born during jury selection. Do you remember that?" I asked.

"Yes, I do," Mike said. "You came in and mentioned it to the judge without the jury there. You came in and said, 'I'm a father again. My wife had a baby!' You asked if you could leave early. Tyson agreed and we shut down at 4 o'clock or whatever it was. I remember that you were very happy about your new son."

"That juxtaposition was interesting," I said. "Here we were in a life-and-death trial. Other people's children had been murdered and now my guy was facing death. There were all these heavy-duty life-and-death issues. At the same time, I was present when a new life was born — my own son. It was surreal. Now that all these years have passed and I have three children, I can appreciate in a whole new way how the victims' families must have felt."

After hours spent reminiscing in that booth at The Cheesecake Factory, Beth and Denise had to get back to work. We all said good-bye, pledging to keep in touch. After the almost literal trial-by-fire we had all experienced together, I would always feel connected to these people in a way that couldn't be duplicated under any other circumstances.

Tommy Felts
Alleged Participant in the Tringali, Leahy and Robertson Murders; Murder Victim

Over a decade after the Fernandez trial, a convicted murderer named Bobby Young pled guilty to the Tommy Felts murder. He received a sentence of only 17 years. This sentence was "concurrent and conterminous" with the earlier sentence he was already serving for murdering the renowned Cigarette powerboat champion, Don Aronow. Receiving a *concurrent* sentence meant that the 17 years would run simultaneously with his other sentence. The fact that it was *conterminous* meant that the sentence was backdated retroactively to begin with the other sentence, which had begun years earlier.

According to H. Dohn Williams, the high-powered criminal defense attorney for Bobby Young, Felts had tortured a Colombian's family members while attempting to extort money during a drug rip-off. As retaliation for the torture of his family members, the Colombian hired killer Bobby Young to execute not only Felts, but also Felts' family. Bobby Young didn't execute the innocent family members but he did go after Felts, spraying him with machine gun fire as he drove on Stirling Road.

Young's prosecutor, who offered him the sweet concurrent and conterminous 17-year sentence, was none other than Cindy Imperato. She made this deal with him shortly before she took the bench as a Broward Circuit Court Judge. In fairness to Cindy, however, her case against Young had begun to unravel when H. Dohn Williams prevailed in his motion to suppress an important statement in the case. Without that statement, it was uncertain that the state could prevail at trial. So, Cindy must have felt that 17 years — the sentence that might have been imposed had they gone to trial without that statement — was better than nothing.

Charles Mitchell "Mitch" Hall   Charlinda Draudt
Alleged Murder Victims of Gil Fernandez and Bert Christie

While researching the book, I was contacted by Paul Sullivan, who had been a good friend of murder victim Mitch Hall.

"Mitch simply repeated something he heard that apparently shouldn't have been repeated," Sullivan said, explaining why his friend was dead.

Hall sometimes did carpentry work at the Apollo Gym and was believed to overhear someone talking about being responsible for the murder of William Halpern. Although the *Sun-Sentinel* reported that Mitch called the BSO and the Miramar Police Department saying he knew who killed Halpern, Sullivan said instead that Mitch had only told his neighbor, who was a Miramar police officer.

According to Sullivan, "Mitch was dead within 24 hours after talking to his neighbor."

Hall's girlfriend, Charlinda Draudt, who was killed as well, was thought to be "collateral damage." She was dead because she was in the wrong place at the wrong time — by Hall's side. Sullivan is convinced that a leak — one that *might* have come from the Miramar Police Department — is responsible for the tragic deaths of Mitch and Charlinda.

Sullivan also wanted to set the record straight about his friend's integrity. He said that during the trial, The *Miami Herald* reported that Mitch was a cocaine dealer, based on information provided by police. But he claims that Mitch was not a dealer. He said he was a good guy who wasn't tied to the crimes that linked the rest of the murder victims.

Sullivan, who also wasn't involved in the crimes but was close to several of the victims through the gym, was warned by BSO shortly after the murders to leave the area for his own safety. He took their advice and moved to Minnesota. He finally returned to South Florida in 2005.

Nick Navarro
Former Broward County Sheriff

I made an appointment to see "Sheriff Nick" and hear what he might have to say about the Fernandez case after all these years.

"Sheriff Nick! Thank you for seeing me."

"It's my pleasure, John. You and I have known each other for a long time."

It was true. I had gotten to know Nick Navarro pretty well after the Fernandez trial, when I represented officers who were reprimanded for police conduct issues. One was a Fort Lauderdale detective who was fired for performing what was perceived to be a racist skit. The officer and I were on the radio quite a bit during that time and the sheriff supported our cause. Upon successful completion of the case, the officer resigned and was awarded back pay and pension rights, and his badge and gun were returned. Later, when the sheriff went into private business and started the Navarro Group and Navarro Security, Sheriff Nick offered the officer a position.

"My wife showed me your brochure and we also looked at your Web site," said the sheriff. "We saw that you've won a lot of murder cases. That made me curious. Why on earth did you choose to write a book about a case you lost?"

"I knew if my first book was about one of my wins, my detractors would say I'd written it just to brag about myself. And I wanted this book to be about more than just a trial. I really believe Gil has transformed and the book was a good way to chronicle that transformation."

"And it's an interesting story, too. Come to think of it, that's a pretty good reason to write a book," he said in a friendly way.

Then we got down to talking about the nuts and bolts of the Fernandez case.

"Yes, I remember it was a turf thing, as I recall," replied Sheriff Nick. "If I remember correctly, the State Attorneys Offices didn't want it. Back then, Michael Satz ran the Broward office and Janet Reno ran Dade. Neither would commit to taking the case, so we went over to the Office of Statewide Prosecution."

Brian Cavanagh, the chief of the State Attorney's Office homicide division, also had told me this in 2006. But it was nice to have the sheriff confirm it, too.

There was never a more relentless and tougher street-cop sheriff than Nick Navarro back in his heyday. Had it not been for Sheriff Nick, it's doubtful that Gil would ever have been indicted. That's ironic, because I found out during my meeting with him that my pastor O.S. Hawkins and Sheriff Nick are good friends. When O.S. came to the closing arguments and encouraged me with his "I pick door number 3" note, I had no idea that he also was a friend of the persistent and determined sheriff.

What a small world it is. During our meeting, Sheriff Nick pulled out some photo albums and asked me, "Have you ever been to Christ's tomb, John?"

"Yes, I have. I went there with my family on a trip with my old pastor O.S. Hawkins, who once was pastor of the First Baptist Church in Fort

Lauderdale," I exclaimed, as I looked at the photos of the Holy Land he showed me.

"You did?" Navarro asked, excitedly. "Tell O.S. I said hello. He and I are friends."

It struck me as ironic that Gil shares the same faith as Nick, who was once his dogged pursuer. Nick told me that he wishes Gil only the best in his prison ministry now: "There's no personal judgment or hostility any more. Gil appears to be genuine from everything I hear. He can do a lot of good in there, and I wish him and his family the very best."

Judy Williams
Juror

I ran into Judy Williams, one of the trial jurors, at a Broward County Starbucks, 12 years after the verdict. As Judy walked past my table, I looked up and noticed her looking at me. She stopped and said, "Don't I know you from somewhere?"

She looked familiar to me, too, but neither of us could remember from where. I thought she might have been one of the parents from my kids' school.

She said, "No, that's not it," as she shook her head. We discussed several other ways we might have met. After a few minutes, neither of us could recall, so I headed out the door to sit at an outside table. Just a few minutes later, she burst through the door, realizing who I was.

She said excitedly, "I remember how I know you!"

At that exact moment, I remembered how I knew her, too. "Yes, I remember, too, you were a juror on the Fernandez case!"

We talked about several issues involving the trial and then I asked her, "Do you remember the vote count in the life-or-death phase of the trial?" I asked.

"Only two jurors voted to recommend the death penalty," she answered.

I was so excited to have the opportunity to ask her the question I felt like screaming in the courtroom right after the trial: "What do you think you guys would have done if you hadn't had the opportunity to choose 'guilty, without a firearm' on the verdict form?"

I reminded her there were myriad options listed on the verdict form, with the first two being the most significant to this case. The first option actually read, "The Defendant is Guilty of First Degree Murder, *with* a firearm," and the second was, "The Defendant is Guilty of First Degree Murder, *without* a firearm." The victims had been shot to death, so it never made any sense that

Gil or anyone could be guilty of murdering them *without* a firearm. Even though there were several projectiles pulled from the victims' bodies, the jury nonetheless decided that Gil Fernandez was "Guilty of First Degree Murder, *without* a firearm."

We both agreed it was obvious that it would be impossible for a person to shoot someone without a firearm. I asked what she thought the jury would have done if they had been given the opportunity to convict Gil without this option.

After only a short hesitation, her unforgettable response was, "We knew the gun was never found, so we probably would have had to find him 'not guilty.'"

I could only shake my head because even though I had suspected this all these years, there was nothing I could do about it.

Judy admitted that the jurors repeatedly discussed the possibility of a life sentence as opposed to the death penalty during the guilt versus innocence phase of their deliberations — before their guilty verdict was even rendered. They were specifically instructed *not* to consider possible penalties during their deliberation as to guilt or innocence. The fact that they discussed the penalty at the wrong time was in direct opposition to the judge's instructions and therefore illegal.

She also confirmed several of the fears I had during the trial. She said the jurors felt nonverbal pressure from the victims' families, and that the families were sitting far too close to the jury box. She also remarked that the jurors discussed that it seemed like Judge Tyson didn't like the defense. Her remark validated my perception at the time of the trial. I knew it was happening and I objected on the record that Tyson was playing favorites. But I couldn't stop the judge's facial gestures and the inflection in his voice. These subtle factors continually communicated his displeasure with the defense.

As Judy and I walked to our cars, we talked about the fact that Gil has led hundreds of men to Christianity in prison, including four guards. We also talked about what happened to Mike Carbone, Bert Christie and other people connected to the trial. I asked her to call me one day, as I'd love to learn more about her view of the jury deliberation process. As a lawyer, I never really get the opportunity to know what goes on in the jury room. I would love to pick her brain.

Luana Tringali
Sister of Victim Al Tringali

Is Gil Fernandez truly repentant?

"I think he's got you fooled, too," replied Luana Tringali.

Luana called me in December 2005, after she learned from her cousin Frank Lanzana that I was planning to release a book about Gil Fernandez and the case. She left me a voicemail that grieved my spirit, big time.

"You're as low as Fernandez," she said bitterly, "and you're only doing this to make money. You can spin it any way you want but that's all you're doing."

Listening to that voicemail was hard, to say the least.

Nice things

Luana's cousin Frank and I had been introduced at a local Rotary Club luncheon at the Riverside Hotel on Las Olas Boulevard a couple months earlier. We struck up a friendship of sorts and agreed to meet at a coffee shop near the hair salon he owns in Fort Lauderdale.

I asked for Frank's help so I could say some nice things in the book about his cousin, Al Tringali. As I informed Frank, all the police reports and newspaper stories referred to Al and the other victims only as "drug dealers." But I was sure these guys had many positive aspects to them, too. Frank agreed to meet to help me portray the good things about his cousin. But Luana didn't believe that was what I wanted to do.

I let Cindy Imperato and Frank know about the angry call. Cindy still had a connection to Luana — and not just because she was one of the prosecutors on the case. She also had developed a friendship with Luana.

Cindy and Frank agreed to reach out to Luana and tell her that I really did appear to be trying to do the right thing, however belatedly. Luana was far from convinced. Cindy and Luana then had lunch together. Thankfully, Luana called me again and left a second message, in which she sounded serious but not angry. In her message, she told me to call her at home and gave me options for precise times. It wasn't a request.

I was grateful for the opportunity to relate to her in a much more positive way. When I called her, she wasn't there, so it was my turn to leave a message. I tried to assure her that I didn't want to hurt her any more than she already had been by everything that happened since her brother's murder in 1983. She then returned my call.

"Thank you for calling me, Luana," I said, sincerely grateful for the chance to speak to her.

"I'm still having nightmares over this whole thing," she said. "I wish Fernandez had gotten the death penalty, so I could know he was dead. I wouldn't have to worry about him getting out one day."

"Luana," I said, "this book is just as much about Gil's transformation and redemption as it is about the old days. I've received many letters from Gil since he's been in prison. They're replete with scriptures and encouragement. He actually lifts me up. There's no way anyone can fake that so consistently over the 15 years since his arrest."

"What redemption are you talking about?" she asked. "He's never confessed to any of these murders. He's never taken responsibility. That's why I still think he's evil.

"I looked at his sweet parents in the courtroom and thought, 'he's a mistake.' If he really *were* repentant like you say, his heart would have changed and he would have confessed to all the evil he did."

I wished Luana knew the Gil I know now. I couldn't imagine her feeling this way if she did. But then I thought about her pain and realized I was asking way too much of her to see another side of him. Why should she? After all, she's the one still living with the agony caused by the person she believes murdered her brother on that April Fools night in 1983.

No wonder she has nightmares, even after all these years.

The Final Appeal

Recently I gave Gil the news that attorney Mike Gelety had agreed to accelerate the filing of another appeal on his behalf, most likely the last one he would ever have. Getting Mike Gelety on board to write and argue this final, exhaustive appeal was a real blessing.

"Mike Gelety is renowned as being one of the best appellate lawyers in the business, so this final look-see is as good a shot as you're ever going to get."

Gil nodded in agreement.

"After seven state and federal appeals, we'll be lucky if we can get another appellate court to consider any of this. But Gelety agrees we've got a couple of good arguments relating to the fundamental unfairness during the trial."

"I know this is the last go-round, but that's OK. God's got it," Gil said. "On all the other appeals, I kept getting in the way. Then, inside my spirit, I heard Him clear as a whistle. I remember it clearly; it was a Thursday in the spring of 2002. God said, 'You've never asked me for help.'

"I sat up straighter and looked at my cellmate, who hadn't said anything. Then I heard Him again in my spirit again, saying, 'You've never asked me for help.'

"I said, 'Lord, if that's you, what do you mean I've never asked you for help? I've always asked you for your help when I did my appeals.'

"Then His spirit spoke to me again: 'That's just it; *you* did the papers and then you asked me to bless what you did. *I* will do it, I just want you to trust me.'"

"You didn't hear Him audibly, did you?" I asked.

Gil replied, "No. I heard His spirit within my spirit. It was as clear as a whistle, like I said. And I'll never forget because it was count time and we're supposed to sit up on our bunks for the head count. But I dropped to my knees right there and said, 'Lord if that's you, I'm asking you to help me.'

"Then you came to visit me on April 3, 2003, John. I'll never forget it. It was a Thursday again and you said, 'Give me your appeal papers and I'll get it done for you.' That had to be from God, John. Remember, I told you I still owed you $9,000 from the trial? You took out a paper and wrote across it, 'paid in full.' That had to be from the Lord, John. He's got it, and I'm not getting in His way this time."

"You've got a lot of strength and faith, Gil, but I don't want to get your hopes up," I said.

"It's got nothing to do with you, John. You can't get my hopes up and you can't get my hopes down. My hope is in the Lord and I'm just gonna trust

Him, like He told me. That's it. You and Gelety are doing your part but He's got it."

"OK, that works for me. There's not a whole lot I can do besides what I've already done in hooking you up with Gelety. He's the best."

"You can feel free to walk from this whole thing now if you want," Gil said with a peaceful smile.

"No way. I might not have told you, but I've run a few marathons in the last few years. Look at this picture I carry of my three kids jumping the rope at the 26-mile mark at the Palm Beach marathon. They ran the last two-tenths of a mile with me across the finish line. See the joy on their faces? That's what this is like with you and me. Do you think I'm going to run 25 miles with you on this deal and then quit before running that last mile? No, my friend, you and I are crossing that finish line together."

"Whadeva you say, running man."

Then he changed the subject. "By the way, thanks for the money you sent. I put it to good use for some of the guys in here who don't have anything."

"When did I send you money?" I asked.

"You gave Michael Moses $100 to give to me. Michael's always sending me something. I love that guy. He's for real."

I was proud of Michael for sending the money, along with his own. I'd forgotten all about it, but Michael hadn't and neither had Gil.

"What did you buy with the money?" I asked him.

"I bought stuff for some of the inmates. The prison gives them one toilet paper roll and one razor a week, and they get toothpaste once every two weeks. The toothbrushes the prison system hands out are cheap pieces of garbage. I wouldn't use them to brush a dog's teeth. And they don't give you any deodorant or shampoo, either. We have to buy this stuff if we want it, and it's a rip-off at the canteen. I call the canteen the 'strong-arm store,' because they shake inmates down for too much money for this stuff.

"That's how I use most of the money I get. I buy these poor guys decent toothbrushes, toothpaste, shampoo and deodorant, because they have nobody to give them anything. I also use the money to contribute to the ministries that give me my books."

He had me laughing at the line about the strong-arm store. But then I got serious when I thought about him donating the same money that others donate to him. He could have easily used it to get junk food or get whatever else the money would buy, but instead he took care of other prisoners. The thought of this humbled and impressed me.

"Wow, that's kind of you to do that, Gil," I said.

"You'd do it, too, John. What am I gonna do, let some guy go without a decent toothbrush so I can have more M&Ms? Come on."

Letters from Gil Fernandez

I asked Gil Fernandez for permission to include excerpts of his letters in this book and he gave me the green light without hesitation. Here are just a few examples of the many he has authorized me to share:

February 5, 2006

Dear John,

Thank you for coming to see me. God bless you. I pray this letter finds you rested up and in God's peace, the peace that passes all human understanding.

As far as the questions you want me to answer…God put this book in your heart to write — then you write it from your heart, not your mind. Since He put it in your heart, He can help you way better than I can. Smile, for I am. You don't need my input — you need the Holy Spirit's input. Whatever you say good or bad about me, or anything at all, so be it!!!! ☺ Amen. So run with it. I will still read your rough copy, but I can't promise I will add or take away. Again, thank you for respecting my decision to not contact my wife.

I'll read with an open heart and allow God to do the rest. Amen. He's the best and He doesn't mess up. ☺ Amen. They might think I'm junk but God doesn't, for He doesn't make junk. I am fearfully and wonderfully made by Him and that's all that counts.

As always I pray this letter finds you doing well in every area of your life. As I write you I know the battle rages within and without, but remember Jesus loves you and you're a soldier under His watchful eye. Now that's enough to get up and run once around your office and shout glory!! Amen.

Today I tell you @ 6:41 AM "<u>Be strong and Be thou courageous, and Fear Not</u>!!!! "For the Lord our God is with you wherever you go!" "He has not given you a spirit of fear, but of love, power and a sound mind." And if He be for you, what devils in hell can stand against you. Amen. No conflict… No conquest, <u>simple but true</u>. Without a battle there can be no victory. <u>Duh</u>! ☹ Our disappointments are His opportunities to be <u>glorified</u>.

<u>So stand</u>, Brother John <u>in His might</u>. Don't say it… Just do it! Amen. <u>He loves you</u> and cares for you. He has many plans for you and <u>none of them include failure</u>! Amen. Smile, for the joy of the Lord is your strength. Amen.

The Lord has started a prayer group in my room every afternoon — 7 days a week. We average 10 men or more in a cramped room. We give testimonies, sing and pray. When I got there, 2-3 men went to church on Sat. afternoons & Sundays. Now out of 96 men we get 10-15 men to attend church. That's not incredible, that's God, and the best is yet to come.

So I thank you for the money and I ask God to return it to you 100 fold in every area of your life in Jesus' name. Overflow, like never before. Amen.

Love always, your brother and servant,

Gil

December 2004 Christmas card

Dear John and Family,

It's that time again; when the world discombobulates the true meaning of this season. Though the world has taken it and turned it around from Him, Him, Him to me, me, me, myself and I…

We are washed as well as fueled now for flight beyond a shadow of a doubt. He is the reason for the season. Approximately 2000 years ago, He came as the Lamb of God who takes away the sins of the world. Next time, He comes as the Lion of Judah, on a white stallion to judge the world of their sin.

He will be known as the King of Kings and Lord of Lords, and his reward will be with him. Pretty profound, huh? That's not even scratching the depth of what awaits us in Christ and those out of Christ. That's why our heartbeat this Christmas should be to be the Light to those lost around us. We have the greatest gift to give — not diamonds, cars, furs, extravagant clothes, money, jewelry, and that's all good. But what we have is life changing and for eternity. All those things will pass. You know it and I'm a prime example!!!

Dom Perignon, Pouilly-Fuisse, cocaine, wine and women can't even come close to the high Jesus gives. The finest clothes and cars don't match up to being clothed in Christ and riding in the ultimate ride: His hands. Amen.

So this Christmas remember Him, as approximately 2000 years ago He remembered you on an old wooden cross at Calvary. Amen.

May He do for you and your family the impossible, unimaginable, improbable and inconceivable this holiday season.

Love you, bro. He's good, all the time, no matter what.

Love always, your brother,

Gil

This letter was written to me after I disclosed to Gil my serious concerns for a family member who was struggling with real difficulties that were affecting my whole family.

August 23, 2005

Dear Brother John,

God bless you and protect you, soldier, as I pen these few lines of brotherly love and encouragement. I received your letter yesterday. I have read it several times and sought the Lord.

It's 4:35 A.M. and I could be sleeping but I feel in my heart to fellowship with you this morning via mail and through the power of the Holy Spirit. As I pen these few lines, I pray He, our comforter, guide, standby, advocate, intercessor, One called alongside to help... yes the "Parakletos," would wrap you up in His anointing, touch you and take you to a new level in Him, this moment in Jesus name.

I don't come with a ton of scriptures or any fancy clichés this morning. I come in love as always... but just as brother to brother. The Bible says a brother is born for adversity. It appears the forms of adversity are escalating in your life. So, your brother is here for you in deed, thought and prayer.

I appreciate your honesty and candor... and your openness. The first step to victory is to confess: I'm powerless, I have issues and I need your help, Lord. The most awesome prayer we could ever say is "Lord help me." Simple but true. No one likes to pray as much and as long as I do, but know that even your older brother; in moments of despair, loneliness, fear, doubt, anxiety, etc, etc; in pools of tears with a snotty nose has just cried out with that simple request "Lord help me!!!!!"

I laugh because people all the time ask me, "You Gil?!!! Go through those things? Heck, yeah. What am I, Super-Christian? No way, Jose. The difference is, I stand up. John, I have gone through many a sleepless night fighting the good fight of faith against the devil. Yes, I have also fought God on many occasions and lost every match with Him!!!! The word says, "There is no counsel (no fight, no reasoning) no wisdom, nor understanding against the Lord (Proverbs 21:30) Amen. God is undefeated and always will be. So, smile if you're fighting Him. You can't win, so give in... Take it from me.

The things you go through and are going through don't move me. The enemy knows your calling and he has to try to derail you. (James 1, all of it; 1 Peter 1, all of it) Do you think he is going to sit back, watch you and not do anything about it? John, that defeated punk is in a quandary. He knows his time is short. So smile, bro… where much has been given to you, much is required from you. It's an honor to be tested and tried. "Weeping may endure for the night but joy cometh in the morning." (Psalm 30:5) Your morning is coming, expect it. Amen.

Hey, I'm preaching myself happy!!!! I pray you feel this joy right now — 8/23/05, 8:03 A.M. — that I'm experiencing. Amen. John, to get through, you got to grow and go through. Your breakthroughs are on the horizon, on the brink, but you must endure and say it before you see it. Begin to declare the victory, "I can't tell, I know, but He can!!!! And He is better than me or anything else." Amen.

John it's by no form or fashion that you're going through these things. He's permitting them to bring you to a new level in Him. Surrender and submission to Him brings provision. When I see you, I'll go into more detail as the Lord leads. (Read Psalm 28:1-9, emphasis on 6-9. He just gave me that for you. Amen.)

Promotion does not come cheap, nor does it lack persecution. It's part of the price. Amen. I believe I've said enough through Him to get your motor running and begin to run this race with a new vigor and enthusiasm. Know that whenever you set your face as a flint to serve God there are not enough devils in hell to stop you. God has shown me that anything I'm involved in for Him will always bring controversy against religion and tradition. Hey, they kicked me out of the faith-based dorm for teaching on the Holy Spirit, laying hands on the sick and casting out devils. Come on, whenever you roll with me there will either be a revival or a riot. But I'm used to that.

Hey, sometimes it's hard being Ms. Emma's son, but I'm going to be it, so smile, laugh, it comes with promotion in the Lord's army. Amen. Ringo Starr sang a song back when you and I were kids: "It don't come easy." And it don't, but it's worth it. Amen? Amen.

I believe, in Jesus name, I'll see you soon. So until then, know the joy of the Lord is your strength and the world can't take it away. (Jesus said it) so don't you give it up. Amen.

Love always, your brother on the battlefield, in Jesus' name,

Gil

October 4, 2005

Dear John, my Brother and Fellow Soldier in the Army of the Lord…

It's 6 A.M., Tuesday, so I decided to knock you out a few lines of love and encouragement. Thank you so much for the surprise visit yesterday and also for calling my folks. I spoke to them last night and they deeply appreciated hearing from you. Especially my Dad. You know the love of a father to his child; you're one yourself. Seems no matter what age I am or where I'm at, not even prison can change my Dad's and Mom's love for me, "I'm still their baby" even at 52 years old. Their love for me has never wavered.

Now imagine the love of God for us! All we put Him through and His love for us (not our sin) never wavers. Nothing can separate us from the love of God. Paul told us that in Romans 8 through the divine inspiration of the Holy Spirit. Everything we do, hinges on love (1 Corinthians 13). The love chapter is a chapter that should be read not only daily but throughout the day of the born-again believer. I like the amplified version of 1 Corinthians 13. It's rich, and food for the soul. Love... God's love... if we could only allow it to sink in deep into our spirit then allow the Holy Spirit to release it to those around us..."what a wonderful world this would be." (Herman's Hermits sang that song in the 60s.)

There are many things that I never shared with you about the courtroom, Judge Tyson, jurors, prosecutors, police, victims' families and friends, even our side. There was a tremendous spiritual battle going on in that courtroom! And at times it overwhelmed me, though I never let on. At that time, I was a baby in Christ. You must remember I was only saved 11 months before I got arrested. And during those 11 months God used me full-throttle, ministering in many places... churches, jail, the streets, schools, even on TV. Plus all the engagements that were set up for the future. Then my world came crashing down... arrested and facing the death penalty, among all the other accusations they kept drumming up.

All the publicity — you tell me if I'm wrong — but I believe 99.9 percent of Christians, I don't care how long they were saved, would have folded and fell apart in despair and most likely would have given up right there in the county jail. But God sustained me and just let me know to trust in Him. Was it easy?!!! Heck, no ☺ and heck, yeah! The disciplined Spartan-type lifestyle that I led before I knew him helped me. Whatever I did, I did with my all. So, when it came to the foot of the cross I had no problem giving Him my all. If I did it for all the foolishness — bodybuilding, karate, sports, police officer, etc. — had to offer, why couldn't I do it for the One who saved me?! Amen! I've never been afraid of a good fight in the natural. The only thing I really feared in the ring or out of the ring was that I would really hurt them bad. Funny, huh? ☺ I'd say, "This fool doesn't know what he's doing." That's what stopped me many times from getting into fights. I knew what I could do if I wanted to do it!

I chuckle sometimes because we try to think for God, and what God is doing. We do it unintentionally. Instead of saying, I don't understand or know, we try to formulate something just to have an answer or a solution.

Society as a whole screams, "justice, justice, justice" until it's them in the loop. Then they cry "mercy, mercy, mercy." ☺ Many times, we give the devil credit for what God is doing. And vice a versa; we give God credit for what the devil is doing.

I've rambled a little bit but I believe you get the picture! Amen. If not, "it'll come to you" as we say in the chain gang. Know that I love you in the Lord and appreciate you more than you know. I pray God reward you over and above all you could ever think or imagine, according to His riches and glory in Christ Jesus for all you do for me. In Jesus name,

Love always, your brother and servant,

Gil

This letter was written in response to South Florida's devastating visit from Hurricane Wilma.

November 2, 2005

Dear Soldier:

God bless you, John, my friend and brother, as well as co-laborer in the harvest…

The fields are ripe… gulf coast states… So. Fla. areas: Many blame this on God as His judgment. Let's see what the word says… (17) For God sent not His Son into the world to condemn the world; but that the world through Him might be saved. (John 3:17) (10) The thief cometh not, but to steal and to kill, and to destroy: I am come that they (storm victims, pre- and post-) might have life, and that they might have it more abundantly (John 10:10).

There are other scriptures I could name that bust up the fire and brimstone, doom and gloom preachers. God is just. I understand this. These things, catastrophes, we have to realize we live in a sin-sick fallen world run by the prince of the air. He's a liar, the father of lies and a murderer from the beginning of time. We have to realize while in this world we are not going to know everything, nor understand everything as to why good people die, get sick — even Christians. That's why we have to be fully persuaded where we will spend eternity. I don't have all the answers but I know the One who does (read Deut. 29:29).

Sin has ramifications and repercussions. It has a payment and it's death, but it also brings chaos, calamity and confusion. That's why God needs men such as you to be fully equipped. Especially in your position to bring a word from on High for those who are broke, busted and disgusted, tore down from the floor down... so low they have to look up to look down. Amen.

I wanted to write you sooner but the Spirit would not release me till this evening. I pray all is well for you, your family and practice, and that you did not suffer much damage. Being in a place like this you don't hear or see much, so it has truly put me in a position to be fully depending on the leading of the Holy Ghost. Amen. Especially in this spot, no Christian TV. Christian radio, at least 85 percent of the time, has interference. So, I have books, the Bible and constant communication with Him.

I believe Christians are pretty well fat out there... conferences; revivals; concerts here, there, everywhere. Amen. CDs, videos, cassettes, Christian TV. Don't like this place? They can go to that place. If I don't like Charismatics, I can go to Pentecostals, or vice versa. If I don't like Assembly of God, I can go to the Church of God. If I don't like them, I can go to the Word of Faith Church, pick my congregations loud, reserved, black, white, Hispanic, mix, young, old, whatever flavor I like. King James or New King James, maybe NIV preaching or Amplified, man or woman preacher. Decisions, decisions, huh? ☺ I can go on and on but I believe you get the picture. Amen. Go ahead and smile. You know controversy is my middle name. ☺

We want power but no purity; healing but not the healer, revival but, God forbid, the reviver show up! Amen. ☺ Lord, send the latter rain but we scream!!! When thunder and lightning comes with it, Amen. Blessing without The Blesser. Oh, The Blesser shows up, things get uneasy. Be ye holy for I am holy – wait upon God!!!! ☺

That's just some food for thought as you meditate. Didn't have any of this on my mind when I began but He digs into the heart. Amen. Feel pretty good writing so I know something here will encourage you a little deeper in Him. "It's in Him," bro, that we can expect things to happen. In Him is the center of the eye, the center of Peace... in Him! It's in Him... I can resist the devil and that punk must flee. You see when I'm in Him, I've already submitted myself unto and into Him.

Well, let's move on. I believe that should get you into the scriptures about God's judgment and wrath. Amen.

Couple of testimonies to encourage you: The Lord opened the door for me to speak to an old man 33 years in the chain gang; 33 years a homosexual to this day, started here when this place was truly a walking casket just waiting to be filled. As I spoke to him, his eyes watered up. I asked him, "Are you happy?" John he looked at me like a little boy in a cage, his eyes asking, somebody please help me. His response: "Do I really have to answer that question?" I told him I already know the answer. It doesn't take a rocket scientist to figure out the devil has lied to him and bound him up. I believe other opportunities will arise to speak to him. I've planted now, the Holy Spirit will water and increase, in Jesus name.

Today while lifting weights, a brother brought me a man who is having extreme problems with his ex-wife and daughter. He's here on a technical violation and is awaiting release. So I ministered to him, he recommitted his life but the blessing was seeing the Holy Ghost break him down. He broke down crying, brokenness all over him, Holy Ghost surgery. Amen. Be encouraged.

Well, in closing, know that I love you in the Lord. In Jesus, bigger and better things are coming for us. Amen. Expect them. Be waiting to hear from you. Know you're in my prayers and thoughts.

The battle rages and intensifies, but so do we. Amen.

Love always, in Jesus' name,

Gil

December 5, 2005

Dear Brother John,

God bless you. It's 7:10 A.M. and I have not gone to breakfast yet. I have been reading the book *Miracles* by R.W. Shambach. I have enclosed a copy for you to read, not to sit on your desk, drawer or bookshelf. This is about Kingdom business — pertaining to you. So know the words I penned are penned by the Holy Ghost. Amen.

I began reading this book @ 6 A.M. At 6:55 A.M. God dealt with me about your brother, whose name I don't even know. But God does and so does the devil. Well, my faith was so invigorated that I couldn't stand or sit still, so I went to my room. I did not pray for your brother — I spoke to that lying, defeated, punk devil (been to breakfast and I'm back) and commanded him in the name of Jesus to get his hands off your brother, in Jesus name, and proceeded to tell him about himself. Amen.

John, sometimes we pray, other times we speak to the devils of oppression, obsession, possession, spirits of addiction, etc., in Jesus name. That's why it's important to invite the Holy Spirit to have His way and allow the gifts of the Spirit to move, especially the word of knowledge and wisdom. Even though he knows he's defeated, he must be advised and reminded he's trespassing, exposed, uninvited and must go, through the blood of Jesus, by the blood of Jesus and in the blood of Jesus. That's why I always stress to you about the anointing, prayer (tongues) and fasting. Jesus said, "howbeit this kind goeth not out but by prayer and fasting." (Matthew 17:21)

We must be prayed up, stayed up (wound up) and fasted up, for times like these. We are soldiers. Paul told Timothy: (3) thou therefore endure hardness as a good soldier of Jesus Christ. (4) No man that warreth entangle himself with the affairs of this life; that he may please Him (Jesus) who hath chosen him (you) to be a soldier (2 Tim. 2:3,4). Amen. Jesus said (and who better, amen!), "And from the days of John the Baptist until now, the Kingdom of Heaven suffereth violence, and the violent (you) take it by force (Matt. 11:12)." Force is through prayer, fasting and speaking the word (Rom. 4:17) under the power of the Holy Ghost.

We must realize that we don't negotiate with the devil — no, no, no! We kick the table in his face, point our finger in his nose and in Jesus name, command him to put it back — put back my brother's joy, peace, health, mind, right now, in Jesus name! Amen.

Look at John 14:12: "verily, verily (truly, truly) I say unto you, he that believeth on me (not on tradition, doctrine, denomination, philosophy or Doctor Phil!), the works that I do shall he do also; and greater works than these shall he do; because I go unto my Father." Amen. Jesus said it, not me, so if He's lying, let's rip that page out; if not, let's do it. The Bible says, let every man be a liar but let God be the truth! Amen. Amen. I like how He says "verily, verily." He says it twice to get their attention, to let them know this is important. Amen.

Look at God's qualifications in 1 Cor. 1:17-31, vs, 27 and 28: "foolish, weak, base, despised, things that are naught" That's me!!!!!! God doesn't call the qualified; He qualifies the called. I'm about to jump out of this uniform!!!! Amen.

I believe the Holy Ghost has said enough to you. I was a fool for Satan, but now, man, there is no high like the high of being a fool for Jesus. Amen.

Love always + forever, your brother + servant, in Jesus name,

Gil

Photo Gallery

The murder site
Photo courtesy of Colby Katz

Gil Fernandez as a police officer in 1979
Photo courtesy of The Miami Herald Archives

Gil Fernandez and Bert Christie at Bert's birthday party in 1983
Photos courtesy of Vince Forzano

Neli and Gil Fernandez in 1983
Photo courtesy of Vince Forzano

Tommy Felts in 1983
Photo courtesy of Vince Forzano

Gil Fernandez in the Mr. Florida
bodybuilding contest in 1989
Photo courtesy of Brett Knesz

*Gil Fernandez and bodybuilding
champion Lee Haney*
Photo courtesy of Brett Knesz

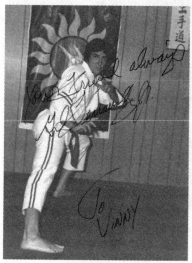

Gil Fernandez
Photo courtesy of Vince Forzano

*Gil Fernandez (left) and
Vince Forzano (middle)*
Photo courtesy of Vince Forzano

John Contini and Gil Fernandez during the 1991 trial
Photo courtesy of The Miami Herald Archives

Louie Vernell and Jim Lewis
Photo courtesy of the Sun-Sentinel

John Contini and Louie Vernell
Photo courtesy of the Sun-Sentinel

Bert Christie
Photo courtesy of the Sun-Sentinel

*Tara Christie flashes the victory sign as
she leaves the courtroom*
Photo courtesy of the Sun-Sentinel

*Gil Fernandez being escorted to court
by Court Deputy Bob Behan*
Photo courtesy of the Sun-Sentinel

*Louie Vernell confers with John Contini
as Gil Fernandez looks on*
Photo courtesy of the Sun-Sentinel

Bert Christie and Louie Vernell
Photo courtesy of the Sun-Sentinel

Gil Fernandez
Photo courtesy of the Sun-Sentinel

Louie Vernell and Bert Christie
Photo courtesy of the Sun-Sentinel

Neli Fernandez
Photo courtesy of The Miami Herald Archives

John Contini in 2004

*John Contini delivering a sermon in 2005 at the New Hope
Christian Fellowship in Port Charlotte, Florida*
Photo courtesy of Paul Szafranski

Judge Cindy Imperato in 2005   *Jim Lewis in 2001*